Phonetics

A Practical Introduction

Speech is the most effective medium humans use to exchange and transmit knowledge, ideas, and experiences. It exists at the physiological level as neural and muscular activity, and subsequent articulatory, acoustic, and auditory events, and as an abstract, rule-governed system at the psychological level. Together, both levels produce communication by speech.

To appreciate speech and its communicative function, all of its characteristics must be understood. This book offers the most comprehensive and accessible coverage of the three areas of phonetics: articulatory, acoustic, and auditory or speech perception.

Students without a linguistics background can be daunted by phonetics, so clear language is used to define linguistics and phonetics concepts with examples and illustrations to ensure understanding. Furthermore, each chapter concludes with comprehension exercises to reinforce understanding.

Online exercises and recordings of speech stimuli from various languages provide additional opportunity to hone perception, production, phonetic transcription skills, and acoustic analysis measurement practice.

RATREE WAYLAND is Associate Professor in the Department of Linguistics of the University of Florida. She received her Ph.D. in Linguistics from Cornell University. Her doctoral research on acoustic and perceptual investigation of breathy and clear phonation in Khmer (Cambodian) spoken in Thailand was sponsored by a Fulbright-Hays Doctoral Dissertation Abroad grant. She was an NIH post-doctoral fellow at the biocommunication laboratory, University of Alabama, conducting research focusing on second language speech learning. She has published extensively on phonetics of various languages, particularly on cross-language perception and production of lexical tones. Her work was supported by grants from the NIH.

Phonetics
A Practical Introduction

RATREE WAYLAND

University of Florida

CAMBRIDGE
UNIVERSITY PRESS

University Printing House, Cambridge CB2 8BS, United Kingdom

One Liberty Plaza, 20th Floor, New York, NY 10006, USA

477 Williamstown Road, Port Melbourne, VIC 3207, Australia

314–321, 3rd Floor, Plot 3, Splendor Forum, Jasola District Centre, New Delhi – 110025, India

79 Anson Road, #06–04/06, Singapore 079906

Cambridge University Press is part of the University of Cambridge.

It furthers the University's mission by disseminating knowledge in the pursuit of education, learning, and research at the highest international levels of excellence.

www.cambridge.org
Information on this title: www.cambridge.org/9781108418348
DOI: 10.1017/9781108289849

First published 2019

Printed in the United Kingdom by TJ International Ltd, Padstow Cornwall 2019

A catalogue record for this publication is available from the British Library.

ISBN 978-1-108-41834-8 Hardback
ISBN 978-1-108-40707-6 Paperback

Additional resources for this publication at www.cambridge.org/WaylandPhonetics

Cambridge University Press has no responsibility for the persistence or accuracy of URLs for external or third-party internet websites referred to in this publication and does not guarantee that any content on such websites is, or will remain, accurate or appropriate.

Brief Contents

Contents

Dr Traci Walker
Human Communication Science
University of Sheffield
362 Mushroom Lane
Sheffield
S10 2TS
United Kingdom

Contact Us

☐ Our Address

Cambridge University Press
University Printing House
Shaftesbury Road
Cambridge CB2 8BS
UK

☐ Order Enquiries

For any enquiries relating to your order or invoice, please contact: Customer Services at the above address or alternatively
Email: customerservices@cambridge.org

☐ Account Enquiries

For any enquiries relating to payments or your account statement, please contact:
Credit Management at the above address or alternatively
Email: customerservices@cambridge.org

☐ All Other Enquiries

Please direct all other enquiries to the following:
Individuals:
Email: directcs@cambridge.org
Phone: +44 (0)1223 326050

Journals:
Email: journals@cambridge.org
Phone: +44 (0)1223 326070

Online Products:
Email: onlinepublications@cambridge.org
Phone: +44 (0)1223 326098

Schools:
Email: educs@
Phone

General Information

☐ Cambridge Website

For our Cambridge Catalogue, online ordering for individuals, sample chapters, email notification service as well as information on the Press worldwide, visit our website at www.cambridge.org

☐ Ordering for Individuals

Please visit www.cambridge.org for a comprehensive catalogue and secure ordering service.

☐ Ordering for Trade Customers

We support trade Electronic Data Interchange (EDI) standards. For more information ask your sales representative for a copy of our EDI leaflet.
For all customers with an existing credit account with us, Pubeasy offers a 24/7 price, availability, and online ordering service and order tracking (see www.pubeasy.com).
Nielsen BookNet Web Services provide a range of electronic ordering methods including EDI (see www.nielsenbooknet.co.uk).

☐ Conditions of Sale

Our Conditions of Sale including our Re
Policy can be found on our web
For Individuals:
http://www
us

Figures

Tables

Preface

Speech is both a physical phenomenon and a symbolic medium used by humans to exchange and transmit knowledge, thoughts, ideas, and experiences. It exists at the physiological level as neural and muscular activity, and as subsequent articulatory, acoustic, and auditory events. At the linguistic and psychological levels, speech is an abstract, rule-governed system. Together, events occurring at both levels bring about communication by speech. To appreciate speech and its communicative function, it is necessary that both of its characteristics, physical and mental or psychological, are understood. This is the overarching goal of this book.

This book is an introduction to fundamental topics in phonetics, including the physics of speech sounds, their articulatory and acoustic descriptions, their transcriptions, and their perception. Analytical tools used to quantify both the articulation and the acoustics of speech sounds are also included. In addition, the basics of phonemic analysis, the method used to examine the abstract, unconscious rules of speech-sound patterning in the mind of a speaker, are also introduced.

The specific aim of this book is to link concepts with hands-on experience. For each chapter, students will encounter concepts presented in a comprehensive but accessible format. In addition to comprehension-checking exercises at the end of the chapter, additional tests and a bank of supplemental materials is available at the book's companion website to reinforce comprehension through hands-on exercises. These materials include recordings of speech stimuli from English and many other languages, including Thai, Chinese, Korean, Arabic, Turkish, Assamese, Dutch, and German, designed to provide students with additional opportunities to hone their perception, production, and phonetic transcription skills and to provide acoustic analysis measurement practice, eliminating the need to acquire recording equipment and a sound booth for high-quality recording. In addition, supplemental acoustic analysis exercises also come with step-by-step instructions on how to perform them using Praat, a free speech acoustic analysis package. Some of these exercises are designed to demonstrate acoustic properties of different speech sounds, while others illustrate the phonetic manifestation of phonological rules (e.g., final devoicing or neutralization of an obstruent's voicing contrast, vowel nasalization, tone sandhi). Additionally, more challenging comprehensive exercises and further research suggestions are provided. Useful URL links to internet resources (e.g., databases, videos) are also included.

In addition to students in introductory courses in linguistic phonetics, students in speech and hearing science, cognitive psychology, and some branches of computer science and electrical engineering may benefit from this book.

The book can be used as the primary source for an introductory undergraduate or graduate course on phonetics, or as a supplement to other materials at the instructor's choosing. Each chapter is largely self-contained in that it leads students through each concept with examples. However, the chapters are sequentially organized by topic: Articulatory phonetics, and phonemic and morphophonemic analyses are covered in Chapters 1–5, Chapters 6–8 present the acoustic properties of speech signals and how they are analyzed, Chapters 9 and 10 discuss hearing and speech perception, and finally, Chapter 11 reviews tools used to quantify articulatory movements and the resulting research findings.

Acknowledgments

This book benefits from the research and ideas of so many linguists and speech scientists, and I am grateful to have learned from them. I want to first and foremost thank my husband, Greg Wayland, without whose continued encouragement, this book would have remained just an idea. I am grateful to Allard Jongman for sparking my interest in phonetics, for his teaching and guidance. I am also in debt to all of my students, past and present, undergraduate and graduate, for their interest and enthusiasm and, more importantly, for making me realize what I needed to do to make phonetics more accessible. I dedicate this book to them. I also want to thank my colleagues M. J. Hardman and Helena Halmari for Jaqaru and Finnish data, respectively, Edith Kaan, Stephanie Wolff, and Michael Gorham for checking some of the data cited, and Caroline Wiltshire for providing references on lexical stress in languages spoken in India. Many people have proofread different versions of this book, including Tom Ratican, Marc Matthews, and Adriana Ojeda. Their assistance is gratefully acknowledged. Lastly, I want to acknowledge the University of Florida for a sabbatical leave to work on the book and my colleagues at the University of Florida Linguistics Department for their moral support.

Ratree Wayland

1

Speech Articulation

Manner and Place

Learning Objectives

By the end of this chapter, you will be able to:

- Identify systems in the body used for speech production, such as
  - The respiratory system
  - The phonation system
  - The articulatory system: the vocal tract
- Describe speech: consonants
- Describe speech: consonants with multiple articulations
- Describe speech: vowels

Introduction

Phoneticians and phonologists are linguists specializing in the study of speech sounds. Phoneticians study their physical properties, whereas phonologists are interested in the structure, organization, and patterns – the more abstract aspects of speech sounds. The division of labor between them is similar to that of an architect (a phonologist) and a builder (a phonetician). The architect is interested in the overall look of the building and its layout, such as the locations of rooms, doors, and windows, as well as the relationship between spaces within the building, whereas a builder focuses on the details of how to construct each part of the building, including the types and sizes of the materials to be used. The analogy is not perfect, but I hope you get the point.

Physical properties of speech sounds can be described in terms of how they are made in the human vocal tract, and this falls under the domain of **articulatory phonetics**. **Acoustic phonetics** focuses on how speech sound propagates or travels, and how its acoustic properties can be measured. Questions on how speech signals are registered and processed by the human auditory system, and

1

which acoustic properties are used to differentiate classes of speech sounds, belong to the domain of auditory phonetics or **speech perception**.

Phoneticians ask questions such as:

- How are speech sounds made?
- What are the speech sounds attested in the world's languages?
- How can they be written down?
- What are their acoustic properties and how can they be measured?
- How are they processed in the ears and perceived or interpreted by the brain?

Phonologists, on the other hand, ask big-picture questions such as:

- How do languages organize speech sounds to differentiate words?
- How are they organized into larger units such as syllables, words, phrases, etc.?
- What are the permissible and impermissible sequences?
- What kinds of modifications occur in permissible and, particularly, in impermissible sequences?

Additionally, such questions as:

- How do children learn how to perceive speech sounds?
- How are speech sounds from a different language learned?

are also of interest, not only to phonologists and phoneticians, but also to cognitive psychologists, among others.

In this chapter, we will take a first step into the study of speech and learn how speech sounds are made by our vocal tract. To do so, it's necessary that we first identify the systems in the body and their roles in the speech production process. Then we will discuss how and where the articulators move to create two main types of speech sounds, namely consonants and vowels.

Systems in Speech Production

In physical terms, speaking is simply the act of making air moving through the mouth and the nose audible to communicate thoughts. It is not a random act, but one that is planned and controlled by the speaker's linguistic knowledge of his or her language and neurally coded in the brain.

As shown in Figure 1.1, speech production begins with a speaker's desire to communicate a thought to a listener. The thought is converted into linguistic representations and coded as neural impulses in the brain. These neural impulses are converted into muscle movements in the vocal tract, generating an outbound acoustic signal. The acoustic signal is picked up by the listener's auditory system and decoded by the brain for meaning. In linguistics, meaning refers to the information (i.e., the concept, the referent, the action, etc.) that the speaker intends to convey to the listener.

Speech production involves three systems in the body: **the respiratory system**, **the phonation system**, and the **articulation system** (Figure 1.2).

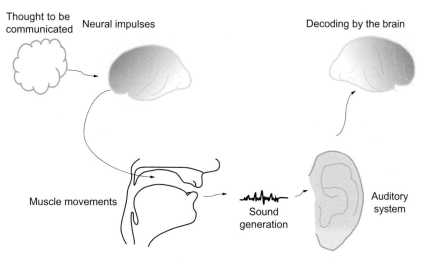

Figure 1.1 Speech production process

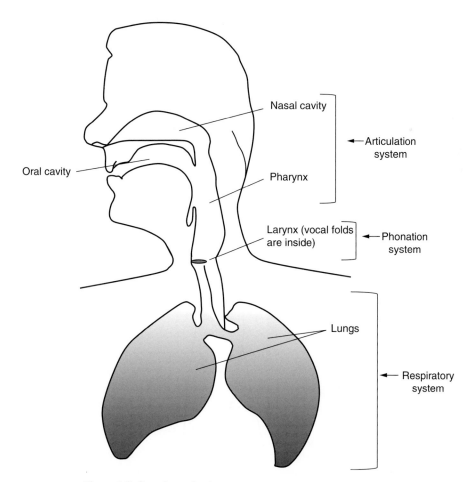

Figure 1.2 Speech production systems

These systems are primarily designed for biological functions such as breathing and eating, and are only secondarily adapted for speech. The respiratory system provides the air supply needed to produce speech. Most speech sounds are powered by pushing air from the lungs upward and outward, that is, the pulmonic airstream. However, many sounds are initiated by moving air trapped inside the vocal tract using the larynx and the tongue. These other airstream mechanisms are discussed more fully in Chapter 2.

The phonation system modifies the airflow as it passes through the larynx. Different adjustments of the vocal folds, two flaps of layered tissue inside the larynx, produce different phonation types, a topic more fully treated in Chapter 2. Finally, the articulation system, which includes the pharyngeal cavity, the mouth, and the nose, performs the final shaping of the airflow before it exits the body. The where and the how of the airflow being shaped are referred to as the place and the manner of speech articulation, respectively. We discuss both later in the chapter. Let's first take a look at each of the three systems in a little more detail.

The Respiratory System

The respiratory system supplies the air needed to initiate speech sounds (see Figure 1.3). It consists of parts of the body that allow us to breathe, including the lungs, the diaphragm, the muscles of the rib cage, and the abdominal muscles. To initiate speech, air has to be drawn in and forced out of the lungs. However, since the lungs do not have muscles of their own, they must rely on muscles of

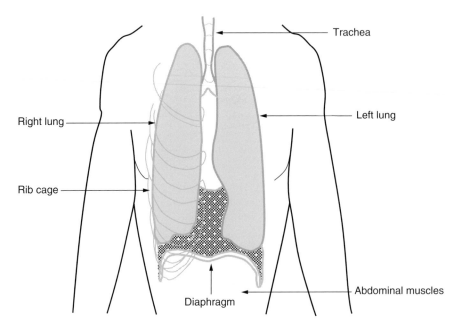

Figure 1.3 The respiratory system

the ribcage and the abdomen to expand or to contract. The diaphragm is a large dome-shaped muscle separating the chest cavity from the stomach. The dome flattens when the diaphragm contracts to allow the lungs to expand during inhalation. Air is squeezed out as the diaphragm and the muscles of both the rib cage and the abdomen contract during exhalation. Air flows upward from the lungs and is then modified by the phonation system.

The Phonation System

The phonation system comprises the larynx and its internal structure. Formed by two major cartilages, the thyroid and the cricoid, the larynx (commonly known as the Adam's apple) sits on a ring of connecting cartilage known as the trachea, or the windpipe (Figure 1.4a). Inside the larynx are the vocal folds (Figure 1.4b, and History Box). They are made up of layers of tissue attached to a pair of **arytenoid** cartilages at the back end, and to the **thyroid** cartilage at the front end. Movements of the arytenoids either bring the vocal folds together (adduct) and close off the airflow from the lungs, or move them apart (abduct) to allow the upward flow of air without obstruction. The spacing between the vocal folds is the **glottis**.

History Box: Vocal Cords

In 1741, Antoine Ferrein, a French anatomist, hypothesized that the ligaments of the larynx are similar to the cords of a violin, and therefore, erroneously called the vocal folds 'cordes vocales' or the vocal cords, the term that is still commonly used today.

Voicing occurs when the air from the lungs pushes the closed vocal folds apart, causing them to vibrate. Sounds produced with vocal fold vibration are **voiced**. In contrast, **voiceless** sounds are those made without vibration of the vocal folds.

An idealized cycle of vocal fold vibration is depicted in Figure 1.5. First, the vocal folds are adducted, closing off the airflow from the lungs (a). Air pressure builds up underneath the closed vocal folds (sub-glottal pressure). When the sub-glottal air pressure becomes greater than the air pressure above the vocal folds (supra-glottal pressure), the vocal folds are pushed apart, from the bottom layer (b) to the top layer (c, d), and set into vibration. According to the myoelastic-aerodynamic theory, the elasticity of the vocal folds and the aerodynamic mechanism known as the *Bernoulli principle* cause the vocal folds to close, again from the bottom layer (e) to the top layer (f, g), and the whole cycle repeats until the air in the lungs is exhausted (see also In Focus). However, current theories contend that the vocal folds would vibrate when there is an asymmetry between the aerodynamic forces created within the glottis and the opening and closing phases of the vocal folds, and that the Bernoulli effect plays only a secondary role.

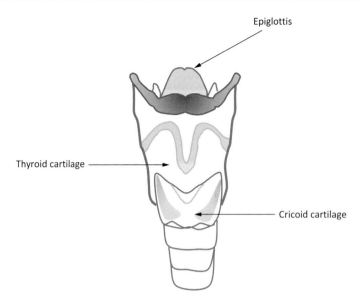

Figure 1.4a   Front view of the larynx

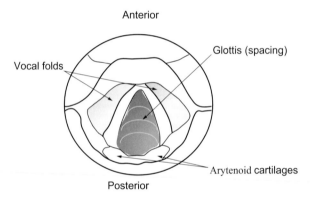

Figure 1.4b   Top view of the larynx

Other modes of voicing are possible with different configurations of the glottis. This is discussed in more detail under phonation types (Chapter 2).

In Focus: Bernoulli Principle

The Bernoulli principle, named after the Swiss-Dutch mathematician Daniel Bernoulli, is invoked to explain why the vocal folds close after they are blown open by the force of sub-glottal pressure. Originally applied to fluid dynamics, the Bernoulli principle states that, for the flow of a fluid that has no viscosity, when the speed of the fluid increases, its pressure or its fluid potential energy decreases. The Bernoulli principle is also applicable to the flow of gas or air. In other words, as the speed of the flow of air increases, the

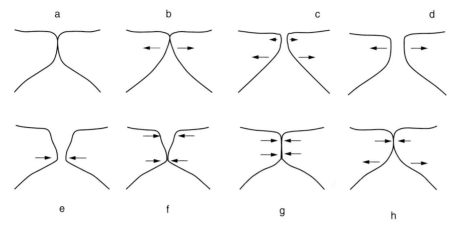

Figure 1.5 Voicing cycle
(Redrawn from Story, B. H. (2002). An overview of the physiology, physics and modeling of the sound source for vowels. Acoustical Science and Technology, 23(4), 195–206, with permission from the author, Dr. Brad Story.)

pressure of the flowing air decreases. In a vocal fold vibratory cycle, to maintain a steady rate of airflow below and above the glottis, the airflow rate at the glottis increases because of the narrowing of the passage, causing a drop in air pressure at the glottis. This drop in air pressure and the elastic property of the vocal folds allow the vocal folds to close. This pattern of the vocal folds closing and opening continues as long as the air supply lasts.

The Articulation System: The Vocal Tract

Airflow through the glottis is further modified inside the vocal tract, which consists of three main cavities: the pharyngeal cavity, the oral cavity, and the nasal cavity (Figure 1.6). The upper surface of the oral cavity contains relatively stationary or **passive articulators**, including the upper lip, the teeth, the alveolar ridge, the hard palate, the soft palate (also called the velum), and the uvula. The lower lip and the tongue are the main mobile or **active articulators** on the lower surface of the vocal tract. Different parts of the tongue are involved in speech production, and it is divided into different areas: tongue tip, blade, front, mid, body, back, and root. Active articulators move toward passive articulators to form varying degrees of constriction, which shape the airflow before it leaves the vocal tract as distinct speech sounds.

Describing Speech Sounds

Air movement can be made audible in a number of ways. It can be blocked, causing the pressure to build up and then suddenly be released. It can be forced to

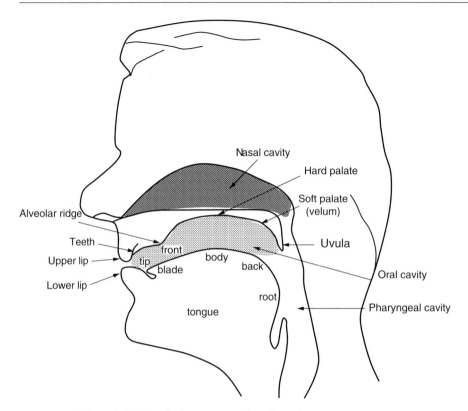

Figure 1.6 The articulatory system (vocal tract)

move fast through a small channel to generate friction or turbulence. Air can also be heard when its molecules vibrate or resonate inside a space such as the body of a guitar or, in the case of speech, the oral cavity. Languages make use of these methods, alone or combined, to make speech sounds audible.

Speech sounds are divided into two broad classes: vowels and consonants. Vibration of air molecules is the main source of energy for vowel sounds, whereas an abrupt release and turbulence alone or in combination with molecule vibration make consonants audible.

Consonants and vowels differ in how they are produced and where they occur in a syllable or a word. In comparison to vowel production, the vocal tract is more constricted, airflow is more obstructed, and less acoustic energy is generated during consonant production. In addition, while consonants can be voiced or voiceless, vowels are commonly voiced. Furthermore, producing a consonant takes a relatively shorter amount of time to complete than producing a vowel. Consequently, consonants are generally shorter and perceptually weaker than vowels.

Besides their articulation, consonants and vowels also differ in number, patterning, and function. Consonants outnumber vowels and tend to occur at the beginning or at the end of a syllable. Vowels more frequently occur at the center of the

Table 1.1 *Differences between vowels and consonants*

Vowels	Consonants
More open vocal tract	Constricted vocal tract
Generally voiced	Can be voiced or voiceless
Higher acoustic energy (perceptually louder)	Less acoustic energy (perceptually softer)
Occur more often at the center of a syllable or a word	Likely occur at edges of a syllable or a word
Function as syllable nuclei	Only some consonants can function as syllable nuclei
Function as the pitch-bearing unit	Only some consonants can bear pitch information
Fewer in number	Larger in number

syllable and function as syllable nuclei. They also serve as the pitch-bearing unit. The differences between vowels and consonants are summarized in Table 1.1.

Consonants

As already mentioned above, consonants are produced with a complete or partial obstruction of airflow. Therefore, one way to describe them is by the amount of airflow obstruction or the size of the oral constriction, commonly referred to as manner of articulation.

Manner of Articulation

Major manners of articulation are plosives, fricatives, approximants, lateral approximants, trills, tap/flaps, and affricates. These consonants are described in the following section with examples drawn from English and other languages. English examples are given in both standard orthography (in italics) and transcribed using the International Phonetic Alphabet (IPA) enclosed in the square brackets []. Examples from other languages are written in the IPA. IPA transcriptions are enclosed in square brackets. Try to memorize each symbol and the sound it represents as you go. We will discuss the IPA chart in Chapter 4.

Plosives are produced with the highest degree of constriction in the vocal tract. The articulators make a complete closure and momentarily block off the airflow before releasing it abruptly. Both oral and nasal plosives occur. For oral plosives, the velum is raised (velic closure) to seal off the nasal cavity so that the air can only exit through the mouth. For nasal plosives, the velum is lowered, and the airflow exits through the nose (Figure 1.7). Plosive sounds such as [p] and [b] in English words *peak* and *beak* are oral while [m] and [n] in *meat* and *neat* are nasal consonants.

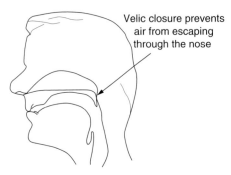

Velic closure prevents
air from escaping
through the nose

Figure 1.7a Oral plosives [p], [b]

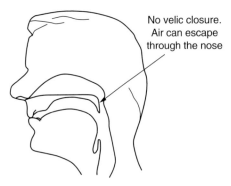

No velic closure.
Air can escape
through the nose

Figure 1.7b Nasal plosive [m]

Figure 1.7 Oral plosives are produced with a raised velum (velic closure) to
prevent air from escaping through the nose while nasal plosives are produced
with the velum lowered allowing air to escape through the nasal cavity

Fricative consonants are produced by two articulators approximating each
other, forming a narrow channel to obstruct the air passage. Turbulent and noisy
hissing or frication occurs as high-pressured airflow is sped up and forced
through the small slit or groove between the articulators. The first consonants
[f, v, θ, ð, s, z, ʃ] in the English words *five, vibe, thigh, thy, sip, zip, ship,* and the
medial consonant [ʒ] in *vision* are fricative consonants (see Figures 1.8a for
labio-dental fricatives [f, v], and 1.8b for post-alveolar fricatives [ʃ, ʒ]).

(Central) approximant consonants are produced when an active articulator
approaches a passive articulator without narrowing the vocal tract to the extent
that a turbulent airstream is produced. The first consonant [j] in the English word
yarn is an example of an approximant consonant produced with the front of the
tongue raised toward the hard palate (Figure 1.9a). The first consonants [w, ɹ] in
wide and *ride* are the other two English approximants. For [w], the back of the
tongue is raised toward the velum (soft palate) with lip rounding (see also
"Complex Consonants" below) (Figure 1.9b). For, [ɹ], there are many ways to

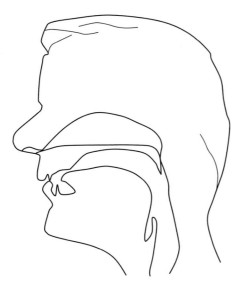

Figure 1.8a Labio-dental fricatives [f, v]

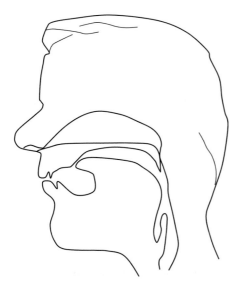

Figure 1.8b Post-alveolar fricatives [ʃ, ʒ]

Figure 1.8 Close approximation of two articulators, forming a narrow passage
to obstruct the airflow, results in frication noise generation as pressured airflow
is sped up and forced through the small slit during fricative production

produce it. The so-called bunched [ɹ] is produced with the tongue body bunched
up toward the hard palate while the tongue tip is kept low underneath the alveolar
or post-alveolar region (Figure 1.9c).

Lateral approximants are produced in such a way that the airstream is
obstructed at a point along the center of the oral tract; a closure between one

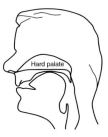

Figure 1.9a Palatal [j]

Figure 1.9b Labio-velar [w]

Figure 1.9c Alveolar [ɹ]

Figure 1.9 Palatal, labio-velar, and alveolar approximants produced with an approximation between the tongue and a passive articulator without generating a turbulent airstream

or both sides of the tongue and the roof of the mouth is incomplete, allowing the air to flow freely over the sides of the tongue. The only lateral sound in English is the [l] sound in *lie*.

Trill consonants are produced when an articulator is set into vibration by a strong airstream. The Spanish 'r' in a syllable-initial position, as in *rojo* 'red', is an example of an alveolar trill [r], in which the tip of the tongue is set into vibration. This sound doesn't occur in American English.

Unlike trills, **a tap** or **a flap** is produced by a single contact between the articulators. In English, most American English speakers produce the 't' sound in *better* and *Betty*, for example, as an alveolar tap [ɾ], with the tip of the tongue making a single brief contact with the alveolar ridge. Commonly, the terms *tap* and *flap* are used interchangeably even though they are

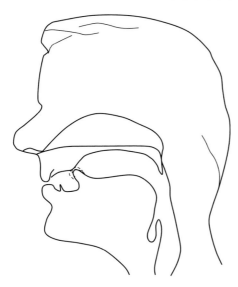

Figure 1.10 Alveolar trill [r] is produced with the tip of the tongue being set into vibration by a strong airstream

technically different. A tap is produced with a single up-and-down motion of the tongue tip touching the alveolar ridge. On the other hand, for a flap the bunched tongue tip swings past the alveolar ridge on its way down. However, the distinction is not consistently maintained, and the term *flap* is preferred for English.

An affricate is the sequence of a plosive released as a fricative. The airflow is completely blocked and then gradually released through a small opening between the articulators. The English affricates are the first and last sounds [t͡ʃ, d͡ʒ] in **chirp** and *judge*.

Major Grouping of Manner of Articulation

Plosives, affricates, and fricatives are grouped together and referred to as **obstruents** because their production involves a substantial amount of airflow obstruction. Approximants are further divided into **liquids** (e.g., English [ɹ] in *rain* and [l] in *lane*) to capture their smoothness, and **glides** (e.g., English [j] in *yawn* and [w] in *wind*) for their gliding motions. In addition, nasals and approximants (and vowels) together are referred to as **sonorants.** They are produced without a complete obstruction of the vocal tract, or frication, are generally voiced, and are louder than obstruents.

Place of Articulation

The constriction or approximation of the articulators involved in consonant production may occur at different locations inside the oral cavity. Thus, besides being differentiated based on the size of the constriction or manner of

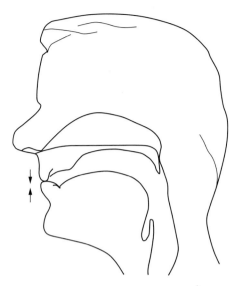

Figure 1.11 Bilabial oral plosive [p], [pʰ], or [b] produced with a complete closure between the upper and lower lips

articulation, consonants are also described in terms of the location of the con-striction, or place of articulation.

Bilabial consonants are made by the upper and the lower lips approximating each other to obstruct the airflow before it leaves the vocal tract. The first consonants [pʰ, b, m] in *pie*, *by*, and *my* are examples of bilabial consonants in English and are found in most of the world's languages (see Figure 1.11 for a bilabial plosive [p], [pʰ], or [b]). The most interesting and rare bilabial sound is the bilabial trill [ʙ]. It occurs as a pre-nasalized [ᵐʙ] in Kele [ᵐʙulim] 'face', and in Titan [ᵐʙulei] 'rat' (Ladefoged & Disner, 2012); both of these languages are spoken in Papua New Guinea. It is produced with the lips loosely close together for the [m] and are then blown apart for the trill.

Next are the bilabial fricatives [ɸ, β]. These two sounds are found in Ewe [éɸá] 'he polished' and [èβló] 'mushroom', and in Venda [ɸima] 'measure' and [βiŋga] 'to marry' (Ladefoged & Disner, 2012). Ewe is spoken in West Africa and Venda in South Africa and Zimbabwe. Japanese has only [ɸ] as in [ɸɯ] 'minus'.

Labio-dental consonants are produced by raising the lower lip until it nearly touches the upper teeth, resulting in a near-complete obstruction of the airflow (see Figure 1.12). The first sounds [f] and [v] in *fine* and *vine* are examples of labio-dental consonants in English. The labio-dental flap [ⱱ] was the last sound to be added to the IPA chart in 2005. It is found in Mono, which is spoken in the northwestern part of the Democratic Republic of the Congo, as in [ⱱa] 'send', for example (Olson & Hajek, 1999). The labio-dental nasal [ɱ] can be heard as a variant of the English 'm' and 'n' sounds in *triumph*, *comfort*, *confront*, *confer*,

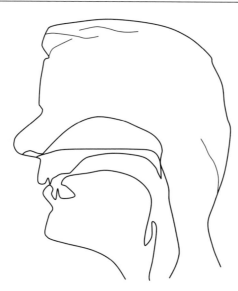

Figure 1.12 Labio-dental fricative [f] and [v] produced with a near-complete obstruction of the airflow by the lower lip and the upper teeth

etc. Another labio-dental sound is the approximant [ʋ]. It is found in Tamil [ʋaj] 'mouth', and Dutch [ʋɑŋ] 'cheek'.

Dental consonants are formed when the tip or the blade of the tongue makes contact with the back of the upper front teeth to obstruct airflow. The first consonants in the British English words *thigh* [θ] and *thy* [ð] are produced in this manner. However, these sounds are produced with the tongue stuck out between the upper and the lower front teeth in most American English dialects. As such, they may be called **interdental** consonants to distinguish them from dental consonants. However, in American English, 't' and 'd' sounds, which are normally produced at the alveolar place of articulation as in *tie* and *die*, may be produced as dental consonants in *eighth* [t̪] and *width* [d̪] before an interdental fricative [θ].

Alveolar consonants are produced when the tongue tip or tongue blade touches or approximates the alveolar ridge to momentarily obstruct the flow of air through the vocal tract. The first consonants [t, d, n, ɹ, s, z, l] in *tan*, *Dan*, *nine*, *ran*, *sign*, *zeal*, and *lie* are examples of alveolar consonants in English. The alveolar lateral fricatives [ɬ, ɮ] are produced with the airflow being blocked through the center of the oral cavity, but the airflow is allowed to escape noisily through a small gap between the sides of the tongue and the upper molars. Both are found in Zulu, as in [ɮálà] 'play' and [ɬânzà] 'vomit'; but only voiceless [ɬ] occurs in Welsh [peɬ] 'far', [ɬaɬ] 'other' (Ladefoged & Disner, 2012).

Retroflex consonants are produced by raising and curling the tip of the tongue such that the underside of the tongue tip touches or approaches the back part of

Figure 1.13a Dental [t̪] or [d̪]

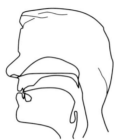

Figure 1.13b Interdental [θ] or [ð]

Figure 1.13 Dental plosive and interdental fricative

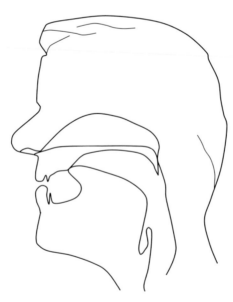

Figure 1.14 Alveolar plosive [t] or [d]

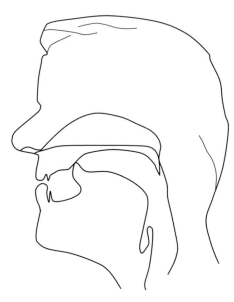

Figure 1.15 Retroflex [ʈ] or [ɖ] produced with tongue tip raised and curled toward the back part of the alveolar ridge

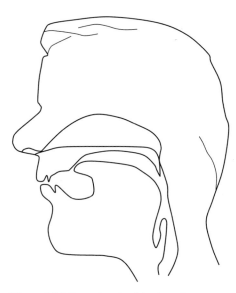

Figure 1.16 Post-alveolar fricative [ʃ]

the alveolar ridge. Retroflex sounds are not common in English. However, some native speakers of American English may produce the 'r' sound in *rye*, *ride*, *ire* or *air* as a retroflex. In addition, a 't' or a 'd' before an 'r' as in *try* or *address* may also be pronounced as a retroflex [ʈ] and [ɖ] for some American English

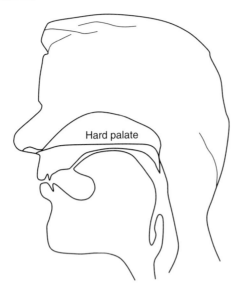

Figure 1.17 Palatal approximant [j]

speakers. Retroflex consonants are common in languages spoken in India, such as Hindi, Tamil, and Malayalam.

Besides plain retroflex consonants [ʈ, ɖ], these languages also have voiceless aspirated and voiced aspirated retroflexes [ʈʰ, ɖʰ]. Hindi retroflex consonants are shown below (Ladefoged & Disner, 2012).

      [ɖɑl] 'branch'   [ʈʰɑl] 'wood shop'
      [ʈɑl] 'postpone' [ɖʰɑl] 'shield'

Retroflex [ɳ] is found in Malayalam [kʌɳɳi] 'link in chain', and lateral approximant retroflex [ɭ] is found in Korean as in [paɭ] 'foot' and in Tamil [puɭi] 'tamarind' (Ladefoged & Disner, 2012).

The articulation of **post-alveolar** consonants involves the tongue blade and the back of the alveolar ridge. Try to say the words *shine*, *shore*, or *shop*. You will notice that during the articulation of the first consonants [ʃ] in these words, the back of your tongue is close to the back of the alveolar ridge.

Palatal consonant production involves the front (not the tip) of the tongue raised toward the hard palate (see Figure 1.6 for the difference between tongue front and tongue tip). The first consonant [j] in *you* is an example of a central palatal approximant in English. A lateral palatal approximant is found in (European) Spanish [poʎo] 'chicken', Italian [fiʎo] 'son' (Ladefoged & Disner, 2012), and Greek [iʎos] 'sun'. Palatal plosives do exist, but are rare because it's difficult to limit tongue contact to just the palatal region without also touching the back part of the alveolar ridge (post-alveolar region) and producing post-alveolar affricates [ʧ, ʤ] instead. Both voiced and voiceless palatal plosives [c, ɟ] occur in Hungarian [ɔcɔ] 'gather', and [cɟɔ] 'his dream' (Ladefoged & Disner, 2012). Voiced and voiceless fricatives [ç, j] occur in Greek [çɛri] 'hand' and [jɛri] 'old

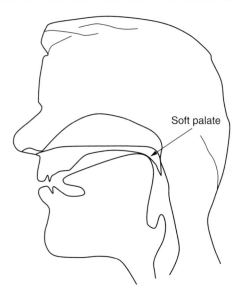

Figure 1.18 Velar plosives [k, g] produced with the tongue raised toward the velum or soft palate

men'. On the other hand, palatal nasal [ɲ] is relatively more common. It's found in Hungarian [ɔɲɔ] 'mother', French [aɲo] *agneau* 'lamb', Lao [ɲúŋ] 'mosquito', and Spanish [seɲor] *señor* 'sir' (Ladefoged & Disner, 2012).

Velar consonants are formed with the back of the tongue raised toward the soft palate. The first consonant sounds [k, g] in *kite*, *king*, *good*, and *gang*, and the final sound [ŋ] in *sing* are examples of velar consonants in English. Velar voiced and voiceless fricatives [x, ɣ] are found in German [buːx] 'book', Vietnamese [xɔ́] 'be difficult' and [ɣɑ̀] 'chicken', and Greek [xɔmɑ] 'soil' and [ɣɔmɑ] 'eraser'. The voiced velar lateral approximant [ʟ] is not a well-known sound. It's found in Melpa [paʟa] 'fence' (Ladefoged & Disner, 2012) and Mid-Waghi [aʟaʟe] 'dizzy' (Ladefoged et al., 1977). Both of these languages are spoken in Papua New Guinea. Voiced velar approximant [ɰ] is found in Tiwi [ŋaɰɰa] 'we', an aboriginal language spoken on the Tiwi Islands, Australia.

Uvular consonants are produced when the back of tongue is raised toward the uvula. Uvular sounds do not occur in English. French has voiced uvular fricative [ʁ] as in [ʁoz] 'rose' and Hebrew has voiceless uvular fricative [χ] as in [χimia] 'chemistry'. However, both can also be found in Aleut [qiɣaχ] 'grass' spoken in the Aleutian Islands (Ladefoged & Disner, 2012).

Uvular voiceless and voiced plosives [q, ɢ] are rare. [q] is found in Quechua [qaʎu] 'tongue' (Ladefoged & Disner, 2012) and Arabic [qitˤ] 'cat' and [qalb] 'heart', and Ket, a Siberian language has [ɢ] as in [baŋɢuk] 'cave in the ground' (Georg, 2007).

The uvular nasal is rare. Japanese has it in word-final position in [nihõɴ] 'Japan' and [sãɴ] 'three', for example (Vance, 2008), when the words are produced before a pause (Aoyama, 2003).

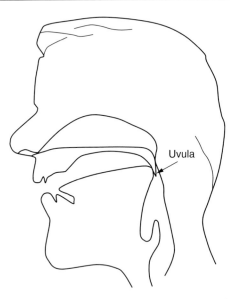

Figure 1.19 Uvular plosives [q, ɢ] produced with a closure between the back of the tongue and the uvula.

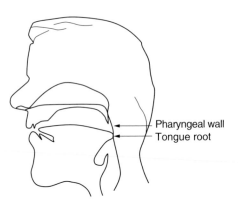

Figure 1.20 Pharyngeal fricatives [ʕ] or [ħ] produced with a close approximation between the back of the tongue and the back wall of the pharynx

Pharyngeal consonants are not very common among the world's languages. They are produced by pulling the back of the tongue toward the back wall of the pharynx. Complete contact between the root of the tongue and the pharynx wall is very difficult to achieve for most people. Thus, pharyngeal plosives have not yet been found in the world's languages. Pharyngeal nasals are also impossible since the approximation between the root of the tongue and the pharynx wall would essentially block the air from flowing through the nose. The only pharyngeal sounds documented so far are voiced [ʕ] and voiceless [ħ] pharyngeal fricatives, both of which occur in Arabic, as in [ʕaaj] 'ivory' and [ħaar] 'hot' (Jarrah, 2013), and Hebrew, as in [ʕor] 'skin' and [ħole] 'humid'.

Table 1.2 *Summary of place of articulation*

Place of Articulation	Active Articulator	Passive Articulator	Examples from English
Bilabial	Upper and lower lips	None	beat, peak, meet
Labio-dental	Lower lip	Upper front teeth	five, vowel
(inter) Dental	Tongue tip	Upper front teeth	thy, think
Alveolar	Tongue tip or blade	Alveolar ridge	tie, die
Post-alveolar	Tongue tip or blade	Behind alveolar ridge	shop, assure
Retroflex	Tongue tip	Hard palate	rye, ride (for some speakers)
Palatal	Tongue front	Hard palate	yes, youth
Velar	Tongue back	Soft palate	keep, good
Uvular	Tongue back	Uvula	
Pharyngeal	Tongue root	Pharyngeal wall	
Glottal	Vocal folds	None	't' in button
Epiglottal	Root of epiglottis	Pharyngeal wall	

Glottal sounds are produced with a constriction deep down in the throat, and thus only a few types of consonants can be made. A glottal stop is made with a constriction at the glottis. The vocal folds are brought together to momentarily shut off the airflow and then audibly released. In American English, most speakers produce a glottal stop [ʔ] in the middle of the words *button* and at the beginning of the exclamation *uh-oh*. In Thai, [ʔ] occurs as an initial consonant in [ʔiŋ] 'to lean (against something)', for example.

The English 'h' sound in *head* is a voiceless glottal fricative [h], but becomes (breathy) voiced [ɦ] when it occurs between two vowels as in *ahead* (see also Chapter 4).

Epiglottal sounds are produced by a constriction between the root of the epiglottis and the lowest part of the pharynx. Fricatives can be produced in this location. Some speakers of Arabic produce epiglottal fricatives [ʕ, ʜ] instead of pharyngeal fricatives [ʕ, ħ]. Additionally, some of the languages of the Caucasus contrast between pharyngeal and epiglottal sounds. The Burkixan dialect of Agul spoken in Dakestan, USSR, contrasts voiced [ʕ] and voiceless [ħ] pharyngeal fricatives with voiceless epiglottal stops [ʡ] and fricatives [ʜ] as in [muʕˤ] 'bridge', [muħ] 'barn', [sɛʡ] 'measure' and [mɛʜ] 'whey' (http://phonetics.ucla .edu/appendix/languages/agul/agul.html).

Table 1.2 summarizes places of articulation with their passive and active articulators. Examples from English are included in the last column. Please refer back to the text for non-English examples.

Further Grouping of Places of Articulation

Similar to manner of articulation, places of articulation may be grouped together to form broader classes. **Labials** refer to all sounds whose production involves the lip(s) (e.g., labial, labio-dental); **coronals** are sounds produced with constrictions made by the tongue tip and blade or the front part of the tongue body (e.g., (inter)dental, alveolar, post-alveolar, retroflex); **dorsals** are produced with the tongue body (palatal, velar, uvular); **pharyngeals** are made with the tongue root (pharyngeal, epiglottal), and finally, **laryngeals** are sounds produced with constriction at the glottis (glottal). Palatal consonants may be considered either coronal or dorsal depending on the extent of the constriction.

Voicing

Besides manner and place of articulation, consonants may be produced with or without vocal fold vibration, resulting in voiced or voiceless sounds, respectively. While both voiced and voiceless sounds are found for some classes of consonants, other classes tend to be mostly voiced. Plosives and fricatives can be voiced or voiceless, but nasals, trills, taps/flaps and approximants are usually voiced.

A simple test to see if the vocal folds are vibrating is to place your hand on your throat while producing the sounds. Try producing the [s] sound in *sip* and alternate it with the [z] sound in *zip*. You should feel the vibration of your vocal folds during the [z] sound, but not during the [s] sound. Other modes of vocal fold vibration are discussed under phonation types in Chapter 2.

Consonants with Multiple Articulations

Thus far, we have described mostly consonants that are produced with a single constriction at a single location in the vocal tract. However, some consonants are produced with two constrictions at two different locations. They are divided into two types depending on whether the two articulations are simultaneous or in sequence. A **contour consonant** is produced with a sequence of two articulations, whereas both articulations are made simultaneously in a **complex consonant**.

Contour Consonants

Contour consonants, such as English affricates [t͡ʃ] and [d͡ʒ] in *chin* and *gin*, are produced with two consecutive articulations, namely a plosive followed by a fricative of the same or similar place of articulation. Besides the two post-alveolar affricates in English, other affricates are also possible, including a bilabial [p͡ɸ] in *pfanne* 'pan' and an alveolar [t͡s] *zahl* 'number' in German, and a palatal [c͡ç] [c͡ça:n] 'a plate/dish' in Thai. Despite being produced with two different articulations and represented by two IPA symbols, affricates behave like single consonants. They occur in contexts where only a single segment is permissible, such as the beginning of a word. For example, a plosive + fricative sequence such as [p͡s] in *psychology* from Greek is not permitted at word onset so [p͡s] is reduced to [s], an allowable word-onset segment in English. To native speakers of English, an affricate feels like a single segment just as an 's' sound does. Though not consistently practiced, a tie bar is used in an affricate transcription to reflect its single segment status, thus [t͡ʃ], [d͡z], [p͡ɸ], etc. In fact, post-alveolar affricates [t͡ʃ] and [d͡ʒ] are sometimes transcribed with a single symbol [č] and [ǰ] respectively.

Other contour consonants are pre-nasalized plosives [ᵐb, ⁿd, ᵑg] produced initially with the velum lowered part-way through the segment, but finished with an oral release. Lateral released plosives [tˡ, dˡ] begin with an oral closure, but end with air being released through the sides of the tongue. Nasal released [tⁿ, dⁿ] plosives start off as regular plosives, but the airflow is released through the nose at the end.

Complex Consonants

Complex consonants have two articulations at the same time with the same or different degrees of constriction. If they are of the same degree, both are considered primary articulations. If they are of different degrees, the one with a higher degree of closure (e.g., a plosive or a fricative) is considered primary while the other (e.g., an approximant) is considered a secondary articulation. Examples of complex consonants with two primary articulations are the Ewe labio-velar [k͡p] and [g͡b] in [k͡pɔ́] 'to see' and [g͡bɔ̃] 'goat' ([́] represents a high tone, and [̃] nasalization). Ewe has three tones: high, mid, and low. Ewe also distinguishes an oral from a nasal vowel where air exits through the nose rather than the mouth. We discuss tones in Chapter 3 and vowel nasalization later in this chapter under vowel description.

Swedish has a dorso-palatal fricative [ɧ], a simultaneous post-alveolar [ʃ], and velar [x] fricatives, as in [ɧok] 'chunk' (http://phonetics.ucla.edu/appendix/lan guages/swedish/swedish.htm).

The English [w] sound in *wind* is an example of a complex consonant produced with two simultaneous approximants: labial, between the lips, and velar between the tongue and the velum. A voiceless labio-velar fricative [ʍ] can be heard instead of [w] for words that begin with 'wh', such as *white, which, what* among some speakers of American English.

Secondary Articulation

A consonant is also considered complex if its production involves a secondary articulation. The [kʷ] in *coop*, for instance, is produced with a secondary articulation. In this case, the primary articulation is the plosive produced at the velum while the secondary articulation is the addition of lip rounding in anticipation of the vowel [u] (compare the position of the back of your tongue and your lips when you say the first consonant in the words *coop* and *keep*; the back of the tongue is advanced toward the hard palate and the lips are not rounded for the latter). Four types of secondary articulation have been identified in the world's languages, as described below.

Labialization is the addition of a [w] or an [u]-like articulation to the primary articulation. In American English, it is often conditioned by the following segment, particularly the [u] vowel, as in [tʷub] *tube*, [sʷup] *soup*, and [kʷup] *coop*, making it difficult to differentiate from a sequence of two consonants, as in [twɪn] *twin*, [swup] *swoop*, and [kwɪk] *quick*. The difference lies in the relative timing of the two articulatory gestures. In a secondary articulation, the two articulations occur simultaneously, whereas in the sequence of two segments, the [w] articulation starts later and partially overlaps with the first articulation. Unlike in English, labialization is contrastive in some languages. For example, [àkʷá] means 'a roundabout way', but [àká] means 'someone has been bitten' in Twi, a Niger-Congo language spoken in Ghana. It is also contrastive in Bura, spoken in Nigeria, as shown below.

Contrastive labialization in Bura, spoken in Nigeria (from http://phonetics.ucla.edu/appendix/languages/bura/bura.html)

[bàrà]	'to want'	[bʷà]	'part'	[kàlà]	'to bite'
[pàkà]	'to search'	[pʷàrà]	'to escort'	[kʷàrà]	'donkey'

Palatalization involves a second constriction formed by the front of the tongue rising toward the palate or a palatal [j]-like articulation to the primary articulation. Palatalization is contrastive in Russian, as in [zof] 'call' vs. [zʲof] 'yawn'. In English, a palatalized [lʲ] may occur in word-initial position, as in *leaf*.

Contrastive palatalization in Russian (from http://phonetics.ucla.edu/appendix/languages/russian/russian.html)

[sok]	'juice'	[sʲok]	'he lashed'
[sof]	'call'	[sʲof]	'yawn'
[mal]	'little'	[mʲal]	'crumple'

Velarization is the addition of a raising of the back of the tongue toward the velum giving rise to a 'dark' auditory sensation. It is indicated by either [ˠ] or [˜]. In English, [ɫ] is velarized in post-vocalic position as in [fiɫ] *feel* and [spɪɫ] *spill*. This is referred to as 'dark [ɫ]', as opposed to 'light [l]' in prevocalic position, as in *lip* and *lack* (see also Chapter 4). However, velarization is contrastive in Marshallese spoken in the Marshall Islands, as in [ɫaɫ] 'knock' and [laɫ] 'earth' (van de Weijer, 2011).

Pharyngealization is the addition of a back tongue lowering and a retraction of the tongue root toward the pharyngeal wall to the primary articulation. The same diacritic used to indicate velarization can also be used for pharyngealization since languages don't usually contrast between these two types of secondary articulation. Pharyngealization can also be indicated by [ˤ]. Some dialects of Arabic contrast plain with pharyngealized consonants. For example, in Syrian Arabic, a plain [d] [dal] 'he pointed' is contrasted with a pharyngealized [dˤ] in [dˤal] 'he stayed'. More examples of a contrast between plain and pharyngealized consonants are given below.

Contrastive pharyngealization in Arabic (van de Weijer, 2011)

[safir]	'ambassador'	[sˤafiːr]	'whistle'
[dam]	'blood'	[dˤam]	'gloss'
[tiːn]	'fig'	[tˤiːn]	'mud'

In summary, consonants are described based on how much the airflow is obstructed, where it is obstructed, and whether or not the vocal folds are vibrating. Most consonants are produced with one constriction in the oral cavity, but some involve a sequence of two articulations, while others involve two simultaneous articulations – either two primary articulations or a primary and a secondary articulation. Secondary articulations are often conditioned by surrounding segments in English, but are contrastive in other languages. We turn next to vowel description.

Vowels

Vowels are produced without a complete closure between the tongue and any part of the roof of the mouth. The airflow is, therefore, never completely obstructed during vowel production. Vowels are also mostly voiced. The basic articulatory description of vowels includes degree of tongue height or vertical tongue position, location of the highest point of the tongue in the mouth or horizontal tongue position, and lip positions.

A diagram known as a vowel quadrilateral similar to the one shown in Figure 1.21 was traditionally treated as a graphical representation of the area in the oral cavity within which the highest point of the tongue is located during vowel production. For example, the quality of the vowel represented by the dot on the diagram is produced with the highest point of the tongue placed as close to the roof of the mouth as possible and as front as possible in the oral cavity without the airflow being substantially obstructed to incur friction. Lip position is not represented in the diagram. However, the tongue and lip positions alone do not fully determine the perceived quality of a vowel. Instead, the configuration of

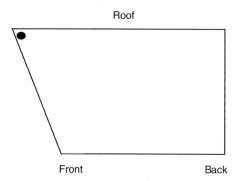

Figure 1.21 Vowel quadrilateral

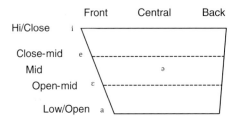

Figure 1.22 Vowel height

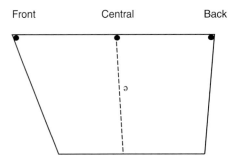

Figure 1.23 Vowel front and backness

the whole vocal tract has to be taken into account. Thus, even though we will continue to discuss vowel location in the quadrilateral with reference to tongue position, the vowel quadrilateral should be treated as representing an auditory space rather than an accurate description of vowel production.

Vowel Height

The height of a vowel refers to the distance between the highest point of the tongue and the roof of the mouth. A close vowel (also called a high vowel) such as [i] in the English word *pea* is produced with the tongue raised close to the roof of the mouth. A vowel produced with a slight amount of tongue raising, leaving a relatively wide gap in the oral cavity like the vowel [ɑ] in the word *pot*, is called a low or an open vowel. A mid vowel is produced with a tongue height that is intermediate between a low and a close vowel. An example of a mid vowel in English is the schwa vowel [ə] in the first syllable of *ago*. Vowels in between close and mid are called half-close, close-mid, or hi-mid, interchangeably. Vowels between mid and low are called half-open, low-mid, or open-mid.

Vowel Front and Backness

The location of the highest point of the tongue in the horizontal plane divides vowels into front, central, and back vowels. A front vowel [i] in English *pea* is

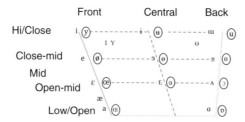

Figure 1.24 Rounded vowels

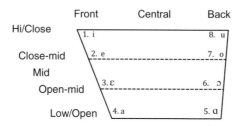

Figure 1.25 Cardinal vowels

produced with the front part of the tongue raised toward the hard palate. A back vowel [u] in *boot* is made with the back of the tongue raised toward the velum (soft palate). A mid, central vowel, the schwa, [ə] heard in the first syllable of the word *ago,* is produced with the center part of the tongue slightly raised toward the area between the hard and the soft palate.

Lip Position

Lip configuration is the third dimension in vowel production. A vowel can be produced with different degrees of lip rounding. A rounded vowel such as [u] in *shoe* is produced with a smaller mouth opening than an unrounded vowel such as [i] in *she*. Lip position is not represented in the vowel diagram. However, when shown in pairs, the symbol on the right (circled) represents a rounded vowel (see Figure 1.24).

Cardinal Vowels

Cardinal vowels are a set of language-independent vowels invented and developed by Daniel Jones, Professor of Phonetics at University College of London from 1921 to 1947. They were intended to be used as references or landmarks in the auditory space to which the vowels of the world's languages could be related. There are two sets of cardinal vowels. The primary set comprises four front and four back vowels, numbered 1–8. Numbers 1–5 are unrounded and 6–8 are rounded. The secondary set, numbered 9–16, are the reverse of the primary set in lip position. Numbers 9–13 are rounded and 14–16 are unrounded. Figure 1.25 shows the cardinal vowels on the vowel quadrilateral.

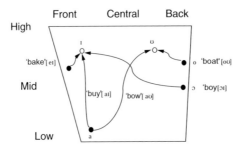

Figure 1.26 American English diphthongs

Cardinal vowel 1 has the quality of a vowel produced with the most front and closest tongue position without audible friction, and vowel 5 with the most back and most open position of the tongue that does not produce audible friction. Equidistance between cardinal vowels is auditorily, and not articulatorily, determined. Since cardinal vowels are auditorily determined, they must be learned initially from Daniel Jones himself and subsequently from a teacher who knows them, or from a recording.

Monophthong vs. Diphthong

The quality of a vowel may change within a syllable. The vowels in *buy*, *boy*, and *how* in English exhibit such a quality change. For *buy*, the quality of the vowel changes from a low to a close vowel [aɪ]. These vowels are called **diphthongs**. On the other hand, vowels produced with a relatively stable quality throughout the syllable are known as **monophthongs**. Both types of vowels exist in most of the world's languages. Figure 1.26 shows the origins and the targets of diphthongs in English, [aɪ], [ɔɪ], [aʊ], [eɪ] and [oʊ] as in *buy, boy, bow, bake*, and *boat*. Notice that the distance between the origins and the targets for [eɪ] and [oʊ] are less drastic than the first three, and are not always treated as true diphthongs, but rather as diphthongized vowels (see also Chapter 4).

Besides height, backness, and rounding, vowels may be differentiated based on how long they are sustained, the tension of the vocal tract muscles, and whether air simultaneously flows through the nose, etc.

Long and Short Vowels

Some vowels are inherently longer than others. In English, the [i] vowel in *peat* is inherently longer than the [ɪ] in [*pit*]. Similarly, the vowel [u] in *boot* is inherently longer than the [ʊ] in *book*. However, note that variation in vowel duration in English is always accompanied by a difference in quality determined by tongue height, tongue backness, and lip rounding, as described above. Variation in duration alone does not change an English word's meaning. For instance, the referent of the word *pit* as 'a large hole in the ground' remains the

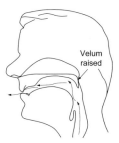

Figure 1.27a Oral vowel

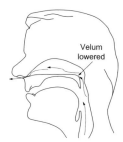

Figure 1.27b Nasal vowel
Figure 1.27 Nasal and oral vowel articulation

same regardless the duration of the vowel, as long as its quality remains [ɪ]. However, vowel length is contrastive in Thai: [pʰan] 'to wrap around', and [pʰaːn] 'pedestal'. [ː] indicates longer vowel duration (see Vowel Length Contrast in Chapter 3).

Oral and Nasal Vowels

Vowels are mostly produced with the velum in a raised position, forcing the airflow to exit only through the oral channel. A vowel produced in this manner is called an oral vowel (Figure 1.27a). A nasal vowel, on the other hand, is produced with the velum in a lowered position, allowing the airflow to divert and exit through the nose. French makes a distinction between oral and nasal vowels in the words [bo] *beau* 'beautiful' and [bõ] *bon* 'good'. English vowels are usually oral, but often become nasalized before a nasal consonant as in [kʰæ̃n] *can*, [bæ̃n] *ban*, and [tʰæ̃n] *tan*. Nasalization is indicated by [˜] (see also Chapter 8).

Tense and Lax Vowels

Vowels are not all produced with an equal amount of muscular tension. One may feel a greater facial and tongue-body tension in saying the [i] vowel in *beat* than the vowel [ɪ] in *bit*. Similarly, the vowel [u] in *boot* is produced

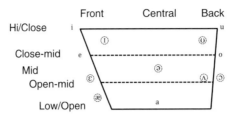

Figure 1.28 Tense and lax vowels

with a greater amount of muscular effort than the [ʊ] vowel in *book*. The first vowels in each of these two pairs of words are labeled tense vowels and the second vowels are lax vowels. However, notice that the difference in vocal tension is also accompanied by differences in duration and quality. Tense vowels are generally longer and higher in auditory quality than their lax counter parts.

In English, besides articulation differences, tense and lax vowels also differ in their distribution. Unlike tense vowels, lax vowels require that a consonant come after it, as in the words *bin*, *chin*, *book*, and *cook*. No such requirement is needed for a tense vowel, as seen in the words *bee*, *see*, *say*, *shoe*, *spa*, *law*, *go*, and *who*. In addition, lax vowels such as [ɪ, ɛ, ʊ] are preferred before a final consonant [ʃ] as in *fish*, *mesh*, and *push*. Tense and lax (circled) vowels in English are shown in Figure 1.28 (see Chapter 5 for further discussion). Diphthongs are not shown in the figure, but all diphthongs are considered tense.

Rhotacized, Rhotic, or r-Colored Vowels

The vowel [ɚ] in the American English words *bird*, *nurse*, and *purse* is made with a simultaneous tongue body bunching or tongue tip curling similar to those found during the [ɹ] 'r' consonant production. This rare type of vowel is known as a rhotacized, rhotic, or r-colored vowel. Many English vowels may be rhotacized before an 'r' as in *bored*, *beard*, and *bear*. Notice, however, that in these latter examples, there is a slight lag between the tongue gesture for the vowel and the 'r' gesture. For this reason, they may be transcribed as a sequence of vowel + 'r' [ɔɹ], [iɹ], and [eɹ] rather than a rhotacized [ɔ˞], [ɨ˞], and [e˞]. See further discussion on the effect of the 'r' sound on its preceding vowels in Chapter 4.

In sum, individual vowels are described in terms of tongue height, tongue backness, and lip position. They can also be further grouped into broad classes such as monophthong–diphthong, tense–lax, long–short, oral–nasals, and rhotic–non-rhotic.

In the next chapter, we discuss how different airstream mechanisms are initiated to produce different speech sounds, and the different ways in which the airstream can be modified at the larynx resulting in speech sounds with different phonation types.

Chapter Summary

- The three systems involved in speech production are the respiratory, phonation, and articulation systems.
- Consonants are produced with a more constricted vocal tract than vowels.
- Individual consonants are described based on the size and place of the constriction as well as the presence or absence of vocal vibration.
- Broad classes of consonants based on their manner of articulation are obstruents, sonorants, liquids, and glides.
- Consonants produced at different places of articulation may be grouped into three broader classes: coronal, dorsal, and guttural.
- Contour consonants are produced with a sequence of two articulations.
- Complex consonants are produced with a secondary articulation. Major types of secondary articulations are labialization, palatalization, velarization, and pharyngealization.
- Three dimensions used to describe individual vowels are tongue height, backness, and lip rounding.
- Vowels can be further grouped into broader classes: monophthong vs. diphthong, tense vs. lax, long vs. short, oral vs. nasal, and rhotic vs. non-rhotic vowels.
- Cardinal vowels are a set of language-independent vowels used as landmarks in the auditory space to which the vowels of the world's languages can be related.

Review Exercises

Exercise 1.1: In the following exercises, be careful to listen to the sounds of the words and not be confused by spellings. **Circle** the word(s) that. . .

    a. *begin* with a *bilabial* consonant: write mitt pit knit fit sit bit

    b. *begin* with a *velar* consonant: cot pot lot dot knot got

    c. *begin* with a *labio-dental* consonant: pet set fete bet met vet

    d. *begin* with an *alveolar* consonant: sip zip nip hip lip tip dip

    e. *begin* with an *alveolo-palatal (post-alveolar)* consonant: thigh sigh shy tie lie high

    f. *end* with a *fricative* consonant: face bush bring rave rough high breathe

    g. *end* with a *nasal* consonant: hinge main leaf rang dumb palm paint

    h. *end* with a *plosive* consonant: sip graph sock crag hide lit sigh

    i. *end* with a *velar* consonant: sing think bang sand rogue bark tough

j. *end* with a *labio-dental* consonant: rough bought dough enough rave taste shaft

Exercise 1.2: Below are some English words. **Circle** the words in which the consonant in the *middle* is *voiced* and **underline** the words in which the consonant in the *middle* is *voiceless*.

middle   seizure   fussy   leisure   baking   coughing
dodging   balloon   vision   bacon   casual   rolling

Exercise 1.3: When the sounds in the English words below are reversed, they make another word. What is the new word in each case, after reversing the sounds?

e.g., net [nɛt] = <u>ten</u> [tɛn]

a. tone _____
b. buck _____
c. mate _____
d. stop _____
e. stack _____
f. pan _____
g. pool _____
h. wrap _____
j. cap _____
k. peak _____

Exercise 1.4: For the following English words, **circle** the words for which the place of articulation of all the consonant sounds in the word is the same.
a. cake
b. took
c. mint
d. debt
e. set
f. palm
g. gang
h. five
i. bumper
j. cope

Exercise 1.5: In the following sets of English words, the sound of the vowel is the same in every case but one. Circle the word that has a different vowel sound.

a.   pen   said   death   mess   mean
b.   meat   steak   weak   theme   green

c.	sane	paid	eight	lace	mast
d.	ton	toast	both	note	toes
e.	hoot	good	moon	grew	suit
f.	dud	died	mine	eye	guy
g.	heat	peak	pie	seek	shield
h.	pack	rake	rat	fad	cat
i.	road	post	horse	phone	coast
j.	some	hum	musk	mood	rush

Exercise 1.6: What English words could result from changing the vowel of the following words?

   a. pan _____
   b. suck _____
   c. choose _____
   d. tell _____
   e. bought _____
   f. fool _____
   g. teeth _____
   h. come _____
   i. pop _____
   j. loose _____

References and Further Reading

Many examples provided in this chapter are drawn from Peter Ladefoged's books listed below and from the website www.phonetics.ucla.edu where audio files for some examples can be found. The website is also a rich source of examples for different types of sounds from the world's languages. *A Practical Introduction to Phonetics* by J. C. Catford is recommended for a more detailed discussion on similar topics covered.

Aoyama, K. (2003). Perception of syllable-initial and syllable-final nasals in English by Korean and Japanese speakers. *Second Language Research*, 19(3), 251–265.

Catford, J. C. (2001). *A Practical Introduction to Phonetics*, 2nd edn. Oxford: Oxford University Press.

Georg, S. (2007). *A Descriptive Grammar of Ket (Yenisei-Ostyak)*. Leiden: Brill.

Jarrah, A. S. I. (2013). English loan words spoken by Madinah Hijazi Arabic speakers. *Arab World English Journal*, AWEJ Special issue on Translation, 2, 67–85.

Ladefoged, P., & Disner, S. F. (2012). *Vowels and Consonants*, 3rd edn. Oxford: Wiley-Blackwell.

Ladefoged, P., & Johnson, K. (2014). *A Course in Phonetics*. Toronto: Nelson Education.

Ladefoged, P., & Maddieson, I. (1996). *The Sounds of the World's Languages*. Oxford: Blackwell.

Ladefoged, P., Cochran, A., & Disner, S. (1977). Laterals and trills. *Journal of the International Phonetic Association*, 7(2), 46–54.

Mufleh, J. (2013). Arabic fricative consonants. *International Journal of Humanities and Social Science*, 3(21), 220–224.

Olson, K. S., & Hajek, J. (1999). The phonetic status of the labial flap. *Journal of the International Phonetic Association*, 29(2), 101–114.

Stevens, K. N. (1977). Physics of laryngeal behavior and larynx modes. *Phonetica*, 34(4), 264–279.

Story, B. H. (2002). An overview of the physiology, physics and modeling of the sound source for vowels. *Acoustical Science and Technology*, 23(4), 195–206.

Titze, I. R. (1976). On the mechanics of vocal-fold vibration. *The Journal of the Acoustical Society of America*, 60(6), 1366–1380.

Titze, I. R. (1988). The physics of small-amplitude oscillation of the vocal folds. *The Journal of the Acoustical Society of America*, 83(4), 1536–1552.

van de Weijer, Jeroen. (2011). Secondary and double articulation. In Marc van Oostendorp, Colin J. Edwards, Elizabeth Hume, & Keren Rice (eds.), *The Blackwell Companion to Phonology*. Hoboken, NJ: John Wiley & Sons.

Van den Berg, J. (1958). Myoelastic-aerodynamic theory of voice production. *Journal of Speech, Language, and Hearing Research*, 1(3), 227–244.

Vance, Timothy J. (2008). *The Sounds of Japanese*. Cambridge: Cambridge University Press.

2

Airstream Mechanisms and Phonation Types

Learning Objectives

By the end of this chapter, you will be able to:

- Distinguish different airstream mechanisms used to produce consonants in the world's languages, namely:
  - Pulmonic airstream
  - Non-pulmonic airstreams
- Describe ways in which airflow is modified at the larynx (phonation types) to differentiate meaning in the world's languages, such as:
  - Voiceless
  - Voiced
  - Breathy
  - Creaky

Introduction

As mentioned in Chapter 1, there are a number of ways that air movement can be made audible to produce speech. It can be set into vibration, blocked then suddenly released, or forced through a narrow opening to produce friction. Vowels are typically made with vibrated and frictionless airflow pushed upward from the lungs (pulmonic airstream). Most consonants are also powered by lung air. In fact, all consonants in English are made with an upward and outward flow of air from the lungs. However, a different body of air may be set in motion to produce many consonant sounds found in the world's languages. In this chapter, airstream mechanisms, or the different ways in which air is moved to produce consonants, are described. The names of airstream mechanisms denote the location where the air movement is initiated and the direction of its movement during speech production.

Pulmonic Airstream

The most common airstream mechanism used to produce speech sounds in all of the world's languages is the **pulmonic egressive** mechanism (Figure 2.1) with air from the lungs being compressed and pushed upward out of the body. The speech sounds used to distinguish the meanings of words in English are produced exclusively by interrupting the outward flow of air from the lungs during exhalation. (Henceforth, a word's meaning refers to the referent, the concept, the action etc. denoted by the word.)

The pulmonic ingressive airstream mechanism is rarely employed in the world's languages as it is extremely difficult to produce speech sounds during inhalation (but see Fact box below).

Fact: Swedish 'Yes'

The Swedish word for 'yes' is produced by sucking the air inside the mouth with lip rounding and tongue position similar to English [ʃ] in *shoe*. This pulmonic ingressive airflow is also used by some other Scandinavian languages to produce short responses such as 'yes' and 'no'. An example from English is a gasping 'huh' to signal surprise or shock. This airstream mechanism is rarely used to produce a contrast in meaning.

Non-Pulmonic Airstreams

Besides the pulmonic airstream, two other types of airstreams are also used in the production of consonants in the world's languages. They are the *glottalic* and the *velaric* airstream mechanisms.

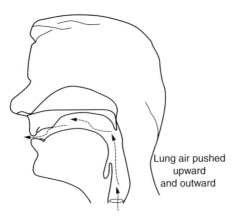

Lung air pushed
upward
and outward

Figure 2.1 Pulmonic egressive airstream mechanism with air from the lungs being compressed and pushed upward and outward

Glottalic Airstream

In the glottalic airstream mechanism, air movement is initiated above the glottis. To initiate air movement, the glottis is closed. The velum is also raised to seal off the nasal passage. Simultaneously, a closure is formed inside the vocal tract above the glottis. It is the air body trapped above the closed glottis and this oral closure that is moved to initiate the sound. Both **glottalic ingressive** and **glottalic egressive** airstreams are used in the world's languages.

For the *glottalic egressive airstream*, the larynx, with the glottis closed, is raised, causing the air pressure inside the vocal tract to increase. The raised larynx acts like an air piston, so that when the oral closure is released, a cork-like popping sound is distinctly audible. The consonants produced with this airstream mechanism are called **ejectives**. Figure 2.2 shows step-by-step how a bilabial ejective [p'] is made.

Ejectives are found in a few languages, including K'echi spoken in Guatemala, Lakhota, Navajo, Quechua (Ladefoged & Disner, 2012), and Montana Salish (http://phonetics.ucla.edu/appendix/languages/montana/montana.html). We include ejectives from Navajo in Table 2.1.

Table 2.1 *Navajo ejectives*

[**t'**ah]	'wait'
[**ts'**ah]	'sage brush'
[niʃ**tɬ'**aː]	'left'
[**tʃ'**ah]	'hat'
[**k'**aːʔ]	'arrow'

(http://phonetics.ucla.edu/course/
chapter11/navajo/navajo.html)

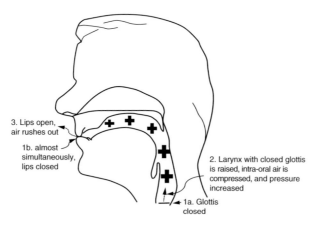

Figure 2.2 Glottalic egressive airstream mechanism for a bilabial ejective [p']

For the *glottalic ingressive airstream*, the larynx is lowered instead of raised, intra-oral air is rarefied, causing the pressure to decrease. Outside air rushes in, instead of out, upon the release of the oral closure. Consonants produced with this airstream mechanism are called **implosives**. However, most implosives found in the world's languages are voiced, suggesting that the vocal folds leak and are set into vibration by lung air during larynx lowering. Consequently, intra-oral air pressure decreases only slightly and a small influx of air rushes in after the oral closure release. Figure 2.3 shows the sequence of events during the production of a bilabial implosive [ɓ].

Sindhi has voiced bilabial, retroflex, palatal, and velar implosives as shown in Table 2.2.

On the other hand, (Owerri) Igbo, spoken in Southeastern Nigeria, has both voiced, voiced aspirated, and voiceless implosives as shown in Table 2.3. See 'In Focus' for preferences for implosives and ejectives among the world's languages.

Table 2.2 *Sindhi implosives*

[ɓani]	'field'
[ɗinu]	'festival'
[ʃatu]	'illiterate'
[ɠanu]	'handle'

(Ladefoged & Disner, 2012)

Table 2.3 *Implosives in (Owerri) Igbo*

Voiced	[íɓa]	'to dance'
Voiceless	[íɓ̥a]	'to gather'
Voiced aspirated	[íɓʱa]	'to peel'

(Ladefoged & Disner, 2012)

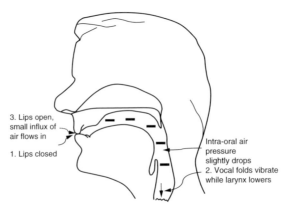

Figure 2.3 Glottalic ingressive airstream mechanism for a bilabial implosive [ɓ]

In Focus: Universal Preferences for Implosives and Ejectives

It was first noted by Haudricourt (1950) and later confirmed by Greenberg (1970) that implosives and ejectives exhibit the opposite tendencies for place of articulation among the world's languages. For implosives, the preferred order is labial, alveolar, and velar, whereas the opposite is true for ejectives, suggesting that compression is favored for back articulation while rarefaction is preferred for front articulation. However, phonetic explanation for these tendencies remains inconclusive (Javkin, 1977).

Velaric Airstream

Many languages in Africa have consonants referred to as **clicks**. Clicks are produced with air trapped between a closure at the velum (soft palate) and the roof of the mouth, and another anterior closure. Once the two closures are formed, the tongue body lowers, increasing the size of the cavity and thus lowering the air pressure. Air from outside rushes in when the anterior closure is opened, producing a distinctive click sound upon its release.

The *velaric ingressive* airstream mechanism just described generates basic click consonants, which are voiceless. However, clicks can be accompanied by voicing or nasality if, simultaneously with basic click production, lung air rises to vibrate the vocal folds and the velum lowers to let the air pass through the nasal cavity. Many African languages make a contrast between voiced and voiceless clicks, and oral versus nasalized clicks. A click sound is made among English speakers, but not as a speech sound. A tsk! tsk!, the sound of disapproval made by English speakers, is an example of a dental click. Figure 2.4 below shows step-by-step how a voiceless alveolar click [!] is made.

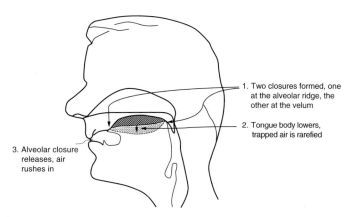

Figure 2.4 Velaric ingressive airstream mechanism for a voiceless alveolar click [!]

Table 2.4 *Zulu clicks*

	Dental	(post)alveolar	Alveolar lateral
Voiceless	[k∣áːgà]	[k!àːk!á]	[k∥áːgà]
Unaspirated	'to whitewash'	'to undo'	'put into a fix'
Voiceless	[k∣ʰàːgá]	[k!ʰàːk!ʰà]	[k∥ʰáːgà]
Aspirated	'to identify'	'to rip open'	'to link horses'
Voiced	[g∣òːɓá]	[g!òːɓá]	[g∥òːɓá]
	'to grease'	'to milk'	'to beat'
Nasalized	[ìsìːŋ∣é]	[ìsìːŋ!é]	[ìsìːŋ∥éːlè]
	'kind of spear'	'rump'	'left hand'

(http://phonetics.ucla.edu/course/chapter11/zulu/zulu.html)

Table 2.5 *Summary of airstream mechanisms*

Airstream mechanism	Air body used	Airflow direction	Consonants produced
Pulmonic egressive	Lung air	Up and outward	Plosives
Glottalic egressive	Air trapped above larynx and in the mouth	Outward	Ejectives
Glottalic ingressive	Air trapped above larynx and in the mouth	Inward	Implosives
Velaric ingressive	Air trapped between the velum and a front constriction	Inward	Clicks

Clicks are well known in languages spoken in Africa, particularly Zulu and Xhosa. Zulu has dental, (post)alveolar, and alveolar lateral clicks. They can be voiceless unaspirated, voiceless aspirated, voiced, or nasalized. Note that the [k], [g] and [ŋ] indicate that the clicks are voiceless, voiced, and nasalized, respectively. Zulu clicks are illustrated in Table 2.4.

To our knowledge, a *velaric egressive* airstream mechanism is not employed to produce speech sounds in any languages.

Table 2.5 summarizes the airstream mechanisms used to produce speech sounds. This includes the location of the body of air used to initiate the flow, flow direction, and the resultant consonants.

Phonation Types

Phonation refers to how the airflow passes through the vocal folds to produce sound. Modal phonation or regular voicing previously discussed (Chapter 1) is one form of this process. Note that the term voice quality is also used to refer to

Table 2.6 *Phonation types*

Phonation type	Position of the vocal folds	Vocal fold vibration	Airflow
Voiceless	Far apart	No	Non-turbulent (laminar) flow
(Modal) voice	Close together	Yes	
Breathy voice	Slightly apart	Yes	Turbulent, noisy flow at high rate
Creaky voice	Tightly together posteriorly, but loosely together anteriorly	Yes anteriorly, No posteriorly	

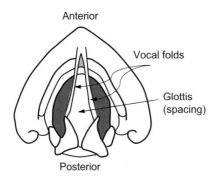

Figure 2.5 State of the glottis during voiceless phonation with the vocal folds far apart

phonation types, but it is often extended to include permanent, non-linguistic, individual voice characteristics such as nasality, raspiness, roughness, harshness, and whispery.

Phonation types are determined by several factors, including the position of the vocal folds, the size and shape of the glottis, the rate of airflow, and whether the vocal folds are vibrating. Major phonation types that affect word meaning in the world's languages are shown in Table 2.6.

Voiceless

Voiceless refers to the absence of vocal fold vibration. This phonation type is produced with the vocal folds far apart (Figure 2.5) to allow lung air to flow through the glottis without generating turbulence. Voiceless sounds are produced with the glottis opened to a similar size as that which occurs during normal breathing.

A lack of airflow through the glottis (thus an absence of vocal fold vibration) due to a complete adduction (closure) of the vocal folds also produces voiceless sounds. For example, a glottal stop [ʔ] is always voiceless because it is produced

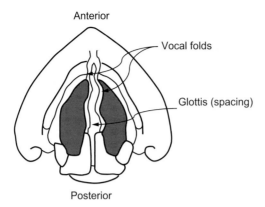

Figure 2.6 State of the glottis during modal voice phonation with the vocal folds set into vibration for most or all of their length

with a complete obstruction of airflow through the glottis (see also Chapter 1: Place of Articulation: Glottal).

(Modal) Voice

Modal voiced sounds are produced with normal phonation or voicing with the vocal folds vibrating along most or all of their entire length (Figure 2.6). The optimal combination of airflow and vocal fold tension produces maximum vibration during this phonation type (see Chapter 1 for stages of the vibratory cycle of modal voicing). Vowel sounds are mostly voiced except in some phonetic contexts, such as between two voiceless consonants. In Japanese, [i] and [ɯ] are voiceless between two voiceless consonants in [çi̥to] 'person' and [ɸɯ̥kɯ] 'clothes' but are otherwise voiced. [◌̥] denotes voiceless. In English, the first vowel in *potato* is usually voiceless. Voiced often contrasts with voiceless to change word meaning in most, if not all, of the world's languages.

Breathy Voice

Breathy voice, or murmur, is produced when the vocal folds are vibrating while remaining apart (Figure 2.7). Lung air becomes turbulent and noisy as it continuously flows through the glottis, giving the sound its husky quality. Breathy voice contrasts with modal voice in Gujarati spoken mainly in Gujarat state, India, as in [kan] 'ear' vs. [ka̤n] 'Krishna' (Ladefoged & Disner, 2012). [◌̤] symbolizes a breathy phonation. Breathiness is not used to contrast meaning in English.

Creaky Voice

Also known as creak, laryngealization, glottalization, or vocal fry, creaky voice is produced with the posterior portion of the vocal folds held tightly together

Anterior

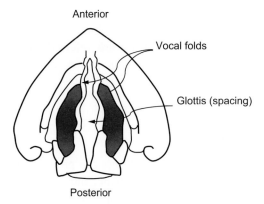

Vocal folds

Glottis (spacing)

Posterior

Figure 2.7 State of the glottis during breathy phonation with the vocal folds vibrating while being apart

Anterior

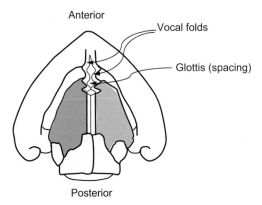

Vocal folds

Glottis (spacing)

Posterior

Figure 2.8 State of the glottis during creaky phonation with the vocal folds held tightly together along the posterior while the anterior is vibrating at a slow rate

while the anterior section is slack and vibrating at a very slow rate. Mazatec contrasts creaky and breathy voiced vowels as in [ndæ̰] 'buttocks' and [ndæ̤] 'horse' (http://phonetics.ucla.edu/vowels/chapter12/mazatec.html). Creaky voice is not employed by English to change word meaning.

Breathy and creaky voice may serve a non-linguistic (paralinguistic) function in English. An utterance produced with breathy voice may sound rather sensual, and at the time of this writing, creaky voice is used by young American adults, particularly women, to sound educated and upwardly 'mobile'. (See www .youtube.com/watch?v=w7BBNEwyOjw for an entertaining YouTube video on the phenomenon.)

In summary, different configurations of the vocal folds produce different phonation types as airflow passes through them. Common contrastive phonation types are voiced and voiceless. Consonants can be voiced or voiceless, but vowels are generally voiced and become voiceless in some contexts. Breathy and creaky voice represent a contrast in some languages, but not in English.

In Chapter 3, moving beyond vowel and consonant description, we discuss phonological patterns occurring at hierarchically larger linguistic units, namely syllables, words, phrases, and sentences. They are referred to as suprasegmentals or suprasegmental features, and include stress, length, tone, and intonation.

Chapter Summary

- Three major types of airstream mechanisms are used to produce the sounds of the world's languages: pulmonic, glottalic, and velaric.
- The pulmonic egressive airstream mechanism is the most common. Stop consonants produced with this airstream mechanism are called plosives.
- The glottalic egressive airstream mechanism produces ejectives, whereas the glottalic ingressive mechanism produces implosives.
- Ejectives are commonly voiceless while implosives are mostly voiced.
- Consonants known as clicks are produced with velaric ingressive airstream mechanisms.
- Because a click production only employs air trapped in front of the velum inside the mouth, it can be produced with different phonation types because lung air can be simultaneously pushed upward through the glottis. It can also be nasalized if lung air exits through the nasal cavity after passing through the glottis.
- The vocal folds can assume different configurations to modify air from the lungs as it passes through the glottis, resulting in different types of voicing or phonation.
- The four major phonation types employed by the world's languages are voiced, voiceless, breathy, and creaky.

Review Exercises

Exercise 2.1: Explain why it is possible or impossible to make the following sounds.
   a. A voiced uvular click
   b. A voiced velar ejective
   c. An alveolar ejective with a hum
   d. A velar click
   e. A voiceless bilabial implosive

Exercise 2.2: Describe briefly why each of the following airstream mechanisms will or will not be affected in a patient whose larynx was

surgically removed (assume that the air can still flow through
the trachea).
a. Pulmonic egressive
b. Velaric ingressive
c. Glottalic egressive
d. Glottalic ingressive

Exercise 2.3: Draw a diagram and describe the production of the ejective [t']. Make sure to label the sequence of events. What are the differences (name two) between the articulation of this sound and the implosive [ɓ]?

Exercise 2.4: What is the Bernoulli effect and why is it important in speech production?

Exercise 2.5: Explain why and how each of the following phonation types will or will not be affected in a patient whose vocal folds cannot be closed.
a. Voiceless
b. (modal) Voice
c. Breathy voice
d. Creaky voice

Exercise 2.6: Place the four phonation types listed in Table 2.6 on a continuum based on the size of the glottal aperture from the most opened to the most closed

Most opened ◄——————————————————————► Most closed

References and Further Reading

Airstream mechanisms and phonation types with actual pictures of the states of the glottis for all four phonations are discussed in Peter's Ladefoged's *A Course in Phonetics*. Some sound files of examples included in the chapter are available at www.phonetics.ucla.edu. Gordon and Ladefoged's article listed in the references is recommended for a survey of cross-linguistic use of phonation type.

Gordon, M., & Ladefoged, P. (2001). Phonation type: A cross-linguistic overview. *Journal of Phonetics*, 29, 383–406.

Greenberg, J. H. (1970). Some generalizations concerning glottalic consonants, especially implosives. *International Journal of American Linguistics*, 36(2), 123–145.

Haudricourt, A. G. (1950). *Les consonnes préglottalisées en Indochine*. Paris: C. Klincksieck.

Javkin, H. (1977, September). Towards a phonetic explanation for universal preferences in implosives and ejectives. In *Annual Meeting of the Berkeley Linguistics Society* (Vol. 3, pp. 559–565).

Ladefoged, P. (2004). *A Course in Phonetics*, 5th edn. Independence, KY: Thomson Wadsworth.

Ladefoged, P., & Disner, S. F. (2012). *Vowels and Consonants*, 3rd edn. Oxford: Wiley-Blackwell.

Laver, J. (2001). *The Phonetic Description of Voice Quality*. Cambridge: Cambridge University Press.

Roy, N., Merrill, R. M., Gray, S. D., & Smith, E. M. (2005). Voice disorders in the general population: Prevalence, risk factors, and occupational impact. *The Laryngoscope*, 115(11), 1988–1995.

Roy, N., Merrill, R. M., Thibeault, S., Parsa, R. A., Gray, S. D., & Smith, E. M. (2004). Prevalence of voice disorders in teachers and the general population. *Journal of Speech, Language, and Hearing Research*, 47(2), 281–293.

3   Suprasegmentals

Introduction

Thus far, we have focused on the phonetic description of segments, namely vowels and consonants. However, in speaking, we don't just simply string vowels and consonants together. Instead, these speech segments are hierarchically organized into larger linguistic units such as syllables, words, phrases, and sentences to communicate meaning. Phonological patterns described in these larger linguistic units are known as suprasegmentals and include **stress** (syllable prominence), **length** (duration), **tone** (pitch level or contour on a syllable), and **intonation** (pitch movement in a sentence). Importantly, suprasegmental features are relative. They are defined in relation to other items in the utterance. For example, a syllable is considered stressed because it is acoustically and perceptually more salient in comparison to other syllables in the same word. In English, the second syllable in *to exPORT* is stressed. It is produced with a higher pitch, a longer duration, and a greater acoustic intensity (perceived as loudness) than the first syllable, and most of these perceptual cues are implemented on the vowel.

In languages with contrastive vowel or consonant length, the same syllable produced with relatively longer or shorter vowel or consonant duration has different meaning.

In tone languages such as Mandarin Chinese, the same syllable [ma] produced with different pitch height or pitch contour will have different lexical referents or meanings: with a high-level pitch, it means 'mother', but with a high-rising pitch, it means 'hemp'. Finally, pitch movements in a sentence in English let the listener know whether the utterance is a question or a statement. For example, upon hearing *Are you coming?* produced with a rising pitch, the listener knows that a yes–no response is required, whereas *I have been there*, produced with a falling pitch will be taken as a statement and an answer is not necessary.

Because they affect the prosody (Greek *prosoidia*) or the melody of an utterance, suprasegmental features, particularly intonation, are also called prosodic features. We will begin our discussion with an introduction of the syllable since it is the linguistic domain of most suprasegmentals, including stress and rhythm, length, and tone.

Syllable

A syllable is the smallest possible unit of speech. Every utterance contains at least one syllable. It consists minimally of a **nucleus** and an optional **onset** (consonants preceding the nucleus) and a **coda** (consonants following the vowel). The nucleus and the coda together form the **rime** of the syllable. Syllable structures for the English words *eye* (VV) and *pick* (CVC), where V represents a vowel and C a consonant, are shown in (1).

1.   Syllable structures for the English words *eye* (VV) and *pick* (CVC)

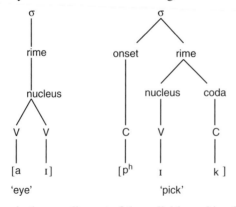

The nucleus is the vocalic part of the syllable and is often occupied by a vowel or sometimes a syllabic consonant (typically a sonorant), as in [bʌ.ʔn̩] *button*, where the syllabic [n̩] occupies the nucleus position of the second syllable (see In Focus for syllabic consonants in Berber, and Chapter 4 for more examples of syllabic consonants in English). [.] represents a syllable break.

2.   Syllabic consonant nucleus in the English word *button* [bʌʔn̩]

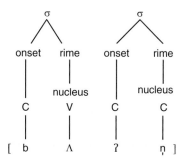

In Focus: Syllabic Consonants

It's more common among the world's language to allow sonorant consonants (e.g., nasals, liquids, and glides) to occupy the nucleus position of the syllable when a vowel is not available. Interestingly, however, obstruents may also serve as syllable nuclei in Tashlhiyt, a dialect of Berber spoken in Morocco (Dell & Elmedlaoui, 1988; Ridouane, 2008), but see Coleman (1999) for an alternative account.

Syllabic obstruents in Tashlhiyt Berber

[tftktstt]   'you sprained it (feminine)'
[utχk]   'I struck you'
[r̩ks̩x]   'I hid'

The acceptable number and type of consonants that can occur at the onset and coda vary from language to language. For example, while Greek allows [ps] in syllable-onset position, English does not. Similarly, while English allows the sequence [ld] in coda position, Thai does not. A syllable with a coda is called a **closed** syllable and a syllable without a coda is called an **open** syllable.

Syllable Weight

A syllable can also be heavy or light depending on the number and type of segments it contains, and languages vary in how syllable weight is computed. As a general trend, languages treat a syllable as light if its rime contains only a vowel with or without an onset consonant (C_0V); (C_0) represents none to any number of consonants. On the other hand, heavy syllables generally contain a long vowel (C_0VV) and/or a coda consonant (C_0VC, C_0VVC).

3.   Diagrams of heavy and light syllables

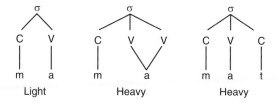

Some languages, including Huasteco, treat syllables closed with a consonant (C_0VC) as light, while only those with a long vowel are considered heavy (C_0VV) (Blevins, 1995).

In English, a syllable containing a tense vowel (C_0VV), a diphthong (C_0VV), or a lax vowel and more than one coda consonant (C_0VCC) is heavy, while a syllable with a lax vowel and no coda consonant (C_0V) is considered light. Interestingly, a syllable with a lax vowel and one coda consonant (C_0VC) may be treated as a heavy syllable in stress assignment rules on polysyllabic nouns, but as a light syllable in adjective and verb assignment rules (see English Stress below). Examples of English syllables are shown in (4).

4.   Some English syllable structures

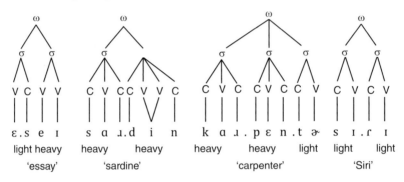

The existence and importance of a syllable unit is evident in writing. In Japanese writing systems (Katakana), for example, there is a symbol for each syllable. Children can also easily be taught to identify syllables in their native tongue. Moreover, native speakers often agree on the number of syllables counted in a word. When a disagreement occurs, it may be attributed to dialectal differences (i.e., American vs. British English) in the way certain words are produced. For example, *history* may be produced with two syllables in American English, but some British English speakers produce the word with three syllables.

Despite evidence of its existence, the syllable remains difficult to define, on both phonetic and phonological grounds. The notion of a chest pulse as an articulatory phonetic correlate of a syllable has been proposed. It was hypothesized that each syllable corresponds to a chest pulse or a contraction of the muscles of the rib cage that pushes air out of the lungs. However, a careful investigation of these groups of muscles revealed that this is not always the case.

Phonological definitions of a syllable have often been circular: A syllable consists of a nucleus and a number of preceding and following consonants. But the nucleus of a syllable cannot be identified before the syllable itself. Thus, a syllable nucleus has to be identified on some other basis.

Sonority

One proposal is to use the sonority of a segment as the locator of a syllable nucleus. Physical correlates of sonority include acoustic intensity, intra-oral air pressure, total amount of airflow, and duration. Being produced with a more open vocal tract, vowels generally have greater sonority, and are louder than consonants. Thus, vowels are more likely to occupy the nucleus position of a syllable. Among vowels, low vowels are more sonorous than high vowels. Among consonants, approximants and nasals are more sonorous than oral stops and fricatives. The full sonority scale is shown in (5) below (see Fact box on sonority plateau).

5.   Sonority scale

Most sonorous ↑ Low vowels

Mid vowels

High vowels and glides

Flaps

Laterals

Nasals

Voiced fricatives

Voiceless fricatives

Voiced affricates

Voiceless affricates

Voiced stops

Least sonorous | Voiceless stops

Fact: Sonority Plateau

A sonority plateau occurs when two adjacent sounds have similar sonority, resulting in a plateau rather than a clear sonority peak or valley, and it is one of the explanations for why native speakers disagree on the number of syllables in a word. For example, due to a lack of a clear sonority valley between the vowel and the following [ɹ], *hire*, *fire*, *hour*, and *our* may be considered one-syllable words by some, but as two-syllable words by others, even when their pronunciations are exactly the same.

As already mentioned, besides vowels, sonorant consonants such as nasals, liquids, and glides may also serve as a syllable nucleus in English. Thus, one possible definition of a syllable is that peaks of syllabicity or nucleus coincide with peaks of sonority. This would help explain why the number of syllables often coincides with the number of vowels (or syllabic consonants) and why people agree on the number of syllables in the majority of words. For example, in *pocket* and *compensate*, there are clearly sonority peaks corresponding to each vowel: two for *pocket* and three for *compensate*. This is illustrated in (6).

6.   Sonority profiles of *pocket* and *compensate*

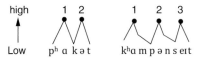

A sonority-based theory of syllables cannot, however, explain why a single-syllable word such as *speak* has two sonority peaks; one for [s] and the other for [i] as shown in (7) below.

7.   Sonority profile of *speak*

In summary, a syllable is the smallest possible unit of speech. It is difficult to define, particularly on phonetic grounds, but its importance in linguistic discussion, particularly for suprasegmentals (discussed in more detail in the following sections) is undeniable. Structurally, it has to have a nucleus. It may also contain an onset and a coda. The acceptable type and number of segments that can occur at onset and coda positions vary from language to language.

Stress

Stress refers to increased prominence placed on a certain syllable in a word, or on a certain word in a phrase or a sentence. Stress placed on a given syllable in a word is called lexical or word stress, whereas emphasis placed on a word in a larger linguistic unit such as a phrase or a sentence is referred to as sentence or prosodic stress. Let's look at stress at the word level first.

Word-Level Stress

Word-level stress refers to the phonological patterning of prominence among syllables in multisyllabic words. Even though phonetic cues used to signal syllable prominence are realized on a segment within the syllable (typically the vowel), the pattern itself is described at the syllable level: a stressed vs. an unstressed syllable.

In a given word, the syllable that receives stress is perceptually more prominent or salient than other syllables, and is phonetically associated with increased duration, greater amount of acoustic intensity (perceived as loudness), higher or lower rate of vocal fold vibration (fundamental frequency, perceived as pitch), higher degree of precision of segmental articulation, particularly that of vowels, and greater acoustic energy in the high-frequency relative to low-frequency region (spectral tilt). Various combinations and degrees of these acoustic markers are used by the world's languages to indicate stress. In English, a stressed syllable is longer, higher in pitch, and contains a fully realized vowel quality, while an unstressed syllable is produced with a centralized (schwa-like) vowel quality with shorter duration, and a lesser degree of intensity. However, vowel reduction is not a marker of stress in languages like Spanish. In addition, a lower, rather than a higher, fundamental frequency cues syllable prominence in languages like Bengali, Hindi, Oriya, Assamese, and Indian English (Hayes & Lahiri, 1991; Mahanta, 2009; Verma, 2005; Pickering & Wiltshire, 2000; Wiltshire & Moon, 2003).

Although relatively rare, stress can be contrastive. For example, a few noun–verb pairs in English differ only in their stress pattern: *a **permit**, to **permit***; *an **object**, to **object***, etc. Stress patterns also differentiate the compound noun *a **hot**dog* from the phrase *a hot **dog***; *a **green**house* from *a green **house**; a **light**house* from *a light **house***, etc. in English. Other English word pairs such as *trustee–trusty* and ***bellow–below*** also differ only in stress.

In Russian, ***muka*** with stress on the first syllable means 'torture', but *mu**ka*** with stress on the second syllable means 'flour'. In Dutch, ***voor**komen* means 'to occur' but *voor**komen*** means to 'prevent'; *bedelen* means 'to give someone his or her part', but *be**delen*** means 'to beg'. In German, ***um**fahren* means 'to drive over someone', whereas *um**fahren*** means 'to drive around something'. In Italian, ***prin**cipi* means 'princes', whereas *prin**cipi*** means 'principles'. Finally, in Mandarin Chinese, ***dong*** *xi* means 'East–West' but *dong **xi*** means 'thing, stuff'.

Most languages have stress. However, Japanese is considered a stressless language because it lacks a stress system such as that described for English and other languages. In Japanese, a syllable is made prominent or accented not by a combination of pitch, loudness, and duration cues like the ones used to signal stress, but only by a sharp drop in pitch from a relatively high (H) to a relatively low pitch (L) between syllables. The location in the word where this pitch drop occurs has to be memorized and is contrastive for limited pairs or sets of Japanese words. For example, in ***ha**shi* (HL) 'chopsticks', the first syllable *ha*, marked with a high tone (H), is accented because the pitch falls after it, whereas the second syllable *shi* is accented in *ha**shi*** (LH) 'bridge' as in *hashiga* (LHL) because the pitch drops on the subject marker 'ga'. On the other hand, *hashi* (LH) 'edge' is considered accentless because the pitch stays high after the second syllable as in *hashiga* (LHH). For this reason, Japanese is called a pitch-accent language and English, in contrast, may be called a stress language (see Pitch Accent below for further discussion).

Stress patterns vary from language to language. In some languages, stress is always fixed on a certain syllable in a word. In Czech, Georgian, and Finnish, for example, stress is usually placed on the first syllable regardless of how many syllables there are in the word. In French, the last syllable is usually stressed, but Polish and Swahili prefer stress on the penultimate (one before last) syllable.

Unlike these languages, stress placement in English is not always predictable, and must be learned. For instance, there is no rule to explain why stress falls on the first syllable in ***buf**falo* (Spanish or Portuguese *búfalo*; Latin *bufalus*) but on the second syllable in *buf**foon*** (French *buffon*; Latin *buffo*).

While the word's historical origin may play a role, learners often don't have access to this knowledge (Zsiga, 2013). The term **lexical** or **free stress** is used when a stress pattern is unpredictable and must be memorized. On the other hand, the term **parametric stress** is used when a stress pattern is predictable by rules.

English Stress

The English stress system is mostly parametric, a complicated one with rules and sub-rules. Only a few will be discussed here. By default, monosyllables are always stressed. For disyllables, as seen earlier, nouns prefer first syllable primary stress, whereas verbs prefer final syllable primary stress. More examples are given in (8).

8.　　　Stress on English disyllabic noun–verb pairs

Noun	Verb
object	ob**ject**
permit	per**mit**
conduct	con**duct**
record	re**cord**
insult	in**sult**
consult	con**sult**
present	pre**sent**

Syllable weight plays a crucial role in English primary-stress assignment. For polysyllabic nouns, the weight of the syllable before last (penultimate) is the deciding factor (Zsiga, 2013). If the penultimate syllable is heavy because it contains a long vowel (9a) or a coda consonant (9b), it is stressed. If it is light, then the stress skips to the second before the last syllable or the antepenult, as in (9c). In other words, primary-stress assignment on multisyllabic nouns follows the following steps:

    a.　Scan the noun from the end, but ignore the last syllable.
    b.　Stress the penult if it is heavy. That is, if it contains a tense vowel or a diphthong (9a), or a lax vowel and a final consonant (9b).
    c.　If the penult is light, stress the antepenult (9c).

9.　　　English stress on polysyllabic nouns

a	b	c
ulti**ma**tum	ex**pan**sion	**sy**llable
di**plo**ma	ad**dic**tion	**ca**mera
pa**pa**ya	a**gen**da	**co**conut
i**llu**sion	re**luc**tance	**in**finity
co**he**sion	e**nact**ment	**sa**nity

Some exceptions are con**sent**, **event**, pa**rade**, ter**rain**, cha**rade**, **cha**racter, **anec**-dote, etc. See if you can come up with more exceptions.

For disyllabic verbs and adjectives, the weight of the last or ultimate syllable determines stress location (Zsiga, 2013). If it is heavy (i.e., containing a tense vowel which is considered long) (10d, 11d), or a vowel plus two or more coda consonants) (10e, 11e), then it is stressed as shown. However, if it contains a lax vowel and only one coda consonant (10f, 11f), the stress moves to the penultimate syllable.

That is, primary stress on disyllabic verbs and adjectives is determined by the following:

1. Scan the verb or the adjective from the end including the last syllable.
2. If the last syllable is heavy, stress it (10, 11 d, e).
3. If the last syllable is light, stress the penult (10, 11 f).

10.   English disyllabic verb stress

d	e	f
de**lay**	se**lect**	**re**lish
por**tray**	pre**serve**	**can**cel
re**ply**	re**venge**	**ed**it
sup**pose**	re**pent**	**vis**it
de**ceive**	de**fend**	**sen**tence
re**veal**	ex**pand**	**lim**it
pe**ruse**	re**solve**	**pub**lish

11.   English disyllabic adjective stress

d	e	f
pre**cise**	o**vert**	**hand**ful
an**tique**	ab**rupt**	**pre**cious
re**mote**	a**dept**	**hand**some
pre**mier**	su**perb**	**fran**tic
ex**treme**	cor**rect**	**cle**ver
mi**nute**	oc**cult**	**rig**id
se**cure**	ab**rupt**	**neu**tral

For polysyllabic verbs with three or more syllables, if the final syllable is heavy, then stress is placed on the antepenultimate syllable as in (12) (Zsiga, 2013).

12.   English polysyllabic verbs with antepenultimate stress

concentrate	re**pu**diate
fumigate	so**lid**ify
in**ti**midate	**em**phasize

infuriate   **im**plement
mo**no**polize   **gra**duate
constitute   **im**plement

Degrees of Stress

Stress is a system of relative prominence with possible multiple perceived degrees. Consider the word *psychology*. The second syllable is the most prominent. The first syllable contains a diphthong, but not as long and loud as the second syllable, whereas the last two syllables are short and soft. We can say, then, that the second syllable carries the word's primary stress, the first syllable has secondary stress and the last two syllables are unstressed. The IPA provides diacritics for primary stress [ˈ] and secondary stress [ˌ], while an unstressed syllable is unmarked. The question of how many levels of stress are linguistically relevant remains a subject of debate, and up to four levels of stress have been proposed for English. However, everyone agrees that there is one main stress on every English word.

Foot

Besides the syllable, the foot is another linguistic unit relevant to a discussion of stress patterns. A foot is a higher-order linguistic unit containing a stressed syllable and any number of unstressed syllables. Two types of foot structure, namely trochaic (13a) and iambic (13b), are particularly useful in the description of stress patterns in English.

A trochaic foot consists of a stressed or a strong syllable followed by an unstressed or a weak syllable, while an iambic foot comprises an unstressed syllable followed by a stressed syllable. For example, *termination* [ˌtʰɚ.mɪ.ˈneɪ.ʃn̩] contains two trochaic feet ***termi*** [ˌtʰɚ.mɪ] and ***nation*** [ˈneɪ.ʃn̩], with stressed syllables ***ter*** [tʰɚ] and ***na*** [neɪ] alternating with unstressed syllables *mi* [mɪ] and *tion* [ʃn̩]. On the other hand, *monopolize* [mə.ˈnɑ.pə.laɪz] contains two iambic feet ***mono*** [mə.ˈnɑ] and ***polize*** [pə.laɪz], with unstressed syllables *mo* [mə] and *po* [pə] followed by stressed syllables ***no*** [ˈnɑ] and ***lize*** [laɪz] (13).

13.   Foot structure at word level

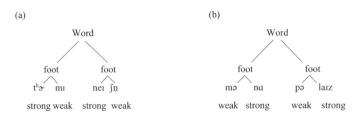

Rhythm

Alternation of strong and weak syllables or foot structure creates different rhythms at the sentence level, and forms the basis for different linguistic rhythmic types. For example, *Mary's eating peanuts* consists of three trochaic feet: *Mary's*, *eating* and *peanuts*. On the other hand, *The burglar ran away* could illustrate three iambic feet: *the bur*, *glar ran*, and *away*. This is shown in (14).

14.   Foot structure at sentence level

Mary's eating peanuts.   The bur glar ran away.

Stress-Timed

English, German, and other Germanic languages are called **stress-timed languages**. It is claimed that the intervals between stressed syllables are equal in duration (isochrony). In other words, each foot is equal in length in stress-timed languages. In the examples above, the time interval between the stressed syllable *Ma* in *Mary's* and *eat* is purported to be the same as the one from *eat* to *pea*. Similarly, the temporal distance between *bur* and *ran* is the same as from *ran* to *way*.

Syllable-Timed

In contrast to stress-timed languages, syllables, both stressed and unstressed, occur at regular time intervals in **syllable-timed languages** such as Spanish and French. In other words, stressed and unstressed syllables are of equal duration, and it is the isochrony of the syllables that determines rhythm in these languages. As mentioned earlier, vowel quality is not reduced in unstressed syllables in Spanish. Thus, the difference in duration between stressed and unstressed syllables in this language is reduced and may contribute to the perception of regular intervals.

However, empirical support is not found for isochrony of either inter-stress intervals or syllables in stress-timed and syllable-timed languages. In stress-timed languages, inter-stress intervals are found to vary depending on the number of intervening unstressed syllables, the phonetic content of these syllables, and, more importantly, the speaker's intention. Speakers may vary the rhythm of an utterance to maximally transmit his or her message without adhering to the equal spacing of the stressed syllable rule. Similarly, in syllable-timed languages like French and Spanish, syllable duration is not found to be constant.

Mora-Timed

Another type of rhythm has been proposed for languages like Japanese. These are called **mora-timed languages**. A mora (μ) is a temporal unit. Although the difference between a mora and a syllable is not always straightforward, syllables with long vowels or long consonants are said to have more morae than syllables with a short vowel. For example, *hashi* [ha.ʃi] 'edge' contains two syllables and two morae, but [too.kyoo] 'Tokyo' contains two syllables but four morae [to.o. kyo.o] as illustrated in (15).

15.   Moraic structure of Japanese words

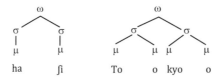

Words with four morae are supposedly twice as long as words with two morae. Thus, the total duration of an utterance in Japanese depends on the number of morae it contains, and mora isochrony (equal duration of morae) determines linguistic rhythm in Japanese. There is evidence in support of the mora as a structural and psychological unit important to the description of Japanese word structure and rhythm. However, more recent research suggests that the mora may not be a direct temporal unit in Japanese. The duration of morae varies and word duration correlates strongly with syllable structure, but only weakly with the number of morae. The number of segments a word contains also predicts word duration.

In sum, three classes of linguistic rhythm or timing have been proposed: stressed-timed, syllable-timed, and mora-timed. The notion of isochrony plays an important role in the search for empirical evidence for rhythmic grouping. It has been hypothesized that stress-timed languages should have inter-stress intervals of roughly constant duration, whereas syllable-timed and mora-timed languages should have syllables and morae of constant duration, respectively. However, empirical evidence has lent little support to this hypothesis.

Motivated by the observations that stress-timed languages allow vowel reduction in unstressed syllables and more complex syllables with a longer string of consonants than syllable-timed languages, more current and popular approaches to the rhythmic classification of languages are based on the duration taken up by vowels and consonants in a sentence. This approach shows that languages are clustered in groups that resemble rhythm classes, with English, Dutch, and Polish as stress-timed languages, French, Spanish, Italian, and Catalan as syllable-timed languages, and Japanese as a mora-timed language. However, this result merely suggests rhythmic similarities and differences across these languages, and not necessarily a full-fledged, empirically based rhythmic typology. It is likely that with more languages analyzed, what emerges will be a rhythmic continuum rather than distinct rhythmic classes.

Sentence-Level Stress

Certain syllables in a word that already carry word stress may receive additional stress because of the word's function in the sentence. For example, in the sentence *My father baked me cookies*, the syllable *fa* in *father* receives additional stress besides the word stress it is already carrying to signal that it is the topic of the sentence. The added prominence placed on a syllable by either a high or a low pitch configuration to make it more prominent than others in a phrase or a sentence is known as a **pitch accent** (not to be confused with pitch accent in Japanese discussed below).

In English and other stress-timed languages, only stressed syllables may be accented. In other words, only syllables that already carry word-level stress are promoted to pitch-accent status at a phrasal or sentence level. In the utterance, *My father baked me cookies*, seen above, a high pitch accent placed on *fa* brings a narrow focus to *father* and invokes contrastive interpretation (i.e., not my mother) in the discourse. A high pitch accent is represented by H*, where H stands for high tone and * indicates alignment with the stressed syllable. L% represents the falling pitch at the end of the phrase.

16.   High pitch accent
                   H*   L%
         My **fa**ther baked me cookies.

Contrastive focus can also be conveyed by a low pitch accent. For example, in the utterance ***Mary cooked dinner?*** a low pitch accent is placed on the first syllable in *Mary* to convey a contrastive interpretation (i.e., I thought it was Susan's turn). L* denotes low tone aligned with the stressed syllable and H% represents a high tone at the end of the phrase to indicate a question.

17.   Low-pitch accent
         L*   H%
         Mary cooked dinner?

In a non-contrastive reading of an English declarative sentence, the pitch accent typically falls on the last word of the phrase. For example,

18.   Default pitch accent on the final content word of a phrase.
                          H* L%
         My father baked me **coo**kies.

By default, this utterance could be the answer to a general question *what happened?* with *broad focus* on the whole utterance. It can also indicate a narrow focus on *cookies* as in an answer to the question *What did your father bake you?* However, if the pitch accent shifts to a different word, then only a narrow focus reading is possible, as in (19).

19.   Non-final pitch accent indicates narrow contrastive focus.
                     H*   L%
         My father baked **me** cookies.

The pitch accent on *me* is used here to indicate that it was *me* for whom *my father* baked the cookies this time instead of *my younger sister* for whom he usually baked them.

If the pitch accent moves to *baked* as in (20), then the contrastive narrow-focus interpretation is that my father didn't 'buy' the cookies (as he usually does) this time.

20.   H*   L%
        My father **baked** me cookies.

More than one word in an utterance can be accented. The utterance represented in (21) below contains three salient words: *father*, *Bangkok*, and *business*, each associated with a pitch accent. The most accented syllable is said to carry the **nuclear pitch** accent, a special type of pitch accent rendering an accented syllable the most prominent among accented syllables.

21.   H*   H*   H* L%
        My **fa**ther   went to **Bang**kok   for **BUS**iness
             pre-nuclear   pre-nuclear accent   nuclear accent
             accent

In this sentence, the first syllable in ***BUS**iness* is the most accented syllable (also known as the **tonic syllable**) and bears the sentence's nuclear pitch accent. The other two accented syllables, the first syllables in ***fa**ther* and ***Bang**kok*, are said to carry pre-nuclear accents. The word with a pitch accent (in an utterance with only one salient word) or a nuclear accent (in an utterance with multiple salient words) is normally taken to be the stressed word of the sentence.

In summary, word-level prominence is called lexical stress. A stressed syllable in a word may be longer in duration, have higher or lower pitch, have fuller vowel quality, and have greater high-frequency relative to low-frequency energy than an unstressed syllable. The acoustic correlates of stress vary from language to language depending in part on their other roles in the language.

Alternation of stressed and unstressed syllables creates prominent peaks or beats, giving rise to a perception of linguistic rhythm. Three rhythmic classes have been proposed: stress-timed, syllable-timed, and mora-timed.

Sentence-level prominence is signaled by a pitch accent, a high or a low pitch configuration placed on a syllable of a word in the sentence to increase its salience. Any number of pitch accents may occur in an utterance. In stress-timed languages, only stressed syllables may be accented. So-called sentence stress refers to the syllable that carries a nuclear pitch accent. In English, the default location of the nuclear pitch accent is the stressed syllable of the last content word, but it can be shifted to other syllables to satisfy the speaker's desire to highlight certain information to the hearer.

Length

In many languages, vowel and consonant duration may vary without incurring any change in meaning. However, when languages manipulate the duration of a vowel or a consonant to change a word's referent, then those languages possess **contrastive length**.

Vowel Length Contrast

In languages such as Thai and Danish, a word's lexical referent changes with the relative duration of a syllable's vowel. In Thai, the same syllable means 'to share' when produced with a short vowel, but 'a birthmark' when the vowel is long. More examples are shown in Table 3.1 for Thai and Table 3.2 for Danish. Other languages with contrastive vowel length include Japanese, Ewe, and Finnish.

Consonant Length Contrast

In comparison to vowel length contrast, consonant length contrasts are relatively rare. A few languages with a phonemic consonant length contrast include Italian, Japanese, and Finnish. Examples of contrastive pairs from Italian, Japanese, and Finnish are given in Tables 3.3, 3.4, and 3.5.

Table 3.1 *Thai vowel length contrast*

Short vowels		Long vowels	
[pan]	'to share'	[paːn]	'equal to, a birthmark'
[pʰan]	'to wrap around'	[pʰaːn]	'a pedestal'
[kan]	'to protect, mutually'	[kaːn]	'business'

Table 3.2 *Danish vowel length contrast*

Short vowels		Long vowels	
[vilə]	'wild'	[viːlə]	'rest'
[menə]	'rewind'	[meːnə]	'mean'
[lɛse]	'mean'	[lɛːse]	'read'

(http://phonetics.ucla.edu/course/chapter9/danish/danish.html)

Table 3.3 *Italian consonant length contrast*

Short consonant		Long consonant	
[fato]	'fate'	[fatːo]	'done'
[nono]	'nine'	[nonːo]	'grandfather'

Table 3.4 *Japanese consonant length contrast*

Short consonant		Long consonant	
[kako]	'past'	[kakːo]	'bracket'
[saki]	'edge'	[sakːi]	'a little while ago'
[bagu]	'bug'	[bagːu]	'bag'

Table 3.5 *Finnish consonant length contrast*

Short consonant		Long consonant	
[tuli]	'fire'	[tulːi]	'customs'
[kisa]	'competition'	[kisːa]	'cat'
[muta]	'mud'	[mutːa]	'but'

Long consonants are also called **geminates**. Geminate plosives are common. Articulatorily speaking, they are produced with longer closure duration and can be two or three times longer than the single consonant. Consonant length is not contrastive in English. However, duration of English plosives may vary. For example, closure duration and the amount of aspiration of plosive stops may be longer in stressed and pitch-accented syllables.

Tone

Every language uses pitch to convey meaning. In our discussion on stress, we learned that pitch is used to signal prominence, both at the word and the sentence levels. What is pitch? Pitch is an auditory impression of the rate of vocal fold vibration. The faster the vocal folds vibrate, the higher the perceived pitch. The tension of the vocal folds, amount of airflow from the lungs, tongue height, and larynx height are important factors affecting the rate of vocal fold vibration. A higher degree of vocal fold tension, greater volume of airflow from the lung, and higher tongue and larynx height lead to a higher rate of vocal fold vibration, and thus higher perceived pitch.

Lexical Tones

More than two-thirds of the world's languages alter the pitch height or pitch shape of a syllable to change its meaning. They are called **tone languages**. They are divided into two types, register and contour tone languages. In **register tone languages**, the pitch level remains relatively stable throughout the syllable, and the relative pitch height of each syllable within a speaker's pitch range (register) is used to differentiate word meaning. In **contour tone languages**, the pitch shape changes over the syllable and it is pitch movement rather than pitch level that distinguishes word meaning.

Tone languages are found mainly in Africa, East and Southeast Asia, the Pacific, and the Americas. African tone languages are characterized by having fewer contrastive tones than those spoken in East and Southeast Asia. In addition, African tone languages are mainly register tone languages, whereas languages spoken in East and Southeast Asia are contour tone languages.

The simplest tone language has only two possible tones. The Bantu languages such as Ibibio, Shona, Zulu, or Luganda contrast word meaning using either a

Table 3.6 *Ibibio's two tones on monosyllables*

Word	Tone	English Gloss
[má]	H	'like'
[mà]	L	'complete'

Table 3.7 *Shona tone pattern on disyllables*

Word	Tone	English Gloss
[ndèrè]	LL	'day flying chafer'
[ndèré]	LH	'cleanly person'
[ndéré]	HH	'self-willed person'
[ndérè]	HL	'idiophone of stinging'

Table 3.8 *Three tones in monosyllables in Yoruba*

Word	Tone	English gloss
[kó]	H	'to build'
[ko]	M	'to sing'
[kò]	L	'to reject'

Table 3.9 *Six tones on Cantonese monosyllables*

Word	Tone	English gloss
[si]	High-level	'poem'
[si]	Mid-level	'to try'
[si]	Low-level	'matter'
[si]	Low-falling	'time'
[si]	Low-high	'to cause'
[si]	Low-mid	'city'

high ['] level, or a low ['] level tone (see Tables 3.6 and 3.7). Yoruba, Hausa, Igbo, and Nua spoken in Nigeria have three registered tones, high ['], mid [¯] or unmarked, and low ['] (see Table 3.8). Cantonese has six contrastive tones: high-level, mid-level, low-level, low-high, low-mid, and low-falling (Table 3.9). Mandarin Chinese, on the other hand, has four tones: high-level, high-rising, falling-rising, and high-falling (Table 3.10).

Unlike tone languages spoken in East and Southeast Asia, some African tone languages also use tone to signal grammatical changes. It has been claimed that in Igbo, a high tone can be used to express possessive case (Ladefoged, 1975: 253). As seen in the examples provided below, the tone of the second syllable [ba] in 'jaw' changes from a low tone to a high tone in 'monkey's jaw'.

Table 3.10 *Four tones in Mandarin Chinese*

Word	Tone	English gloss
[maː]	High-level	'mother'
[maː]	High-rising	'hemp'
[maː]	Low falling-rising	'horse'
[maː]	High-falling	'scold'

[àgbà]	'jaw'
[èŋwè]	'monkey'
[àgbá èŋwè]	'monkey's jaw'

Another example of grammatical use of tone is from a dialect of Edo called Bini spoken in Nigeria. In Bini, tones are used to signal tenses. An example is given below.

Grammatical tone in Bini (Ladefoged, 1975, pp. 253–254)

a. ì mà 'I show' (habitual)
b. í mà 'I am showing'
c. ì má 'I showed'

Both the subject pronoun and the verb carry a low tone for the timeless, habitual tense. The tone of the pronoun changes from high to low to indicate a present progressive tense, while the tone of the verb changes from low to high to indicate past tense.

As a final note, it is important to know that while pitch is the main acoustic correlate of lexical tone, duration, intensity, and voice quality or phonation type (breathy and creaky) may also serve as secondary perceptual cues to tonal distinction.

Tone Transcription

Tones can be transcribed in many different ways. As seen above, for languages with only two or three contrastive tones, a high tone can be marked by an acute accent over the vowel ['] and a low pitch by a grave accent [`]. A combination of an acute accent followed by a grave accent can be used to transcribe a falling tone [^], while a grave accent followed by an acute accent can be used to transcribe a rising tone [ᵛ]. The mid-level tone is often left unmarked in many languages.

Different tones may also be transcribed by assigning numerical values to a speaker's pitch range, with 5 being the highest and 1 being the lowest (Chao, 1948). For example, a high-level tone may be assigned a value of 55 and a low-level tone may be given an 11 value. Similarly, a high-rising tone could be numerically transcribed as a 35 tone. Moreover, a graphical representation of

Table 3.11 *Tonal contrast in Thai*

Tone number	Description	Pitch	Tone letter	Example	Gloss
1	Low-falling	21		$k^ha{:}^1$	galangal root
2	High-falling	51		$k^ha{:}^2$	I, kill
3	High-rising	45		$k^ha{:}^3$	trade
4	Low-falling-rising	215		$k^ha{:}^4$	leg
5	mid(level)-falling	32		$k^ha{:}^5$	stuck

pitch levels or **tone letters** can also be used along with numerical pitch level values. However, scholars working on Thai prefer tone diacritics as shown in Table 3.11.

In some cases, the tone of a word may change due to the influence of a neighboring tone. This phenomenon is called **tone sandhi**. In Mandarin Chinese, for example, the falling-rising tone (Tone 3) is changed to a high-rising tone (Tone 2) when it is followed by a falling-rising tone (Tone 3). There is also a tonal phenomenon known as **declination** or **down-drift**, mostly found in African tone languages, in which the pitch level of a given tone is lowered over a phrase or a sentence. For example, the pitch level of a low tone at the beginning of a phrase will be higher than the pitch level of another low tone appearing at the end of the phrase. Another pitch-lowering phenomenon is **down-step**. First discovered in and commonly occurring among tone languages in sub-Saharan Africa, it is described as a lowering effect of a preceding low tone on the following high tone, thus setting a lower pitch ceiling for subsequent high tones. The term is also used to describe similar pitch-lowering phenomena associated with intonation in non-tonal languages (see Intonation below).

Pitch Accent

A few of the world's languages, such as Japanese, Norwegian, Swedish, and Serbo-Croatian, are classified as pitch-accent languages. Similar to tone languages, these languages use tone contrastively. However, the number of tones is usually limited, (e.g., two) and the use of the tonal contrast is limited to a certain syllable in a word. Moreover, this tonal contrast only applies to some pairs of words in the language. For example, approximately 500 pairs of bisyllabic words in Swedish can be contrasted by two tones or accents: [an.den] 'duck' has a falling tone on the first syllable, but [an.den] 'spirit' has a falling tone on both syllables. It is the presence of the pitch accent (or lack thereof) on the second syllable that distinguishes meaning between the two words. This system does not apply to monosyllabic words.

Table 3.12 *Tokyo Japanese pitch accent*

Tonal pattern	Word	English gloss
HLL	kákiga	'oyster'
LHL	kakíga	'fence'
LHH	kakígá	'persimmon'

In contrast to Swedish, pitch accent in Tokyo Japanese is not predictable, and is defined as the point at which the pitch falls. As Table 3.12 shows, in 'oyster', the first syllable bears the high pitch accent, marked with a high tone (H), and the pitch starts to fall (L) after this syllable. In 'fence' the second syllable is accented. On the other hand, 'persimmon' is considered unaccented since the pitch doesn't fall after the high tone on the second syllable. The location of the pitch-accented syllable in Tokyo Japanese has to be learned. But once known, the entire pitch pattern of the word is predictable by two rules. First, an accented mora and all morae preceding it are marked by a high tone whereas all morae following it receive a low tone (Reetz & Jongman, 2009). Second, when not accented, the first mora carries a low tone.

Some researchers argue that Japanese possesses the true characteristics of a pitch-accent language, while Swedish does not. Other researchers argue that both languages may be considered pitch-accent languages and that the system and characteristics of a pitch accent may vary from language to language. To date, researchers have yet to agree on a set of defining features of a pitch-accent language.

In sum, all languages manipulate pitch at the syllable level to convey meaning. In tone languages, the pitch pattern associated with each syllable carries its lexical referent and must, therefore, be learned. On the other hand, the location of the pitch-accented syllable in some multisyllabic words conveys the word's meaning in pitch-accent languages and has to be memorized. The pitches of the remaining syllables are, however, predictable and can be derived by rules. Finally, in stress languages such as English, pitch, along with duration, intensity, and vowel quality, is used to signal how prominent a syllable is relative to its neighbors in the same words. Variation in prominence or stress patterns, in turn, is used to differentiate words. English stress is a mixed system with both predictable and unpredictable aspects.

Intonation

Besides the syllable, languages also manipulate pitch at the phrase and the sentence level to convey meaning. This is known as **intonation**. Intonation is the tune of the utterance. It is similar to tone in that pitch is the main object being manipulated. However, the kind of meaning that intonation conveys differs from that of tones. In intonation, the pitch pattern of a word does not affect its lexical referent, but its information status in the discourse may change. Depending on the specific pitch pattern used, the word's referent may be asserted as in (a), queried as in (b), or questioned as in (c).

> a. "I am a lawyer."
> b. "You are a lawyer?"
> c. "A lawyer?" I thought you were a doctor!"

In this example, the word *lawyer* is produced with three different pitch patterns, but its referent remains the same: *a person who studies or practices law*.

In (a), it is produced with **falling intonation**, a general decrease in pitch toward the last word, a phenomenon known as **declination**. It indicates a declarative statement. The **rising intonation** in (b) signals a question that requires a yes or no answer. In (c), the rise-fall-rise intonation indicates surprise.

The high and low pitch configuration or pitch accent of a certain word may create 'ripples' on the overall falling and rising intonation contour of an utterance. Note, however, that a pitch accent associated with a salient syllable in an accented word in an utterance is not the same as a pitch accent associated with a salient syllable in a word in a pitch-accent language such as Japanese discussed earlier. An intonation pitch accent conveys discourse information (i.e., contrastive interpretation), whereas a lexical pitch accent creates a lexical contrast (i.e., changing word meaning).

The stretch of connected speech over which a particular intonation pattern extends is called an **intonation phrase** (IP), a **tone group**, or a **breath group**, etc. marked by [ǀ]. For example, the statement *We will go to Atlanta this weekend* contains one IP, but *We will go to Atlanta this weekend ǀ if the weather is niceǁ* contains two IPs. The onset of the second IP is signaled by a rising pitch on *weekend*. The [ǁ] represents a major intonation group, the end of the sentence in this case. The two IP markers are similar, but not identical to the IPA symbol for a dental [ǀ] and an alveolar [ǁ] click introduced in Chapter 2.

Intonation patterns may be used to differentiate syntactic structures. Consider the following two statements.

> a. Everyone knows ǀ but Linda is cluelessǁ.
> b. Everyone knows Belinda is cluelessǁ.

(Reetz & Jongman, 2009, p. 223)

These two sentences are nearly identical in the make-up of their segments, but one (a) contains two main clauses whereas the other (b) consists of a main clause and an embedded clause. This difference is cued by the absence of pitch rise at the end of the first clause, and thus the number of IPs with which they are produced.

In English, yes–no questions are associated with rising intonation, whereas questions starting with a question word, such as *When are you coming?* are usually produced with the same falling intonation as that of a statement. Similarly, positive tag questions, such as *You are not tired, are you?* have rising intonation, but negative tag questions, *You are tired, aren't you?* have falling intonation.

The relationship between intonation and the meaning it carries is language specific. Nonetheless, some universal trends have been observed. Cross-linguistically, low or falling intonation denotes assertions and finality, whereas rising intonation signals uncertainty and non-finality. Intonation may also be used to convey a speaker's attitude or emotional state such as anger, sadness, jealousy, etc. The use of these intonation patterns may be subtle and subject to dialectal and individual differences. Finally, all languages, including tone languages, use intonation. However, the interaction between tone and intonation is complicated and remains poorly understood since pitch manipulation is involved in both of these prosodic features.

Having described both segments (vowels and consonants) as well as supra-segments (stress, length, tone, and intonation), in the next chapter we discuss how they are written down or transcribed using the International Phonetic Alphabet.

Chapter Summary

- Suprasegmentals are features of linguistic units larger than an individual vowel or consonant.
- The main suprasegmental features are stress, length, tone, and intonation.
- Because they affect a language's rhythm or prosody, they are also referred to as prosodic features.
- Lexical stress is the relative degree of prominence among syllables in a word. The position of a stressed syllable is fixed in some languages, but varies in other languages depending on syllable structure or weight.
- Sentence stress is prominence at the sentence level in which a syllable already carrying lexical stress is accented to signal extra emphasis by the speaker.
- Alternation of stressed and unstressed syllables at the sentence level forms the basis for linguistic rhythms.
- The three known linguistic rhythms are stress-timed, syllable-timed, and mora-timed rhythms.
- The notion of isochrony – equal intervals between stressed syllables, syllables, and morae as perceptual correlates to the three linguistic rhythms – is not fully supported by recent research.
- Languages with contrastive vowel or consonant length vary consonant and vowel duration to change word meaning.
- Languages that use voice pitch to change word meaning are called tone languages.
- Two types of tone languages are register and contour tone languages.
- In pitch-accent languages, voice pitch is also used to contrast meaning in a limited set of words.

- Intonation refers to the use of variation in voice pitch at the phrase or sentence level for both linguistic and non-linguistic purposes.
- The stretch of connected speech over which a particular intonation pattern extends is called an intonation phrase (IP), a tone group, or a breath group.
- The tonic syllable is the syllable that carries the major pitch or nuclear pitch accent in an IP.

Review Exercises

Exercise 3.1: Indicate the number of syllables these words contain.
   a. democracy
   b. pneumonia
   c. numerical
   d. physicality
   e. polygamists
   f. revisionary
   g. higher
   h. hierarchical
   i. hire
   j. optimism

Exercise 3.2: Draw sonority profiles for the following words. Do sonority peaks and/or valleys coincide with the number of syllables you think they contain?

national	wire	realist
mirror	higher	prism
bottom	reality	debatable
lavatory	realism	alienate

Exercise 3.3: Underline the primary stressed syllable in the following English words.
   a. nationality
   b. ambition
   c. meager
   d. aberrant
   e. carriage
   f. detonation
   g. garage
   h. colander
   i. monetary
   j. trigonometric

Exercise 3.4: Find a word with the same number of syllables and stress pattern as the following.

a. pessimistic
b. decree
c. ambidextrous
d. superfluous
e. maniacal
f. pseudonym
g. dormitory
h. ludicrous
i. kimono
j. torrential

Exercise 3.5: For each of the following words, explain why the stress falls where it does.

a. tornado
b. promise
c. consider
d. assure
e. pertain
f. convince
g. procure
h. elicit

References and Further Reading

Aderibigbe, A. G. (nd). Function of Tones: An Overview of Languages in Nigeria. Retrieved on July 5, 2016 from www.academia.edu/2215662/Functions_of_Tone_An_Overview_of_Languages_in_Nigeria.

Akinlabi, A. (2004). Yoruba sound system. In N. Lawal, M. Sadiku, & A. Dopamu (eds.), *Understanding Yoruba Life and Culture* (pp. 453–468). Trenton, NJ/Asmara, Eritrea: Africa World Press. Inc.

Akinlabi, A., & Urua, E. (2000). Tone in Ibibio verbal reduplication. In H. E. Wolff, & O. D. Gensler (eds.), *Proceedings of the 2nd World Congress of African Linguistics* (pp. 279–291). Cologne: Rudiger Koppe Verlag.

Blevins, J. (1995). The syllable in phonological theory. In J. A. Goldsmith (ed.), *The Handbook of Phonological Theory* (pp. 206–244). Cambridge, MA: Blackwell.

Burzio, L. (1994). *Principles of English Stress* (No. 72). Cambridge: Cambridge University Press.

Chao, Y. R. (1948). *Mandarin Primer*. Cambridge: Harvard University Press.

Chomsky, N. (1968). *The Sound Pattern of English*. Cambridge, MA: MIT Press.

Clopper, C. G. (2002). Frequency of stress patterns in English: A computational analysis, *IULC Working Papers Online*, 2(2).

Coleman, J. (1999, August). The nature of vocoids associated with syllabic consonants in Tashlhiyt Berber. In *Proceedings of the XIVth international congress of phonetic sciences* (Vol. 1, pp. 735–738).

Dell, F., & Elmedlaoui, M. (1988). Syllabic consonants in Berber: Some new evidence. *Journal of African Languages and Linguistics*, 10(1), 1–17.

Fox, A. (2002). *Prosodic Features and Prosodic Structure: The Phonology of Suprasegmentals*. Oxford: Oxford University Press.

Gordon, M. (2006). *Syllable Weight: Phonetic, Phonology, Typology*. New York: Routledge.

Hayes, B. (1981). *A Metrical Theory of Stress Rules*. New York: Garland.

Hayes, B. (1995). *Metrical Stress Theory*. Chicago, IL: University of Chicago Press.

Hayes, B., & Lahiri, A. (1991). Bengali intonational phonology. *Natural Language & Linguistic Theory*, 9(1), 47–96.

Kadyamusuma, M. (2012). Effect of linguistic experience on the discrimination of Shona lexical tone. *Southern African Linguistics and Applied Language Studies*, 30(4), 469–485.

Kreidler, C. (1989/2004). *The Pronunciation of English*. Oxford: Blackwell

Ladefoged, P. (1975). *A Course in Phonetics*, 2nd edn. New York: Harcourt Brace Jovanovich.

Lehiste, Ilse, & Lass, Norman J. (1976). Suprasegmental features of speech. *Contemporary Issues in Experimental Phonetics*, 225, 239.

Mahanta, S. (2009). Prominence in Oriya, Bangla and Assamese: A phonetic and phonological investigation. *International Journal of Dravidian Linguistics*, 38(1), 101–128.

Parker, S. G. (2002). *Quantifying the Sonority Hierarchy*. Doctoral dissertation, University of Massachusetts at Amherst.

Pickering, L., & Wiltshire, C. (2000). Pitch accent in Indian-English teaching discourse. *World Englishes*, 19(2), 173–183.

Ramus, F., Nespor, M., & Mehler, J. (1999). Correlates of linguistic rhythm in the speech signal. *Cognition*, 73(3), 265–292.

Reetz, H., & Jongman, A. (2009). *Phonetics: Transcription, Production, Acoustics, and Perception*. West Sussex: Wiley-Blackwell.

Ridouane, R. (2008). Syllables without vowels: phonetic and phonological evidence from Tashlhiyt Berber. *Phonology*, 25(02), 321–359.

Vance, T. (2008). *The Sounds of Japanese*. New York: Cambridge University Press.

Verma, D. (2005). Pitch variation as a correlate of narrow and contrastive focus in Hindi. ECOSAL, Jan 6–8, 2005.

Warner, N., & Arai, T. (2001). The role of the mora in the timing of spontaneous Japanese speech. *The Journal of the Acoustical Society of America*, 109(3), 1144–1156.

Wiltshire, C., & Moon, R. (2003). Phonetic stress in Indian English vs. American English. *World Englishes*, 22(3), 291–303.

Zsiga, Elizabeth C. (2013). *The Sounds of Language*. Oxford: Wiley-Blackwell.

4

Transcribing Speech

Introduction

In Chapter 1, we saw that speech sounds are produced with a number of articulatory attributes according to place, manner, and voicing for consonants, and tongue height, backness, and lip rounding for vowels. However, to describe speech sounds by listing all of their articulatory characteristics would prove daunting and impractical. To describe a simple English word, *beat*, one would have to describe the actions of the lips and the vocal folds for 'b' followed by the tongue movement and position for the vowel 'ea', and end with the position of the tongue and laryngeal action for the final 't'. For this reason, linguists have devised a set of symbols commonly known as the International Phonetic Alphabet (IPA) and use them as shorthand to represent speech sounds. Each IPA symbol represents one speech sound and denotes the articulatory features involved in its production. For example, the [p] symbol represents a voiceless bilabial plosive sound, a sound produced with airflow from the lungs passing through the vocal folds without setting them into motion and then being blocked momentarily behind the closed lips before being released into the atmosphere. More importantly, unlike orthographies which vary from language to language, the IPA allows for a consistent, one-to-one mapping between sounds and symbols. For instance, despite orthographic inconsistencies, the [f] sound in *fin, philosophy*, and *tough* is represented by the same IPA symbol, [f]. However, do note that, unlike a recording, IPA symbols do not provide the truest representation of speech sounds. For instance, the same [pʰ] symbol represents the first sound at the beginning of the English words *pin, pan, pun*, ignoring variation in the amount of aspiration (a puff of air following the release of the lips) due to the following vowels or the context where the words are produced – in isolation, or in different positions in the sentence or by different talkers. That is, IPA symbols do not capture sub-segmental details.

The IPA chart is sanctioned by the International Phonetic Association, also known as the IPA. The mission of the association is to promote the study of phonetics and to provide standards for phonetic transcription of all the world's languages. The IPA also publishes studies on phonetic theory and description through its journal *The Journal of the International Phonetic Association (JIPA)*. In addition, The International Congress of Phonetic Sciences (ICPhS) conference is held every four years under the auspices of the IPA where linguists, notably phoneticians and phonologists from all over the world, gather to share their research findings.

In this chapter, we will begin with an overview of the IPA chart. Next, we discuss how sounds are written down using the IPA. Then we describe IPA transcription of the consonants and vowels of American English.

The International Phonetic Alphabet (IPA)

The IPA chart is modified periodically. The most recent version was published in 2005. It comprises six main groups of symbols: three for consonants, one for vowels, one for suprasegments, and one for diacritics used to further differentiate small differences among vowels and consonants.

Pulmonic Consonants

The first consonant chart contains symbols for consonants produced with the pulmonic airstream mechanism (see Figure 4.1). They are arranged into columns according to their place of articulation, and into rows according to their manner of articulation. In each column, the symbols on the left represent voiceless sounds, and the ones on the right are voiced sounds.

Empty white cells represent sounds that are physically possible but have not yet been attested, whereas empty gray-out cells represent sounds that are considered physically impossible. Take the voiced and voiceless labio-dental plosives, for instance. These two sounds are possible if a complete closure between

CONSONANTS (PULMONIC)

	Bilabial	Labiodental	Dental	Alveolar	Postalveolar	Retroflex	Palatal	Velar	Uvular	Pharyngeal	Glottal
Plosive	p b			t d		ʈ ɖ	c ɟ	k ɡ	q ɢ		ʔ
Nasal	m	ɱ		n		ɳ	ɲ	ŋ	N		
Trill	ʙ			r					ʀ		
Tap or Flap				ɾ		ɽ					
Fricative	ɸ β	f v	θ ð	s z	ʃ ʒ	ʂ ʐ	ç ʝ	x ɣ	χ ʁ	ħ ʕ	h ɦ
Lateral fricative				ɬ ɮ							
Approximant		ʋ		ɹ		ɻ	j	ɰ			
Lateral approximant				l		ɭ	ʎ	ʟ			

Figure 4.1 Pulmonic consonants
Where symbols appear in pairs, the one to the right represents a
voiced consonant. Shaded areas denote articulations judged
impossible.

	Clicks		Voiced implosives		Ejectives
ʘ	Bilabial	ɓ	Bilabial	ʼ	Examples:
ǀ	Dental	ɗ	Dental/alveolar	pʼ	Bilabial
ǃ	(Post)alveolar	ʄ	Palatal	tʼ	Dental/alveolar
ǂ	Palatoalveolar	ɠ	Velar	kʼ	Velar
ǁ	Alveolar lateral	ʛ	Uvular	sʼ	Alveolar fricative

Figure 4.2 Non-pulmonic consonants

the lower lip and the teeth can be made so that the airflow cannot escape. In
contrast, a pharyngeal nasal is impossible since a complete closure at the pharynx
would necessarily block the nasal passage up above.

Non-Pulmonic Consonants

The second set of consonant symbols (non-pulmonic consonants) is placed
below the main consonant chart, and includes symbols representing consonants produced with non-pulmonic airstream mechanisms, which include
clicks, implosives, and ejectives (Figure 4.2, see also Chapter 2: Airstream
Mechanisms).

OTHER SYMBOLS

ʍ	Voiceless labial-velar fricative	ɕ ʑ	Alveolo-palatal fricatives
w	Voiced labial-velar approximant	ɺ	Voiced alveolar lateral flap
ɥ	Voiced labial-palatal approximant	ɧ	Simultaneous ʃ and x
ʜ	Voiceless epiglottal fricative		
ʕ	Voiced epiglottal fricative	Affricates and double articulations can be represented by two symbols joined by a tie bar if necessary. k͡p t͡s
ʡ	Epiglottal plosive	

Figure 4.3 Other symbols

Other Symbols

"Other symbols" are symbols for more complex consonants: those produced with more than one articulation such as voiced and voiceless labio-velar approximants [w, ʍ], and those produced at places of articulation not included in the main chart, e.g., alveolo-palatal fricatives and epiglottals (Figure 4.3). Many of these have already been discussed in Chapter 1.

Alveolo-palatal fricatives [ɕ, ʑ] are found in Polish [ɕali] 'skirt' and [ʑali] 'gasped' (Ladefoged & Disner, 2012). They are produced with the blade of the tongue raised toward the back of the alveolar ridge, but the tongue body raised toward the palate. They are between the retroflex and the palatal on the chart but are left out because of a lack of space. Another symbol not on the main chart is the voiced alveolar lateral flap [ɺ]. It is found in Japanese [kokoɺo] 'heart' instead of a voiced alveolar (central) flap [ɾ] for some speakers.

Vowels

The fourth set of symbols is for vowels (Figure 4.4). Many of these are found in English and they will be covered in the next chapter. Among well-known, non-English vowels is the close front rounded [y]. It occurs in French [vy] 'seen', and in Turkish [kys] 'sulky'. French also has [ø, œ] as in [lø] 'the' and [lœʁ] 'their'. The close central unrounded vowel [ɨ] occurs in Thai [mɨː] 'hand'. It is also frequently used to transcribe the last vowel in American English *wanted* [wãntɨd], *fitted* [fɪtɨd], *cashes* [kʰæʃɨz] and *passes* [pʰæsɨz], for example (see also Chapter 5: Phonemic Analysis). Its rounded counterpart [ʉ] is found in the Oslo dialect of Norwegian [bʉː] 'shack' (http://phonetics.ucla.edu/appendix/languages/norwegian/norwegian.html).

The close and close-mid back unrounded vowels [ɣ, ɯ] are found in Vietnamese [tɤ] 'silk' and [tɯ] 'fourth'. The sound [ɒ] occurs in Khmer (Cambodian) as in [kɒː] 'neck'.

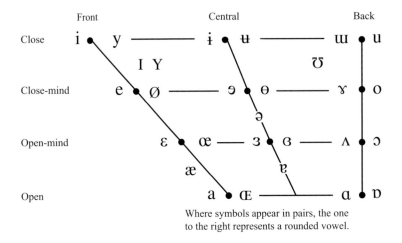

Where symbols appear in pairs, the one
to the right represents a rounded vowel.

Figure 4.4 Vowels

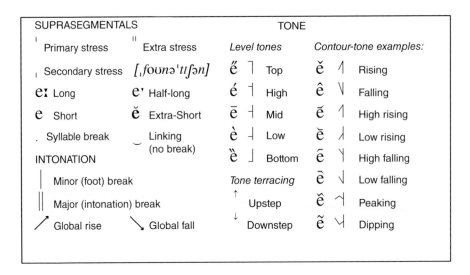

Figure 4.5 Suprasegmentals

Suprasegmentals

The fifth set of symbols are those used to transcribe suprasegmental features, which include stress, length, intonation, and tone already discussed in Chapter 3.

The last set comprises the diacritics that can be used to further denote articulatory details such as phonation type, nasalization, tongue advancement degree, rhoticity, etc., for vowels and secondary articulation for consonants (Figure 4.6).

DIACRITICS   Diacritics may be placed above a symbol with a descender, e.g. ŋ̊

̥	Voiceless	n̥ d̥	̤	Breathy voiced	b̤ a̤	̪	Dental	t̪ d̪
̬	Voiced	s̬ t̬	̰	Creaky voiced	b̰ a̰	̺	Apical	t̺ d̺
ʰ	Aspirated	tʰ dʰ	̼	Linguolabial	t̼ d̼	̻	Laminal	t̻ d̻
̹	More rounded	ɔ̹	ʷ	Labialized	tʷ dʷ	̃	Nasalized	ẽ
̜	Less rounded	ɔ̜	ʲ	Palatalized	tʲ dʲ	ⁿ	Nasal release	dⁿ
̟	Advanced	u̟	ˠ	Velarized	tˠ dˠ	ˡ	Lateral release	dˡ
̠	Retracted	e̠	ˤ	Pharyngealized	tˤ dˤ	̚	No audible release	d̚
̈	Centralized	ë	̴	Velarized or pharyngealized	ɫ			
̽	Mid-centralized	e̽	̝	Raised	e̝	(ɹ̝	= voiced alveolar fricative)	
̩	Syllabic	n̩	̞	Lowered	e̞	(β̞	= voiced bilabial approximant)	
̯	Non-Syllabic	e̯	̘	Advanced Tongue Root	e̘			
˞	Rhoticity	ɚ a˞	̙	Retracted Tongue Root	e̙			

Figure 4.6 Diacritics

Types of Phonetic Transcription

Phonetic transcription refers to the act of writing down speech sounds using a set of printed symbols such as the IPA that we just discussed. Using **narrow transcription**, linguists try to represent as many phonetic details as possible in their transcription, including those that reflect language-, dialect-, and even speaker-specific details. However, only noticeable phonetic features – those necessary for listeners to reproduce a recognizable word – are represented in **broad transcription**.

Phonetic transcription is language specific. Take the voiceless plosives [p, t, k] at the beginning of English words, *pick*, *tick*, and *kick*, for instance. They are produced with aspiration. These same voiceless plosives are produced without aspiration in French. Therefore, in French, they are represented with the same symbols, [p, t, k], in both a broad transcription and a narrow transcription. But in English, they are transcribed as [p, t, k] in a broad transcription, but as [pʰ, tʰ, kʰ] in a narrow transcription.

On the other hand, both sets of symbols are needed for a broad and a narrow transcription of voiceless plosives in Thai. Unlike English, Thai contrasts between voiceless aspirated and voiceless unaspirated plosives, as in [pan] 'to share' vs. [pʰan] 'to wrap around'; [tan] 'a dead end' vs. [tʰan] 'to catch up with'; [kan] 'to prevent/protect' vs. [kʰan] 'itchy'. In this case, [p, t, k] will be used to transcribe the voiceless plosives in the first word of the pair, and [pʰ, tʰ, kʰ] will be used for the second word in both a broad and a narrow transcription.

The difference between a narrow and a broad phonetic transcription is continuous, with many possible intermediate levels of transcription depending on the transcriber's level of training and his or her experience with the language being described, as well as the objective of the transcription. For instance, the English word *pool* may be transcribed as [pʰul], [pʰ*w*ul], [pʰuɫ] or [pʰ*w*uɫ] depending on the number of known phonetic properties the transcriber discerns and/or wishes to convey.

Another type of phonetic transcription is **impressionistic transcription**. This type of transcription is not influenced by the known phonetic properties of the language being described. It is used, for example, when transcribing an unknown language or speech of a clinical patient for diagnostic purposes. Such transcription lacks a word or a syllable boundary since they are not yet known. It should include all discernible phonetic details since their importance and relevance have yet to be determined.

In contrast to phonetic transcription, **phonemic transcription** doesn't represent the actual phonetic realization of speech sounds, but rather how they are treated by native speakers. For example, the English 'p' sound is produced differently in *peak* versus in *speak*. Specifically, the 'p' sound in *peak* is produced with aspiration following the opening of the lips. However, aspiration is absent following the release of the lips for 'p' in *speak*. In a narrow transcription, the 'p' in *peak* will be transcribed as [pʰ], but as a plain [p] in *speak*. However, these two 'p' sounds are treated by native speakers of English as the same sound and would be transcribed by the same symbol /p/ in a phonemic transcription. The different versions of 'p' in this example are known as **allophones**, and the same abstract unit of sound that native speakers think they belong to is referred to as a **phoneme** (see the next chapter for the procedures linguists use to discover the number of phonemes and their allophones). Note that slashes are used to denote a phonemic transcription and square brackets are used for a phonetic transcription.

In a sense, a phonemic transcription is considered broad since it doesn't include phonetic details. On the other hand, unlike a *broad* transcription, it's not considered a phonetic transcription proper since it captures the abstract representation or category of sound rather than its physical execution.

Figure 4.7 below captures the distinction between different types of transcriptions as conceptualized above using the English word *pancake* to illustrate.

In this example, the impressionistic transcription shows the same level of phonetic details as the narrow phonetic transcription but lacks syllable boundaries. The broad transcription lacks diacritics that represent phonetic details such as nasalization of [æ] in anticipation of the following nasal consonant, place assimilation to the following velar plosive of the 'n' in *pan*, and the unreleased nature of the final 'k' in *cake*. The phonemic transcription includes only the six phonemes that make up the word, and is enclosed in slash brackets instead of square brackets.

In summary, narrow and broad phonetic transcriptions differ in how much detail they include. A broad transcription represents only symbols for sounds

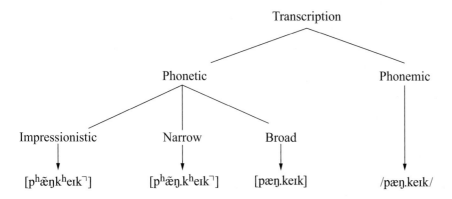

Figure 4.7 Types of transcription

necessary to approximate the pronunciation of the utterance, while a narrow transcription includes phonetic details of the actual realization of the sounds. The amount of detail included varies depending on the transcriber's ability and goals. Impressionistic transcription is narrow transcription that tries to capture the actual pronunciation of the utterance without known phonetic patterns of the language or the speech material being described. On the other hand, phonemic transcription represents contrastive sound units as they are represented in the speaker's mind.

In the next section, we will discuss the IPA symbols needed for both broad and narrow transcriptions of American English consonants and vowels.

Transcribing American English

Now that we are familiar with the IPA and different types of transcription, let's apply this knowledge to transcribing American English. It should be noted that there are many dialects of American English. As such, your transcription may deviate from what's described below depending on the dialect or the speaker you are transcribing. We will begin with consonant transcription followed by vowel transcription.

Consonants

The IPA symbols needed for a broad or phonemic transcription of English are shown in Table 4.1. Note that they should be enclosed in slashes for phonemic transcription.

Narrow Transcription of American English Consonants
Some American English consonants are pronounced differently depending on their phonetic context. Some of these pronunciation variations occur because of the consonant's absolute position in a syllable or a word, but many are due to its

Table 4.1 *The IPA symbols for American English consonants and words that contain them*

IPA	Example word	IPA	Example word
[p]	**sp**ill	[θ]	**th**ink
[b]	**b**ill	[ð]	**th**y
[m]	**m**ill	[s]	**s**ip
[t]	s**t**and	[z]	**z**ip
[d]	**d**ance	[ʃ]	**sh**ip
[n]	**n**ine	[ʒ]	a**z**ure
[k]	s**k**ull	[ʧ]	**ch**in
[g]	**g**ull	[dʒ]	**g**in
[ŋ]	si**ng**	[l]	**l**ip
[f]	**f**ive	[ɹ]	**r**ip
[v]	**v**ibe	[j]	**y**ip
[w]	**w**ipe	[h]	**h**ip

proximity to other segments within an utterance. We will begin our discussion with absolute positional variants, focusing on plosives.

Positional Variants

Aspiration

As mentioned above, all voiceless plosives are aspirated when they occur in word-initial position or before a stressed vowel. These variants of the voiceless plosives are referred to as aspirated plosives and are transcribed with a diacritic [ʰ] (Table 4.2).

Note that the amount of aspiration in plosives before an unstressed vowel in *potato*, *tomato*, and *concur* is much reduced in comparison to before a stressed vowel. Those occurring after 's' or before an unstressed vowel are not aspirated (Table 4.3).

Devoicing

For some American English speakers, voiced plosives may be completely or partially devoiced when they are not surrounded by voiced segments. For example, unlike the second 'b' sound in *baby*, the first 'b' is produced by many speakers without vocal fold vibration during its closure (Table 4.4). Similarly, the 'b' sound in word-final position in *tab* may show only partial voicing during closure. The [˳] diacritic is used to represent a devoiced (voiced) plosive. The [˺] represents unreleased consonants discussed in the next section.

On the other hand, some voiceless consonants become voiced in certain contexts. For instance, the voiceless glottal fricative [h] becomes voiced and breathy when it occurs as an onset consonant of a stressed syllable and is surrounded by vowels (see Table 4.5 for examples).

Table 4.2 *English aspirated plosives*

pan	[pʰæn]
tan	[tʰæn]
can	[kʰæn]
append	[ə.ˈpʰɛ̃nd]
attack	[ə.ˈtʰæk]
accuse	[ə.ˈkʰjuz]
potato	[pʰə.ˈtʰeɪ.ɾoʊ]
tomato	[tʰə.ˈmeɪ.ɾoʊ]
concur	[kʰən.ˈkʰɚ]

Table 4.3 *Unaspirated plosives in English*

span	[spæn]
stand	[stæ̃nd]
scan	[skæn]
maple	[meɪ.pl̩]
tactic	[tʰæk̚.tɪk]
bacon	[beɪ.kn̩]

Table 4.4 *English devoiced plosives*

baby	[b̥eɪ.bi]
tab	[tʰæb̥]
pad	[pʰæd̥]
tag	[tʰæg̥]
bedtimes	[b̥ɛd̥̚tʰaɪmz]
bad things	[b̥æd̥̚θĩŋz]

Consonant Release

English plosives show a few variations depending on how they are released. For voiced plosives, they may be released abruptly, similar to their release in word-initial position. The release may also be gradual, soft, and therefore inaudible. In some cases, however, they may be produced without a release at all when they precede another consonant or in word-final position. No special diacritic is required to represent a release, abrupt or soft, but the [̚] diacritic is used when the release is absent.

Similar to voiced plosives, voiceless plosives may be produced without a release. However, in addition to an abrupt release and a gradual, inaudible release, a puff of air or aspiration may be audible after the release of a voiceless plosive, particularly in enunciation (Table 4.7).

Voiceless plosives are also unreleased when they precede another consonant.

Table 4.5 *English voiced glottal fricatives*

[əˈɦɛd]	'ahead'
[əˈɦɔɪ]	'ahoy'
[ɹiˈɦɝˌsəl]	'rehearsal'
[ɹiˈɦaɪɚ]	'rehire'

Table 4.6 *Unreleased voiced plosives in English*

cab	[kʰæb̥]
Ted	[tʰɛd̥˺]
beg	[b̥ɛg˺]
bagged	[b̥æg˺d̥]
tadpole	[tʰæd˺pʰoʊɫ]
dabbed	[d̥æb˺d̥]

Table 4.7 *Released, unreleased, and aspirated final voiceless plosives in English*

pack	[pʰæk], [pʰæk˺] [pʰækʰ]
cat	[kʰæt], [kʰæt˺] [kʰætʰ]
cake	[kʰeɪk], [kʰeɪk˺] [kʰeɪkʰ]

Flap/Tap/Glottal Plosive

English 't' and 'd' sounds are produced as a flap [ɾ] when they are preceded by a stressed vowel and followed by an unstressed vowel. Compare, for example, the 't' sound in *attack* and *attic*. The 't' in *attic* [ˈæ.ɾɪk] is produced as a flap while the 't' in attack [əˈtʰæk] is realized as a voiceless aspirated [tʰ]. Similarly, 't' in *latter* [ˈlæ.ɾɚ] and 'd' in *ladder* [ˈlæ.ɾɚ] are both produced as a flap. Listeners have to rely on the duration of the preceding vowel [æ] to differentiate between them: the [æ] in *ladder* is longer than that in *latter*. Besides 't' and 'd', 'n' may be produced as a flap in the same context, as in *many* [ˈmæ̃.ɾi], and *money* [ˈmʌ̃.ɾi] (see Table 4.9).

Besides [tʰ], [t], [t'] and [ɾ], the English 't' is often produced as a glottal stop [ʔ] when it occurs word-finally or before a syllabic [n̩] in which speakers bring the vocal folds tightly together after the vowel or the coda of the preceding stressed syllable. In addition, with an intervening consonant, the preceding vowel is often glottalized (creaky) (Table 4.10).

In summary, English plosives exhibit positional variants. Voiceless plosives are aspirated in word-initial position and when they precede a stressed vowel.

Table 4.8 *English unreleased
voiceless plosives preceding another
consonant*

bake pan	[b̥eɪk̚pʰæ̃n]
tapped	[tʰæp̚t]
meatball	[mit̚b̥ɔɬ]
captive	[kʰæp̚tɪv]

Table 4.9 *English flap*

attic	[ˈæ.ɾɪk]
latter	[ˈlæ.ɾɚ]
better	[ˈbɛ.ɾɚ]
beetle	[ˈbi.ɾl̩]
many	[ˈmæ̃.ɾi]
money	[ˈmʌ̃.ɾi]

Table 4.10 *Glottal stop in English*

cat	[kʰæ̃ʔ]
bat	[bæʔ]
beaten	[ˈbi̥.ʔn̩]
button	[ˈbʌ.ʔn̩]
tighten	[ˈtʰaɪ.ʔn̩]
mitten	[ˈmɪ.ʔn̩]
captain	[ˈkʰæp.ʔn̩]
mountain	[ˈmaʊ.ʔn̩]

Voiced plosives may be (partially) devoiced word-initially or word-finally. Both voiced and voiceless plosives may be released or unreleased in word-final position. Voiceless and voiced alveolar plosives /t, d/ are produced as a flap when they occur between a stressed and an unstressed vowel. Finally, a /t/ in word-final position or before a syllabic [n̩] is often produced as a glottal stop.

Besides positional variants, English consonants also exhibit variations due to their relative position with other segments in the utterance. This type of variation will be referred to as contextual variants to contrast them with the positional variants just discussed. The most common phenomenon that leads to consonant variations in English and the world's languages is coarticulation.

Coarticulation
Speech sounds in an utterance are not discretely articulated one at a time. Instead, the articulatory gestures of adjacent sounds are overlapped. This phenomenon is known as **coarticulation**. In English and other languages, coarticulation

Table 4.11 *Anticipatory coarticulation in English*

/tɛnθ/	[tʰɛ̃n̪θ]	'tenth'
/tɹaɪʌmf/	[tʰɹaɪ.ə̃ɱf]	'triumph'
/kʌmfɚt/	[kʰʌ̃ɱ.fɚt̚]	'comfort'
/sændwɪtʃ/	[sæ̃m.wɪtʃ]	'sandwich'
/ɪnkʌm/	[ɪŋ.kʰə̃m]	'income'

Table 4.12 *Perseverative coarticulation in English*

/pleɪ/	[pʰl̥eɪ]	'play'
/pɹeɪ/	[pʰɹ̥eɪ]	'pray'
/skul/	[skʷuɫ]	'school'
/kip/	[k̟ʰip]	'keep'
/kup/	[k̠ʰʷup]	'coop'

introduces variation in consonant (and vowel) production. For example, voiced laterals and central approximants [l] and [ɹ] are completely or partially devoiced after voiceless plosives, as in *play* [pʰl̥eɪ] and *pray* [pʰɹ̥eɪ].

Coarticulation comes in several types depending on the direction and the extent of the overlap. Anticipatory and perseverative coarticulations are differentiated based on the direction of the influence, whereas allophonic versus phonemic coarticulations are distinguished based on the extent of the effect.

In anticipatory (or regressive) coarticulation, a sound's pronunciation is affected by a following sound. For example, the alveolar nasal is produced as a dental nasal in *tenth* because of the dental fricative [θ] that comes after it, as indicated by [̪] in the narrow transcription: [tʰɛ̃n̪θ]. Another example of regressive coarticulation is the realization of the bilabial nasal /m/ as labio-dental [ɱ] in *triumph* [tʰɹaɪ.ə̃ɱf]. More examples of anticipatory coarticulation in English are given in Table 4.11.

On the other hand, the devoicing of [l] and [ɹ] in *play* [pʰl̥eɪ] and *pray* [pʰɹ̥eɪ] above are examples of perseverative (or progressive) coarticulation, where the articulatory feature of a sound is affected by a sound that comes before it. In these two examples, features of the preceding sound persevere to affect the articulation of the following sound. In these cases, the voiceless feature of the [p] carries over to the following approximant sounds. [k̟] in *keep* represents a more forward [k] in comparison to a more retracted [k̠] in *coop*. See more examples of preservative coarticulation in English in Table 4.12.

Based on the extent of its effect, two other types of coarticulation are distinguished: **allophonic** and **phonemic coarticulation**. Allophonic coarticulation occurs when an allophone results from the coarticulatory effect. Most examples discussed above belong to this type of coarticulation, e.g., [l̥], [ɹ̥], [n̪], [ɱ], [k̟] are

Table 4.13 *English light and dark 'l'*

/lʊk/	[lʊk]	'look'	/kul/	[kʰuɫ]	'cool'
/læk/	[læk]	'lack'	/kʌl/	[kʰʌɫ]	'cull'
/leɪk/	[leɪk]	'lake'	/skʌl/	[skʌɫ]	'skull'
/læb/	[læb]	'lab'	/skælp/	[skæɫp]	'scalp'

Table 4.14 *Intrusive glottal stop in English*

cup	[kʰʌʔp]
cut	[kʰʌʔt]
tack	[tʰæʔk]
ice	[ʔaɪs]
aim	[ʔeɪm]
The east	[ðə'ʔist]
He ate	[hi'ʔeɪt]

allophones of /l/, /ɹ/, /n/, /m/, and /k/ respectively. In contrast, the realization of /n/ as [ŋ] in *penguin* [pʰɛ̃ŋ.gwĩn], [ɪŋ.kʰɔ̃m] 'income', and as [m] in [sæ̃m.wɪʧ] 'sandwich' are examples of a phonemic coarticulation since its effect turns one phoneme into another in the language: /n/ to /ŋ/ and /m/ respectively.

Secondary Articulation

In English, coarticulation also leads to a number of secondary articulations, such as labialization, velarization, and palatalization on consonants (also see Chapter 1 Contour Consonants).

Labialization is the addition of lip rounding. For example, 's' in *soon* and *soul* is produced with lip rounding in anticipation of the following close, back, rounded vowel [u]. The [ʷ] diacritic is used to represent labialization, the lip rounding gesture added to the articulation of [s] in narrow transcription: *soon* [sʷun], and *soul* [sʷol].

Velarization is the addition of tongue back raising toward the velum. When preceded by a vowel, the English 'l' sound is often produced with this secondary gesture, and is referred to as a 'dark l'. Compare the 'l' sounds in *lip* and *pill*, for example. The 'l' in *lip*, also known as 'light l', is produced with the tongue tip touching the alveolar ridge with the back of the tongue in a lowered position. The 'l' in *pill*, on the other hand, is produced with the back of the tongue raised toward the velum in addition to the simultaneous tongue-tip gesture. The 'dark l' also occurs when it precedes another consonant, as in *field* [fiɫd], *film* [fɪɫm], *false* [fɔɫs], etc. Velarization is represented by the diacritic [~] through the symbol for [l] or [ˠ] next to the symbol for other velarized consonants. More examples of dark and light 'l' in English are given in Table 4.13.

Palatalization involves an addition of tongue body raising toward the hard palate. English 'l' in *million* is usually produced with this additional tongue gesture. Since this added action is similar to the [i] vowel or a [j]-like gesture, it is represented by the diacritic [ʲ], as shown in the narrow transcription of *million* [mɪlʲən] or *leaf*: [lʲif], *leash*: [lʲiʃ], and *lease* [lʲis], for example. Please note that the term palatalization is also used to describe the process whereby a consonant that is normally produced at a different place of articulation becomes an (alveo) palatal consonant, as when the 't' in *tree* is pronounced as an affricate [t͡ʃ] or when a [d] is pronounced as [dʒ], as in /dɪd ju/ > [dɪdʒə] *did you?*

Consonant Intrusion

Coarticulation can also result in a totally new consonant being inserted. For example, an intrusive [t] is heard between [n] and [s] in *prince* for most American English pronunciations. This happens because the timing of the oral closure release and the raising of the velum, which should happen simultaneously for [s] production, is slightly off. Specifically, the velum is raised first and the oral closure release lags slightly behind, allowing for an oral plosive [t] to occur in between, as represented in the narrow transcription [pʰɹ̃ĩnts]. This intrusive plosive typically shares place of articulation with the preceding nasal but voicing with the following fricative. Other examples of plosive intrusions are [k] in *length* [lɛ̃ŋkθ], *strength* [stɹɛ̃ŋkθ], and [p] in *something* [sʌ̃mpθɪ̃ŋ], *Memphis* [mɛ̃mpfɪs], etc.

The glottal stop [ʔ] is another intrusive consonant. It occurs before a final voiceless plosive [p, t, k] because speakers close their vocal folds after the vowel rather than leaving them open while making the final plosive sounds. A [ʔ] may also appear at the beginning of a word that begins with a vowel or between two words when the first ends with a vowel and the second begins with a vowel as in *the ice* [ðə ˈʔaɪs], and *she aims* [ʃi ˈʔeɪmz], in order to separate them (Reetz & Jongman, 2009). More examples of [ʔ] insertions in English are shown in Table 4.14, and see Fact box on intrusive [ɹ] in some American English speakers.

Fact: Intrusive [ɹ]

[ɹ] is an intrusive consonant among speakers of American English dialect along the east coast in particular, so *Cuba*, *Donna*, and *banana* are produced as *Cuber*, *Donner,* and *bananer* with an [ɚ] vowel on the last syllable. President Kennedy is a famous speaker of this dialect.

Syllabic Consonants

As discussed in Chapter 3, every syllable must contain a nucleus, and this position is usually occupied by a vowel. For example, [æ] and [ɪ] are the nuclei of the first and second syllables, respectively, in the word *panic* [pʰæ.nɪk]. However, sometimes a consonant becomes the nucleus of the syllable because the vowel, usually a schwa [ə] in an unstressed syllable, is not pronounced, as in *button* [bʌ.tn̩] (or [bʌ.ʔn̩]). In this case, the tongue makes contact with the alveolar ridge for [t] (or the vocal folds snap closed for the [ʔ]) and releases as

Table 4.15 *English syllabic consonants*

/batəl/	[batl̩]	'bottle'
/katən/	[kʰaʔn̩]	'cotton'
/bʌtɚ/	[bʌɾɻ̩]	'butter'
/ætəm/	[æɾm̩]	'atom'

[n] without moving because both [t] and [n] share place of articulation. Since there is no intervening vowel, [n] ends up in the nucleus position of the syllable and is referred to as a 'syllabic [n̩]' with the diacritic [ˌ] placed underneath it. Since the syllable nucleus is typically the loudest segment in the syllable, sonorant consonants, particularly [l, ɹ, m, n, ŋ], are typical candidates for this role. In addition, even though schwa deletion occurs most easily when adjacent consonants have the same place of articulation so that a single constriction can be maintained for both consonants, it may also occur when the two consonants have different places of articulation, as in *bottom* [baɾm̩], *taken* [tʰeɪkn̩], [vɪʒn̩] *vision*, and *uncle* [ʌ̃ŋkl̩]. More examples of English syllabic consonants are given in Table 4.15.

A question that often arises is when the syllabic [ɹ̩] or the vowel [ɚ] or [ɝ] should be used in transcription. There is likely more than one answer or preference on this, but a syllabic [ɹ̩] should be used when no vowel is present to serve as the syllable nucleus, whereas [ɚ] and [ɝ] should be used when the r-colored vowel is unstressed and stressed respectively.

Twenty-four IPA symbols are required for a broad or a phonemic transcription of consonants in English. However, the pronunciation of many English consonants varies depending on their absolute positions or their positions relative to other segments in an utterance, and a number of symbols and diacritics are needed to represent their phonetic details in a narrow transcription. In the next section, we discuss transcription of English vowels.

Vowels

Depending on the dialect, fifteen–sixteen vowel symbols are needed for a broad transcription of American English vowels (Tables 4.16 a, b). These include five front vowels [i, ɪ, eɪ/e, ɛ, æ], five back vowels [u, ʊ, oʊ, ɔ, ɑ], three central vowels [ɚ/ɝ, ə, ʌ], and three diphthongs [aɪ, aʊ, ɔɪ]. Some dialects don't distinguish between [ɑ] and [ɔ] so *caught* and *cot* are produced with the same vowel quality, namely [ɑ]. (See In Focus on vowel mergers before /ɹ/.)

The vowels [i, eɪ, ɑ, ɔ, oʊ, u, ɝ, aɪ, aʊ] are tense, and [ɪ, ɛ, æ, ə, ʌ, ʊ] are lax. Tense vowels are longer, located in more extreme positions in the vowel space and can occur in syllables that end in a vowel (open syllables) or in a consonant (closed syllable). Lax vowels are shorter, occupy less extreme positions and can only occur in closed syllables when stressed. Some lax vowels (e.g., ə, ɪ) may occur in unstressed, open syllables as in *China*, *Cuba*, *city*, and *pretty*.

Table 4.16a *American English monophthong vowels*

IPA symbol	tense/lax	Example word	IPA symbol	Tense/lax	Example word
[i]	tense	b**ead**	[ʊ]	lax	b**oo**k
[ɪ]	lax	b**i**d	[ɔ]	tense	b**ough**t
[ɛ]	lax	b**e**d	[ʌ]	lax	h**u**t
[æ]	lax	b**a**d	[ɑ]	tense	h**o**t
[u]	tense	b**oo**ed/ b**oo**t	[ɝ]	tense	b**ir**d
[ə]	lax	**a**bout	[ɚ]	lax	fath**er**

Table 4.16b *American English diphthong and diphthongized vowels*

IPA symbol	tense/lax	Example word
[aɪ]	tense	buy, tie, hide
[aʊ]	tense	cow, loud, how
[ɔɪ]	tense	boy, toy, coin
[eɪ]	tense	bay, bake, cake
[oʊ]	tense	coat, tote, boat

In Focus: Vowel Merger Before /ɹ/

In most dialects of American English, distinctions among some monophthongs disappear before [ɹ]. For example, [e], [ɛ], and [æ] are merged so 'Mary', 'merry', and 'marry' are homophones. Similarly, there is no distinction between [o] and [ɔ] so *wore* and *war* are homophones, so are *for* and *four*. *Beer* can be pronounced as [biɹ] or [bɪɹ], and *poor* can be pronounced as [pʰuɹ], [pʰoʊɹ] or [pʰʊɹ].

Note that some textbooks treat [ɔ] and [ɑ] as lax vowels. But like a tense vowel, both can occur in open syllables, e.g., *law* and *spa*. Additionally, a lax vowel rather than a tense vowel tends to appear before a [ʃ] as in [fɪʃ] *fish*, [kʰæʃ] *cash*, [pʰʊʃ] *push*, and [mɛʃ] *mesh*. In addition, the tense versus lax distinction is absent before a final [ŋ] so *sing* can be pronounced as [sĩŋ] with an [i], [sɪ̃ŋ] with an [ɪ] or somewhere in between. The vowels [aɪ, aʊ, ɔɪ] are considered true diphthongs while [eɪ, oʊ] are called diphthongized vowels. Tongue movements are more substantial in the three true diphthongs than in the two diphthongized vowels. In addition, the diphthongized vowels may be produced with less or no diphthongization in some contexts, i.e., preceding an alveolar approximant [l], as in *bail* and *bowl* and should be transcribed as monophthongs [e] and [o] respectively. In addition, [eɪ] has also become [ɛ] before an [l], particularly in southern dialects of American English, so contrasting pairs such as *sale* ~ *sell*, *fail* ~ *fell*, *hail* ~ *hell* and *tale* ~*tell* are homophones and are pronounced as [sɛɫ], [fɛɫ], [hɛɫ], and [tʰɛɫ] respectively. Furthermore, tense vowels [i] and [u] may also be diphthongized i.e., produced with a [ʲ] and a [ʷ] off-glide as in [biʲd] *bead*, [siʲ] *sea*, [buʷd] *booed* and [tʰuʷ] *two*.

Schwa [ə] is known as the neutral vowel because of its position on the vowel chart and the neutral vocal tract configuration during its production. It occurs only in unstressed syllables, as in *above*, *avoid*, and *alone*. However, even though an unstressed vowel is shorter and more centralized than a stressed vowel, not all of them become schwa. For example, the unstressed vowel in the second syllable of *rabbit*, *manage*, and *childish* is closer to an [ɪ] than a schwa. Since schwa only appears in unstressed syllables and is not contrastive with any other vowels, it is not considered a phoneme.

By convention, the r-colored or rhotacized (see Rhotacization below), open-mid central vowel [ɝ] is used to transcribe the vowel in *fur*, *nurse*, *purse*, and so on, while r-colored schwa [ɚ] is used to represent a similar vowel in an unstressed syllable, such as in *father*, or *mother*. Phonetically speaking, the quality of these two vowels, without the rhotacization, is closer to the schwa [ə] than to the non r-colored [ɜ] in British English [ɜ] *bird*. However, since schwa only occurs in unstressed syllables, r-colored schwa [ɚ] is not used to represent the stressed rhotacized vowel in *fur*, *nurse*, and *purse* mentioned above. Note that, due to their phonetic similarity, some phoneticians do not differentiate between [ɝ] and [ɚ] based on stress.

Finally, in r-less or non-rhotic English dialects such as the Bostonian dialect, [ɹ] is replaced by [ə] so *near* and *hear* are pronounced [nɪə] and [hɪə] to rhyme with *idea*, *via*, *galleria*, *Maria*, *media*, and *India*.

Narrow Transcription of English Vowels

In comparison to consonants, vowel sounds show greater variation across American English dialects. In this section, we will only discuss the influence of following consonants on vowel pronunciation, including nasalization, rhotacization, and vowel lengthening.

Nasalization

American English vowels are typically oral. They are produced with the velum in a raised position so that airflow can only exit through the oral cavity. However, they become nasalized in the context of a following nasal consonant. In this case, the velum is lowered during either the entire articulation or a portion of the vowel before the oral constriction for the nasal is made, thus allowing air to partially exit through the nose. Nasalization is indicated by the [˜] diacritic placed above the vowel, as in *can* [kʰæ̃n], *sum* [sʌ̃m], and *bank* [bæ̃ŋk]. Note that the absence of nasality doesn't affect meaning in English because it is not phonemically contrastive. It just makes the utterance sound non-native to native listeners.

Table 4.17 *French nasal vowels*

[lɛ]	'ugly'	[lɛ̃]	'flax'
[la]	'there'	[lã]	'slow'
[lɔ]	'prize'	[lɔ̃]	'long'

Table 4.18 *Vowel lengthening in English*

[bæk]	'back'	[bæˑg]	'bag'
[feɪs]	'face'	[feɪˑz]	'phase'
[bæʧ]	'batch'	[bæˑʤ]	'badge'
[pʰ̥ɹaɪs]	'price'	[pʰ̥ɹaɪˑz]	'prize'

Interestingly, a distinction between [ɪ] and [ɛ] is often lost before a nasal [n] so *pin* and *pen* and *tin* and *ten* are homophones in American English, particularly the southern dialects.

On the other hand, nasality is phonemic in French (see Table 4.17). For example, [bo] means mean 'beautiful', but [bõ] means 'good'. The term **nasal vowels** is used rather than **nasalized vowels** when nasality is phonemic.

Rhotacization

In addition to nasal consonants, [ɹ] also asserts its influence on a preceding vowel. Vowels affected by [ɹ] are referred to as 'r-colored' or rhotacized vowels (see also Chapter 1 § Rhotacized, Rhotic, or r-Colored Vowels). [ɝ/ɚ] as in *hurt* and *number* are the r-colored or rhotacized vowels in American English, with tongue gestures for the vowel and the [ɹ] occurring simultaneously. This is different from a vowel preceding an [ɹ] as in *bar*, *beer*, and *bored*. Try producing these words yourself. You will notice that, in these cases, tongue gestures for [ɹ] and the vowel are not formed simultaneously – the tongue bunching for [ɹ] occurs slightly after the vowel – and may be treated as a vowel + [ɹ] sequence. Thus, *bar*, *beer*, and *bored* should be transcribed as [bɑɹ], [biɹ], and [bɔɹd] respectively rather than [bɑ˞], [bi˞], and [bɔ˞d].

Vowel Lengthening

In addition to its quality, the duration of a vowel may also be affected by the following consonant. For example, compare the duration of the vowel [æ] in *bad* and *bat*. You will notice that the vowel articulation is held for a longer time in *bad* than in *bat*. This is also true for [ɪ] in *bid* and *bit* or [i] in *bead* and *beat*. In fact, all vowels occurring before a voiced obstruent (plosives, fricatives, and affricates) are longer than vowels that occur before their voiceless counterparts. The extra length is represented by the diacritic [ː] or [ˑ]. To distinguish inherent vowel duration or vowel lengthening induced by consonants from the contrastive vowel length discussed in Chapter 3, a half long diacritic will be used for the former, thus narrow transcriptions of *bead* and *beat* would be [biˑd] and [bɪt], respectively. For diphthongs, the lengthening is realized mostly in the last (off-glide) portion.

Note that American English vowels are also longer in open syllables than in closed syllables, as in:

[siʲˑ] 'see',   [tʰoʊˑ] 'tow'   [sɔˑ] 'saw'   [haɪˑ] 'high'
[sijp] 'seep'   [tʰoʊt] 'tote'   [sɔft] 'soft'   [haɪt] 'height'

In summary, the quality of an English vowel is affected by following nasals, [ɹ], and voiced and voiceless obstruents. A vowel becomes nasalized and rhotacized when it precedes a nasal consonant and [ɹ], respectively. Its duration is relatively longer before a voiced obstruent than before a voiceless obstruent.

Chapter Summary

Linguists use the IPA to transcribe speech. But unlike a recording, the IPA only captures articulatory features at the segment level while sub-segmental details are ignored. Speech may be transcribed with different degrees of detail. An impressionistic transcription aims at noting down every discernible phonetic detail without the influence of previous linguistic knowledge of the speech material being transcribed. A narrow transcription includes the phonetic details of each target phoneme as it is produced in different contexts. A broad transcription provides information to approximate the pronunciation of an utterance, but without its fine phonetic details. Lastly, a phonemic transcription does not represent the actual physical reality, but the abstract sound categories or phonemes in the native speaker's mind.

Approximately twenty-four consonant symbols and fifteen–sixteen vowel symbols are needed for a broad or a phonemic transcription of English. A number of diacritics, however, are necessary for a narrow transcription, as both English consonant and vowel production exhibit positional variation due to the influence of their absolute position in an utterance or the phonetic characteristics of neighboring segments.

As mentioned earlier, phonetic features included in a narrow phonetic transcription are revealed through a phonemic analysis, a process we describe in the next chapter. In addition, a related morphophonemic analysis used to reveal phonetic variations of a morpheme (the smallest meaningful linguistic unit) is also discussed.

Review Exercises

Exercise 4.1: What are the differences between a narrow and a broad transcription? Between a broad and a phonemic transcription?

Exercise 4.2: Name and describe different types of coarticulation and provide your own examples.

Exercise 4.3: Provide a narrow transcription for the following English words according to your own pronunciation.

wishing   strength   traffic   remain   manage
baking   vision   comb   chore   shame

Exercise 4.4: Write American English words that correspond to the following transcriptions:
  a. [ˈʧĩpĩŋ]
  b. [ðiz]
  c. [əˈbaʊt]
  d. [ˈhɪdn̩]
  e. [kw̥ĩn]

Exercise 4.5: Provide a correct transcription for the following English words.

a. grab	[græb]	should be	[	]
b. should	[ʃud]	should be	[	]
c. wrist	[wɹɪst]	should be	[	]
d. strength	[stɹɛ̃nθ]	should be	[	]
e. throw	[thɹoʊ̥]	should be	[	]

References and Further Reading

There are many interactive IPA charts online where you can hear how each IPA symbol is pronounced. We recommend the one by Peter Ladefoged which can be found here www.phonetics.ucla.edu/course/contents.html even though it represents an older (1996) version and a consonant, namely the labio-dental flap [ⱱ], is missing from it.

Ladefoged, P., & Disner, S. F. (2012). *Vowels and Consonants*, 3rd edn. Oxford: Wiley-Blackwell.

Ladefoged, P., & Maddieson, I. (1996). *The Sounds of the World's Languages*. Oxford: Blackwell.

Reetz, H., & Jongman, A. (2009). *Phonetics: Transcription, Production, Acoustics, and Perception* (Vol. 34). West Sussex: John Wiley & Sons.

5

Phonemic and Morphophonemic Analyses

Learning Objectives

By the end of this chapter, you will be able to:

- Describe phonological concepts, such as:
  - Abstraction
  - Predictability
  - Phoneme
  - Allophones
- Recognize contrastive distributions, namely:
  - Contrastive
  - Analogous
- Identify predictable distributions, such as:
  - Complementary
  - Free variation
- Perform basic phonemic and morphophonemic analyses, and compose generalizations capturing allophonic and allomorphic derivations

Introduction

Besides knowing how to produce and perceive sounds in their language, native speakers also know if two sounds distinguish word meaning. That is, they know if two sounds represent a contrast, or if they are just different pronunciations of the same sound. To native English speakers, the different 'p' sounds in *peak* and *speak* are not contrastive. They are positional variants of the same sound. If the 'p' from *speak* were to be replaced by the one from *peak*, or vice versa, they may sound odd or foreign accented, but no new words would be heard. But if the 'p' in *peak* is replaced by the 'b' from *beak*, a native speaker will immediately recognize that a different word has just been said; that is, they will treat the 'p' and the 'b' sounds as members of two distinct sound categories or phonemes, each of which has the power to change a word's meaning. The number and type of phonemes used to distinguish words vary from language to language.

This knowledge is largely subconscious, and cannot, therefore, be directly obtained by asking native speakers. In fact, they are often not aware of the phonetic difference between sounds that they treat as members of the same phoneme (see 'Categorical Perception' discussed in Chapter 10). But we know that they possess this abstract knowledge, in part, because of its generalizability. For instance, if we present native English speakers with English-like words that they haven't heard before, such as *bish*, *pish*, and *spish*, they will likely judge that *bish* and *pish* are two different words. They would also invariably pronounce the 'p' sound in *pish* with aspiration (puff of air following the release of the lip closure), but without it for the 'p' sound in *spish*, revealing their abstract knowledge of the categorical membership of 'b' and 'p' as well as the positional variants of 'p'. The non-word test is a good tool to confirm what we think native speakers know. But how do we find out what they know to begin with?

In this chapter, we discuss a method of phonemic analysis that phonologists use to identify phonemes, their positional variants, and the rules that govern their distributions – the phonological knowledge used to produce and hear one's native language. But before discussing the steps involved in this analytical procedure, it's necessary that we first become familiar with the relevant concepts, including the terms phoneme and allophone we introduced in Chapter 4. We conclude the chapter with a discussion on another type of analysis known as morphophonemic analysis, a method used to discover pronunciation variations of a morpheme, the smallest meaningful linguistic unit. Don't worry if you are not sure what this means at this point. We will go over this procedure in more detail in later sections.

Phonological Concepts

Familiarity with some phonological concepts is crucial for a better understanding of the phonemic analysis process. We will begin with the basic notions of abstraction and predictability, and their phonological parallels: phonemes and allophones.

Abstraction: Predictability – Phoneme and Allophone

As already discussed in Chapter 4, the term *phoneme* refers, not to one sound, but to a family of sounds treated as being the same by native speakers. Just as furniture is a label for a group of objects used to make a space suitable for living or working, phoneme is an abstract label for a group of sounds used to distinguish words in a language. And just as we don't technically build "furniture," but a piece of furniture such as a bed, a chair, a night stand, etc., a phoneme cannot be pronounced. What is produced and heard are the individual members of the phoneme, called *allophones*. (See In Focus for evidence of the reality of phonemes.)

In Focus: The Reality of Phonemes

The most influential paper addressing abstract phonological knowledge, including that of a phoneme, was written by Edward Sapir in the article "The psychological reality of phoneme" published in French under the title "La réalité psychologique des phonèmes" in the *Journal de Psychologie Normale and Pathologique* in 1933. The most cited example was Sapir's recount of his interaction with his informant, John Whitney, a speaker of the Native American language Sarcee spoken in Canada. Specifically, the example involved two words [dìní] 'it makes a sound' and [dìní] 'this one'. To Sapir's trained ears these two words are identical in every way (i.e., homophones), including the low and the high tones on the first and the second syllable, but Whitney insisted that he heard a 't' at the end of [-ni] in 'it makes a sound'. As it turned out, when a suffix [-i] is added, [dìní] 'this one' becomes [dìníː] with the final vowel lengthened, but 'it makes a sound' becomes [dìnítí], with the appearance of Whitney's phantom [t]. Sapir took this to mean that Whitney knew that the phantom 't' is part of the word even when it is not pronounced. That is, in Whitney's mind, the word for 'this one' is represented as /dìní/, but the word for 'it makes a sound' is represented as /dìnít/. (See a discussion on underlying and surface representation in section later in the chapter.)

In Chapter 4, we saw that a voiced plosive such as /d/ in English has multiple variants, namely voiceless [d̥] as in *day*, unreleased [d'] as in *tad* and a flap [ɾ] in *ladder*. These three phones occur in different positions in a word: word- or syllable-initial, word-final, and between a stressed and an unstressed vowel, respectively. The distribution of phones tells us how they are related and treated by the speaker. Phones that occur in a non-overlapping pattern or that can be freely interchanged without affecting meaning are treated as different allophones of the same phoneme. In this example, the three phones [d], [d'] and [ɾ] are considered allophones of the same phoneme /d/. Simply put, they are three different pronunciations of /d/.

Allophones are predictable, but phonemes must be learned and memorized. For instance, besides meaning, there is no rule in English that tells native English speakers to expect a /p/ in *pen*, but a /d/ in *den*. They have to be learned and remembered as part of the identity of the word. In fact, all three sounds making up these two words must be learned.

Let's examine allophones of the phoneme /t/ in English to further illustrate the difference between phonemes and allophones.

Table 5.1 *Allophones of English /t/*

top	[tʰɑpˀ]	kitten	[kʰɪ.ʔn̩]
stop	[stɑpˀ]	spot	[spɑtˀ]
little	[lɪ.ɾl̩]		

Here we see that the letter 't' is pronounced as [tʰ], [t], [ɾ], [ʔ], and [tˀ] depending on where it is in a word. It is pronounced as a voiceless aspirated alveolar plosive [tʰ] in syllable-initial position in *top*, as a voiceless unaspirated alveolar plosive [t] in *stop*, as a voiced alveolar tap [ɾ] in *little*, as a voiceless glottal plosive [ʔ] in *kitten*, and as an unreleased voiceless alveolar plosive [tˀ] in *spot*. If you ask native speakers of English, they would agree that these are simply different pronunciations of 't'. In other words, they are allophones of the same phoneme /t/. The occurrence of each allophone is predictable and can be captured by the generalizations or **allophonic rules**. Allophonic rules for English /t/ are as follows:

Rules:

1. /t/ is aspirated in initial position of a stressed syllable.
2. /t/ becomes a flap [ɾ] when it occurs between a stressed and an unstressed vowel.
3. /t/ is pronounced as a glottal plosive [ʔ] when it precedes a syllabic [n̩].
4. /t/ is pronounced without an oral closure release, [tˀ], when it occurs in word-final position.

Note that some of these rules are not always applied for some speakers, dialects, speaking style, etc. In other words, they are variable. For instance, Rule 4 may not apply when the word is produced in a careful, reading style.

Same Phones but Different Phonemes

It is important to note that the same set of phones may be grouped into different phonemes by different languages. We just saw that [t] and [tʰ] are allophones of the same phoneme in English. However, these two phones are allophones of two separate phonemes in Thai, as shown in Table 5.2. The distribution of [t] and [tʰ] overlaps in Thai: They both can begin a word. Which word begins with a [t] and which begins with a [tʰ] must be learned and memorized. This is also true for [p], [pʰ] and [k], [kʰ].

In comparison, there are no aspirated plosives in Spanish, only voiced [b, d, g] and voiceless unaspirated [p, t, k]. The sounds [p, t, k] are allophones of /p, t, k/ whereas [b, d, g] and [β, ð, ɣ] are allophones of /b, d, g/. The phones [β, ð, ɣ] occur between vowels, and after non-nasal consonants, whereas [b, d, g] appear word-initially, after nasals or after [l] in case of /d/. Native speakers of one language often carry over features of their native phonology into words from a

Table 5.2 *Thai voiceless aspirated and voiceless unaspirated plosives*

Voiceless aspirated		Voiceless unaspirated	
[tʰaː]	'to apply (e.g., paint)'	[taː]	'eye, grandfather'
[pʰaː]	'to accompany'	[paː]	'to throw'
[kʰaː]	'to be stuck'	[kaː]	'a crow'

Table 5.3 *Hindi voiceless velar plosives*

Voiceless unaspirated		Voiceless aspirated	
[kal]	'era'	[kʰal]	'skin'
[kan]	'ear'	[kʰan]	'ruler'

new language. Therefore, *taco* is often pronounced as [tʰɑkoʊ] by English speakers and *baby* is pronounced as [beɪβi] by Spanish speakers.

Identifying Phonemes and Allophones: The Distribution of Speech Sounds

How do we know whether two (or more) phones are treated by native speakers as members of the same phoneme or as different phonemes? The answer is we examine their distribution. Three main distribution patterns between two phones are contrastive, complementary, and free variation.

Contrastive Distribution: Minimal Pairs, Allophones of Different Phonemes

Recall that the main function of phonemes is to distinguish words. Thus, if two sounds occur in the same position in a word, and substituting one with the other changes the word's meaning, then they belong to two different phonemes.

Consider the data from Hindi in Table 5.3. Similar to Thai, both voiceless unaspirated velar plosive [k] and voiceless aspirated plosive [kʰ] may occur word-initially in Hindi, and substituting [k] with [kʰ] will change the meaning of the word from 'era' to 'skin', and from 'ear' to 'ruler'. [k] and [kʰ] are in contrastive distribution with each other, and are therefore allophones of two different phonemes.

Pairs of words that differ only in one segment are called *minimal pairs*. They are the most reliable evidence that two phones are allophones of two separate phonemes, so phonologists like to seek them when they can.

Analogous Distribution: Near-Minimal Pairs, Allophones of Different Phonemes

A minimal pair may not always be found for certain pairs of sounds. For instance, consider the [ð] and [ʒ] sounds in English presented in Table 5.4.

Table 5.4 *Near-minimal pairs in English*

[fɛðɚ]	'feather'	[mɛʒɚ]	'measure'
[niðɚ]	'neither'	[liʒɚ]	'leisure'
[ɹæðɚ]	'rather'	[æʒɚ]	'azure'

Table 5.5 *Jaqaru near-minimal pairs*

[ʃa]	'hello (man to man)'	[miʃi]	'cat'
[saja]	'to stand'	[nisa]	'in just a moment'
[iʃa]	'no, not (principal cause)'		

For each word pair, both sounds occur in word-medial position. They are preceded and followed by the same vowels. However, the initial consonants of the two words also differ. Since there is more than one difference between them, they are not considered a minimal pair, but rather a *near-minimal pair*. To decide whether two phones occurring in such analogous environments belong to the same or different phonemes, we need to consider whether there is any reason to believe that the other difference, namely between the initial consonants in this case, is responsible for the distribution of [ð] and [ʒ]. From the fact that the initial consonants for both sets of words appear to be random, we conclude that the difference between [ð] and [ʒ] is not influenced by the initial consonants and that they are allophones of two different phonemes: /ð/ and /ʒ/.

Let's look at another example of near-minimal pairs from Jaqaru (Table 5.5). We see here that, similar to the English [ð] and [ʒ], no minimal pairs exist for [s] and [ʃ] in this data set. However, we also see that they occur in similar environments: word-initial followed by [a] in 'hello' and 'to stand', and word-medial preceded by [i] and followed by [a] in 'no', and 'in just a moment'. Even though there are other differences (e.g., the presence of [j] and [n] in 'to stand' and 'in just a moment'), there is no good reason to think that they are responsible for the difference between [s] and [ʃ]. It is, therefore, reasonable to conclude that [s] and [ʃ] are allophones of two different phonemes, which means that Jaqaru speakers have to learn and memorize that 'hello' begins with [s], but 'to stand' begins with [ʃ].

Complementary Distribution: Allophones of the Same Phoneme

If one sound occurs where the other sound never occurs, then the two sounds are in non-overlapping or complementary distribution with one another, and are allophones of the same phoneme, as illustrated by the data from Kenyang in Table 5.6.

In Kenyang, minimal pairs can never be found for [q] and [k] because these two sounds do not appear in the same positions in words: [q] appears only after non-high back vowels [ɔ, o, ɑ], while [k] occurs elsewhere. They are in

Table 5.6 *Kenyang [q] and [k]*

[enɔq]	'tree'	[enoq]	'drum'
[eket]	'house'	[ntʃiku]	'I am buying'
[nek]	'rope'	[ejwɑrek]	'sweet potato'
[ŋgɑq]	'knife'	[ekɑq]	'leg'
[mək]	'dirt'	[nɑq]	'brother-in-law'
[ndek]	'European'	[pɔbrik]	'work project'
[betək]	'job'	[bepək]	'to capsize'
[tiku]	(name)	[ku]	'buy!'
[ɑyuk]	(name)	[esikɔŋ]	'pipe'
[kebwep]	'stammering'	[ŋkɔq]	'chicken'
[ŋkɑp]	'money'	[kɔ]	'walk!'

(from Odden, 2005)

complementary distribution. Phones showing this type of distributional pattern are allophones of a single phoneme.

It should be noted that not all phones in complementary distribution are allophones of the same phoneme. For example, in English, [h] can only be found in word- or syllable-initial position, whereas [ŋ] only occurs in word- or syllable-final position, and thus they are in complementary distribution. However, due to their phonetic dissimilarity, it is highly unlikely that they would be treated as each other's variant or allophones of the same phoneme (see also Phonemic Analysis below).

Free Variation: Allophones of the Same Phoneme

In some phonetic contexts, more than one pronunciation of a given sound may be possible. In English, both released [p] and unreleased [p'] occur in the same environment; they can both appear at the end of a word. This is also true for [t] ~ [t'] and [k] ~ [k'].

The choice between [p] and [p'] does not make a difference in meaning. They are in free variation, and are allophones of the same phoneme. However, this is not to say that their occurrence does not depend on stylistic, dialectal, formality, or other considerations.

One should not confuse allophonic free variation with phonemic free variation. Two phones from the same phoneme are interchanged freely in allophonic variation, whereas two phonemes are interchanged in phonemic free variation. In English, [i] and [aɪ] are allophones of different phonemes: /i/ and /aɪ/ (e.g., *he* vs. *high*), but either can be heard on the first syllable of the word *either*. Similarly, [s] and [ʃ] are allophones of separate phonemes, as in *sip* vs. *ship*, but either of them is produced in *enunciate* and *appreciate*.

Underlying and Surface Forms: Abstract vs. Concrete

Underlying forms are abstract representations of sounds stored in the mind/brain of the speaker, while surface forms are the actual realizations of sounds.

Table 5.7 *English released and unreleased voiceless bilabial plosives*

leap	[lip]	leap	[lipʼ]
keep	[kʰip]	keep	[kʰipʼ]
tap	[tʰæp]	tap	[tʰæpʼ]
rip	[ɹip]	rip	[ɹipʼ]

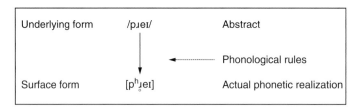

Figure 5.1 Phonological derivation of English *pray*

The distinction is analogous to the difference between phoneme and allophone. The surface form is derived from the underlying form by rules. As diagrammed in Figure 5.1, the underlying form of *pray* is /pɹeɪ/, but its surface form is [pʰɹ̥eɪ] where /p/ is aspirated and /ɹ/ is voiceless because of English aspiration and liquid voicing assimilation rules (Figure 5.1).

Note that the question of how abstract our mental representation of speech sounds is remains a subject of debate. There's evidence to suggest that subphonemic information is available and used by listeners to retrieve words from the lexicon. For instance, words produced by familiar talkers are remembered better and recalled faster, suggesting that some talker-specific phonetic features are stored in our long-term phonological memory.

Natural Classes

Sounds of languages fall into *natural classes*. They are groups of sounds that share some features (phonetic characteristics that distinguish each phoneme of a language from every other phoneme of that language) to the exclusion of other sounds. More importantly, they are affected in the same way by the same environments or contexts, and they exert the same effects on other sounds in the environment. In other words, they participate in similar phonological processes. For instance, voiced plosives [b, d, g] in English form a natural class. As previously discussed (Chapter 4), all vowels in English are lengthened before voiced plosives in comparison to before voiceless plosives [p, t, k], which also form another natural class; so /æ/ in *tab* [tæˑb], *tad* [tæˑd], and *tag* [tæˑg] is longer than in *tap* [tæp], *tat* [tæt] and *tack* [tæk], and so on. It's important to note that since all three voiced plosives participate in the vowel-lengthening process, they

Table 5.8 *English consonant and vowel natural classes*

/p, b, t, d, k, g, ʔ, f, v, θ, ð, s, z, ʃ, ʒ, h, t͡ʃ, d͡ʒ/	=	obstruents
/p, b, t, d, k, g, ʔ, m, n, ŋ/	=	plosives
/p, b, t, d, k, g, ʔ/	=	oral plosives
/m, n, ŋ/	=	nasal plosives
/f, v, θ, ð, s, z, ʃ, ʒ, h/	=	fricatives
/f, v, θ, ð/	=	non-sibilants
/s, z, ʃ, ʒ/	=	sibilants
/v, ð, z, ʒ/	=	voiced fricatives
/m, n, ŋ, l, r, w, j, vowels/	=	sonorants
/r, l/	=	liquids
/w, j/	=	glides
/i, ɪ, e, ɛ, æ/	=	front vowels
/u, ʊ, o, ɔ, a/	=	back vowels

must all be included in the set. Excluding one or more of the members will violate the definition of natural class given above. For instance, with the exclusion of /g/, /b, d/ do not form a natural class, and neither do /g, b/ or /g, d/.

Some examples of natural classes in English are given in Table 5.8.

Other examples of phonological processes that a natural class in American English may undergo are: vowels become nasalized before a nasal consonant, particularly in stressed syllables, as in [pʰɛ̃n] *pen*, [tʰĩn] *tin*, [bʌ̃n] *bun*, [pʰæ̃ndə] *panda*, [bĩŋgoʊ] *bingo*; liquid [l, ɹ] becomes voiceless after a voiceless plosive, e.g., [bleɪd] *blade* vs. [pʰl̥eɪd] *played*, or [bɹeɪ] *bray* vs. [pʰɹ̥eɪ] *pray*; and a nasal place of articulation becomes similar to that of a following consonant, e.g., [hæ̃mbɔɫ] *handball* instead of [hæ̃ndbɔɫ], [kʰʌ̃ɱfɚt], or *comfort* instead of [kʰʌ̃mfɚt].

Phonemic Analysis

Having gone over the relevant terminology and concepts, we now turn to the steps involved in performing a phonemic analysis.

The starting point of a phonemic analysis is a set of phonetic data, collected first hand by you, preferably, or from a reliable secondary source. If a secondary source is used, it is always a good idea to double-check with native speakers to assure the accuracy of the data set, and thus your analysis. From the data, identify a pair or a set of phones that are phonetically similar. The assumption is that sounds with similar phonetic characteristics are more likely to belong to the same phoneme. Recall that the main function of a phoneme is to distinguish words, and naturally, languages would favor using sounds that are phonetically distinct to do the job. For instance, it is more likely that [b] and [k] will be treated as different phonemes and used to contrast words than [d] and [ɾ]. We refer to pairs or sets of phonetically similar sounds whose phonemic status needs to be examined as **suspicious pairs**.

Table 5.9 *Japanese [s] and [ʃ]*

[kesa]	'this morning'	[aʃita]	'tomorrow'
[osoi]	'slow, late'	[ʃimasɯ]	'(I will) do (it)'
[kusarɯ]	'to rot'	[mɯʃi]	'insect'
[ase]	'sweat'	[toʃi]	'year'
[miso]	'soy bean paste'	[hoʃi]	'star'

[s]	[ʃ]
e_a	o_i
o_o	a_i
ɯ_e	#_i
a_e	ɯ_i
i_o	

Figure 5. 2 Distribution of [s] and [ʃ] in Japanese

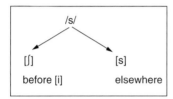

Figure 5.3 Japanese /s/ and its allophones

Let's consider the distributions of [s] and [ʃ] in Japanese data. They are both voiceless fricatives, but differ in their place of articulation, as shown in Table 5.9.

The environments for [s] and [ʃ] are shown in Figure 5.2. When we look at the environments for Japanese [s] and [ʃ] in Figure 5.2, one thing that jumps out is that the vowel following [ʃ] is always an [i]. On the other hand, the environments for [s] have little in common, except for the fact that they are all vowels. This data set thus shows that [s] and [ʃ] are in complementary distribution, where [ʃ] occurs only before [i], and [s] occurs elsewhere. Phones with this pattern of distribution are treated as allophones of the same phoneme.

The Basic Allophone

Next, we need to choose one allophone as the basic form to name the phoneme. A basic allophone is the one with the widest distribution or whose distribution can be described as 'elsewhere'. In this case, this would be the [s]. Thus, we can summarize our analysis as follows: [s] and [ʃ] are in complementary distribution and are allophones of the same phoneme /s/ in Japanese: [ʃ] occurs before [i] and [s] occurs elsewhere. This is diagrammed in Figure 5.3.

Table 5.10 *Oral and nasal vowels in Apinayé*

[api]	'ascend'	[apĩ]	'to kill'
[apɛ]	'lick'	[apɛ̃]	'show'
[apa]	'your arm'	[mã]	'no'
[tono]	'armadillo'	[kõnõ]	'knee'
[puɾu]	'field'	[kũmũ]	'smoke'

(From Ham, 1961)

Table 5.11 *Oral and nasalized vowels in English*

[pʰĩn]	'pin'	[pʰɪt]	'pit'
[pʰæ̃n]	'pan'	[pʰæt]	'pat'
[pʰʌ̃n]	'pun'	[pʰʌd]	'pud'
[kʰĩn]	'keen'	[kʰɪt]	'kit'
[tʰĩn]	'tin'	[tʰɪp]	'tip'

/s/ —————————→ [ʃ] / ___ i

Figure 5.4 Allophonic rule for Japanese /s/

This pattern can also be restated as a generalization: The phoneme /s/ is pronounced [ʃ] before [i], and written as a rule as shown in Figure 5.4.

Consider another example from Apinayé, spoken in central Brazil (Table 5.10). The sounds of interest here are the oral vowel vs. the nasalized vowel. Does Apinayé have two sets of vowel phonemes: oral vs. nasal, or just one set and the other set is derived by rule?

To reach a conclusion, first, we look for minimal pairs, and there are two to be found: 'ascend' vs. 'to kill' and 'lick' vs. 'show'. Based on these, we can conclude that [i] and [ĩ] are allophones of two different phonemes /i/ and /ĩ/, so are [ɛ]~/ɛ/ and [ɛ̃]~/ɛ̃/. The remaining are near-minimal pairs, including 'your arm' vs. 'no', 'armadillo' vs. 'knee', and 'field' vs. 'smoke', and these further suggest that [a]~[ã], [o]~[õ], and [u]~[ũ] are also allophones of separate phonemes, namely /a/, /ã/, /o/, /õ/, and /u/, /ũ/, respectively. That is, nasalization is contrastive in Apinayé. Apinayé speakers have to learn and remember whether a vowel in a word is oral or nasal.

The phonemic status of nasalization in English is, however, different from that of Apinayé, as illustrated in Table 5.11. Unlike Apinayé, no minimal pairs exist in English for nasalization. Nasalized vowels occur before a nasal consonant, while oral vowels occur elsewhere. They are in complementary distribution and are, therefore, allophones of the same phoneme. Unlike Apinayé, nasalization is not contrastive in English. Native English speakers don't have to remember if a vowel in an English word is oral or nasal. Without conscious awareness, they

Table 5.12 *Korean [l] and [ɾ]*

[l]		[ɾ]	
[midal]	'shortage'	[ɾadio]	'radio'
[pal]	'big'	[saɾam]	'person'
[mul]	'water'	[kiɾi]	'road'

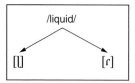

Figure 5.5 Korean liquid phoneme

automatically produce it as a nasalized vowel in the context of a nasal consonant. To differentiate between non-contrastive nasalization in English and contrastive nasalization in Apinayé, we use the terms nasalized vowels vs. nasal vowels, respectively.

No Basic Allophone

What happens if the distribution of two or more allophones is equal, such that one cannot be chosen as basic? Consider the following data set from Korean in Table 5.12. From the data, we see that [l] and [ɾ] are in complementary distribution in Korean and are, therefore, allophones of the same phoneme. Importantly, they are both equally distributed; [ɾ] occurs syllable initially and [l] syllable finally. How do we determine which one is basic? We may choose [l] based on the fact that it is more common than [ɾ] among the world's languages, and it may also be simpler in terms of articulation. We may also choose one based on its frequency of occurrence if known. We may also toss a coin or choose at random. However, linguists consider it unlikely that speakers randomly choose which sound to mentally represent. Another possibility is not to choose either one, and simply call it 'liquid', a family name that both belong to, without giving more weight to one member over the other, as diagrammed in Figure 5.5.

Positional Neutralization

In some cases, two sounds may be contrastive in one position but not in another. For instance, voiced and voiceless obstruents are contrastive in Dutch, but the distinction is lost in word-final position, where they are all voiceless. This is illustrated in Table 5.13.

Table 5.13 *Obstruent final voicing neutralization in Dutch*

/pad/	[pat]	'toad'	/pad/+ən	[padən]	'toads'
/puːz/	[puːs]	'cat'	/puːz/+ən	[puːzən]	'cats'
/lat/	[lat]	'lath'	/lat/+ən	[latən]	'laths'
/vɔs/	[vɔs]	'fox'	/vɔs/+ən	[vɔsən]	'foxes'

(Grijzenhout & Krämer, 2000)

In these examples, we see that Dutch voiceless obstruents /t/ and /s/ are pronounced as [t] and [s] in 'lath, laths' and 'fox, foxes' in both word-final and word-medial positions. On the other hand, due to the final obstruent devoicing rule, voiced obstruents /d/ and /z/ are pronounced as [t] and [s] in word-final position in 'toad' and 'cat'.

A good example of positional neutralization from American English is the contrast between /t/ and /d/. They are allophones of two different phonemes in word-initial and word-final position as in *tip* [tʰɪp] vs. *dip* [dɪp], and *bed* [bɛd] vs. *bet* [bɛt]. However, their phonemic difference becomes neutralized when they occur between two vowels when the following vowel is unstressed, as in *kitty* [kʰɪɾi] vs. *kiddy* [kʰɪɾi]. They are both pronounced as a tap [ɾ], and without context, it may be difficult to decide which word was meant by the speaker.

Morphophonemic Analysis

Depending on their educational background, speakers of a language may know 100,000 words or more. Each word and its meaning has to be learned and memorized, as there is no natural relationship between individual sounds or a sequence of sounds making up a word and its meaning. Ferdinand de Saussure, a Swiss linguist, refers to this arbitrary relationship between sounds and meaning as, "the arbitrariness of the signs." For instance, the four-legged canine animal is encoded with the [dɔg] sound sequence in American English, but with [pero], [ʃjɛ̃], and [mǎː] in Spanish, French, and Thai respectively.

Phonotactics

Besides words, native speakers of a language also know what sequences of sounds are permissible or not in their language. A native English speaker would reject the sequence [sfid] as an English word because [s] and [f] are not allowed to be next to each other to form an onset of an English syllable. Rules for allowable or unallowable combinations of sounds are called phonotactic rules, and they vary from language to language. For instance, the string [-ld] in word-final position as in *mild* and *child* is legal in English but not permissible in Thai. Consequently, native speakers of Thai, like myself, have a hard time producing this consonant sequence in a native-like fashion.

Table 5.14 *English plural morpheme*

[-ɨz]		[-z]		[-s]	
[mæsɨz]	masses	[bægz]	bags	[pʰæks]	packs
[mɛʃɨz]	meshes	[dɔgz]	dogs	[mæts]	mats
[tʃɚtʃɨz]	churches	[dɔlz]	dolls	[mɑps]	mops
[feɪsɨz]	faces	[tʰoʊz]	toes	[tʰɔks]	talks

Phonological Alternations

Words are made up of small meaningful parts called **morphemes**, which could be represented by a single sound or, more frequently, by a string of sounds. For instance, *salt* is a mono-morphemic word made up of one morpheme, but *slowly* consists of two morphemes: the stem *slow* + the suffix *ly*. Just as a phoneme may have a number of predictable variants called allophones, a morpheme may also have one or more variants called allomorphs. Consider the alternation of plural morphemes in English (Table 5.14). Each morphological variant is called **an alternant**.

In this data set, there are three alternants, [-ɨz, -z, -s], signaling the meaning of plurality depending on the ending sound of the stem. The alternant [-s] occurs after a stem ending with a voiceless plosive, [-z] after a voiced segment including a vowel, and [-ɨz] after a fricative or an affricate. This kind of alternation is called **phonological alternation**, a variation conditioned by a sound in the environment. Since all three alternants add the same meaning to the stem they are attached to, we conclude that they are members of the same underlying morpheme. Just as a phonemic analysis reveals the underlying phoneme and its allophones, morphophonemic analysis is performed to reveal an underlying morpheme and its allomorphs.

In this data set, [-z] is considered the basic allomorph as it has the widest distribution. The analysis can be formally stated as follows: the plural morpheme /-z/ is pronounced [-s] or [-ɨz] after a stem ending with a voiceless plosive or an affricate or a fricative, respectively. That is, the plural morpheme /-z/ has three allomorphs [-ɨz, -z, -s]. This is diagrammed in Figure 5.6.

Rules that account for different realizations of the phonological alternation of a morpheme are called *morphophonemic rules*. Notice that morphophonemic rules allow the language to overcome its phonotactic constraints. From the plural data above, we see that the plural morpheme for words ending with a fricative or an affricate is pronounced [-ɨz]. Because a sequence of two affricates or fricatives is not allowed in English, a vowel has to be inserted to break them up to form another syllable for them to be pronounceable. Although English doesn't require that a fricative agree in voicing with its preceding segment (e.g., *false* [fɔls]), having a sequence of consonants with the same phonation type helps ease their articulation. (See the Fact box below on the ingenious test used to examine inflectional morpheme development in young children.)

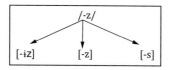

Figure 5.6 English plural morpheme

Fact: The Wug Test

In 1958, Jean Gleason, a psycholinguist, designed an experiment famously known now as the Wug Test to investigate plural (and other) inflectional morpheme acquisition in young children. With this test, Gleason demonstrated that children have tacit knowledge of morphological patterns in English. For example, children were shown a picture of an unknown creature and were told:

> This is a WUG. Now there is another one. There are two of them. There are two_____.

The children automatically referred to them as 'wugs' [wʌɡz] with the plural suffix [-z], suggesting that they are able to extract generalizable rules from the language around them.

Consider another data set from English shown in Table 5.15. The English past-tense morpheme for regular verbs has three alternants, [-d], [-t], [-ɪd]. The phones that precede the [-d] are [z], [aɪ], [b], [l], [n], and [v]. All of these are voiced. The phones that precede the [-t] are [k], [f], [p], [s], [ʃ], and [θ]. All of these are voiceless. The phones that precede the [-ɪd] are [t] and [d]. These are alveolar plosives. Here, [-d] has the broadest distribution and, thus, is the basic allomorph. The analysis can be stated as follows: the past-tense morpheme /-d/ is pronounced as [-t] after voiceless consonants and [-ɪd] after alveolar plosives. The family tree of this morpheme is diagrammed in Figure 5.7.

This morphophonemic rule fixes the problem introduced by the phonotactic constraint of not allowing a cluster of alveolar plosives (e.g., [-td], [-dd]) in word-final position in English.

Some English verbs form the past tense by changing the vowel. For example,

'write'	[ɹaɪt]	'wrote'	[ɹoʊt]
'see'	[si]	'saw'	[sɔ]
'sing'	[sɪŋ]	'sang'	[sæŋ]
'give'	[ɡɪv]	'gave'	[ɡeɪv]

Unlike regular verbs, there is no general rule for past-tense formation of irregular verbs. They have to be memorized.

Table 5.15 *English past-tense morpheme*

[-d]		[-t]		[-ɨd]	
[bʌzd]	buzz**ed**	[beɪkt]	bak**ed**	[lɪftɨd]	lift**ed**
[saɪd]	sigh**ed**	[stʌft]	stuff**ed**	[foʊldɨd]	fold**ed**
[gɹæbd]	grabb**ed**	[dʒʌmpt]	jump**ed**	[hitɨd]	heat**ed**
[kʰɔld]	call**ed**	[kʰɪst]	kiss**ed**	[sitɨd]	seat**ed**
[fænd]	fann**ed**	[wɪʃt]	wish**ed**	[sidɨd]	seed**ed**
[seɪvd]	sav**ed**	[fɹɔθt]	froth**ed**	[skɪdɨd]	skidd**ed**

Table 5.16 *Possessive prefix in Zoque*

[pama]	'clothing'	[mbama]	'my clothing'
[plato]	'plate'	[mblato]	'my plate'
[burru]	'burro'	[mburru]	'my burro'
[tatah]	'father'	[ndatah]	'my father'
[trampa]	'trap'	[ndrampa]	'my trap'
[disko]	'phon.record'	[ndisko]	'my phonograph record'
[kaju]	'horse'	[ŋgaju]	'my horse'
[kwarto]	'room'	[ŋgwarto]	'my room'
[gaju]	'rooster'	[ŋgaju]	'my rooster'
[waka]	'basket'	[nwaka]	'my basket'
[jomo]	'wife'	[njomo]	'my wife'
[ʔane]	'tortilla'	[nʔane]	'my tortilla'
[faha]	'belt'	[faha]	'my belt'
[ʃapun]	'soap'	[ʃapun]	'my soap'
[sʌk]	'bean'	[sʌk]	'my beans'
[ranʧo]	'ranch'	[ranʧo]	'my ranch'
[lawus]	'nail'	[lawus]	'my nail'

(From Roca & Johnson, 1999)

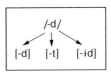

Figure 5.7 English past-tense morpheme

Let's now take a look at the alternations of the possessive prefix in Zoque, spoken in Eastern Central Mexico.

From this data, we see that there are four alternants for the first-person possessive prefix 'my' in Zoque. They are [m-], [n-], [ŋ-], and null, [ø] (the absence of a prefix). Next, we examine their distributions and find that the form

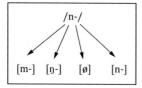

Figure 5.8 Zoque possessive prefix morpheme

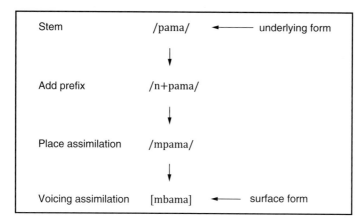

Figure 5.9 Derivation of Zoque possessive morpheme

the prefix takes agrees in place of articulation with the initial consonant of the stem. That is, [m-] appears before stems with initial bilabial plosives, [n-] with initial alveolar plosives, glides, and glottals, and [ŋ-] with initial velars. No prefix is added when the initial consonant of the stem is a fricative or a liquid consonant. So [n-] is the best candidate as the basic allomorph because it has the widest distribution. So we can state our analysis as follows: the morpheme /n-/ is pronounced [m-] before a bilabial, [ŋ-] before a velar, [ø] before a fricative or a liquid (or non-plosive), and [n-] elsewhere. This is diagrammed in Figure 5.8.

Something else also happens after the prefix is added to the stem. The initial consonant of the stem agrees in voicing with the prefix, turning all voiceless initial consonants of the stem into voiced ones. The possessive form of 'my clothing' is derived as diagrammed in Figure 5.9.

It should be observed that when more than one rule is involved, their ordering may matter. In this example, a strict ordering of the place and the voicing assimilation rules is not required to correctly derive the surface form: /pama/ → /n+pama/ → /nbama/ → [mbama].

Interestingly, the constraint that nasals must agree in place of articulation with a following plosive is common across languages, including English. There are exceptions, but in general, in words that contain a nasal + stop sequence, the nasal and the stop typically share the same place of articulation, for instance *camp* [kʰæ̃mp], *chant* [ʧæ̃nt], *lamp* [læ̃mp], *rank* [ɹæ̃ŋk], and so on.

We conclude below with a list of common phonological alternations found in the world's languages. Awareness of these alternation patterns would facilitate phonemic and morphophonemic analyses.

Common Phonological Alternations

1. Local assimilation = adjacent consonants become similar.

   Example: Assimilation of place of articulation in English: /tɛnθ/ → [tɛn̪θ] tenth

2. Distance assimilation = non-adjacent consonants become similar.

   Example: Liquid harmony in Sudanese: /ləga/ + /-ar-/ → [l-al-əga] 'wide (plural)' (Cohn, 1992)

3. Coalescence = two segments become one with features from both.

   Example: /sp/ → [f] in child speech as in /spun/ *spoon* → [fun]

4. Dissimilation = a segment becomes less similar to another segment.

   Example: /f/ → [t] before /θ/ in English /fɪfθ/ *fifth* → [fɪtθ]

5. Lenition = a segment becomes 'weaker' in articulation.

   Example: In Gascon, spoken in Southwest France, voiced bilabial plosive /b/ becomes voiced bilabial fricative [β] in intervocalic position, as in [bux] 'you', but [aβe] 'to have'

6. Fortition = a segment becomes 'stronger' in articulation.

   Example: /v/ → [b] in Betsimisaraka Malagasy, an Austronesian language spoken on the island of Madagascar, as in [vari] 'rice', but [homambari] 'eat rice' (a compound of /homam/ 'eat' +/vari/ 'rice' (O'Neill, 2015)

7. Debucallization = a segment becomes a glottal stop or an [h].

   Example: English /t/ is pronounced as [ʔ] before a syllabic [n̩], as in [bʌʔn̩] *button*

8. Deletion = a segment is deleted.

   Example: English /θ/ is deleted in /fɪfθs/ → [fɪfs] *fifths*

9. Epenthesis = a segment is inserted.

   Example: [t] insertion in English word /pɹɪns/ → [pʰɹ̃ɪnts] *prince*

10. Shortening = a segment is shortened.

    Example: unstressed vowel is reduced to a schwa [ə] in English as in /pitsɑ/ → [pʰitsə] *pizza*

11. Lengthening = a segment is lengthened.

    Example: vowel lengthening before voiced obstruents in English, as in [bæːg] *bag* vs. [bæk] *back*

12. Metathesis = segments switch order.

    Example: /æsk/ *ask* is pronounced as [æks] by some speakers of English

In sum, the phonology of a language includes rules on how a particular phoneme is phonetically realized (i.e., produced) in different positions in a word. On the other hand, the morphology of a language includes rules that affect the pronunciation of a particular morpheme. These rules are internalized and become part of a native speaker's (subconscious) knowledge, guiding his or her production and comprehension.

Now that we are familiar with the articulatory-based description (Chapters 1–2), transcription (Chapter 4), and phonological patterning (Chapter 5) of speech sounds, in the next three chapters (Chapters 6–8), we will discuss sounds as acoustic events. In Chapters 6 and 7, basic acoustic terms and digital signal processing are explained, followed by acoustic descriptions of vowels and consonants in Chapter 8.

Chapter Summary

- Speech sounds are grouped into contrastive units called phonemes.
- Positional variants of a phoneme are called allophones.
- Linguists perform a phonemic analysis to discover the phonemes and allophones of a given language.
- Allophonic rules account for predictable phonetic realizations of phonemes.
- A morpheme is the smallest meaningful linguistic unit.
- Predictable variants of a morpheme are called allomorphs.
- A morphophonemic analysis is performed to uncover allomorphs of morphemes.

- A morphophonemic rule captures different realizations of the phonological alternation of a morpheme.
- Knowledge of common phonological alternations facilitates phonemic and morphophonemic analyses of the world's languages.

Review Exercises

Exercise 5.1: Define minimal pairs and provide examples from English or other languages that you know.

Exercise 5.2: Define and provide examples of "underlying form" versus "surface form."

Provide three examples of phonological alternations in English.

Exercise 5.3: **Phonemic analysis**

Setsawana: Consider the phonemic status of the [l] and [d] sounds in Setsawana (Botsawana). Are they allophones of the same phoneme or different phonemes? If they are allophones of the same phoneme, state the rule.

lefifi	'darkness'	loleme	'tongue'
selɛpɛ	'axe'	molɔmo	'mouth'
xobala	'to read'	mmadi	'reader'
lerumɔ	'spear'	xo3ala	'to marry'
loxadima	'lightning flash'	didʒɔ	'food'
dumɛla	'greetings'	feedi	'sweeper'
lokwalɔ	'letter'	khudu	'tortoise'
mosadi	'woman'	podi	'goat'
badisa	'the herd'	hudi	'wild duck'

(from Odden, 2005)

Turkish: Which vowels are distinct phonemes? What phonetic characteristics are used distinctively in the vowel system?

1. [gɑz] 'gas'   2. [gøz] 'eye'
3. [giz] 'mystery' 4. [gyz] 'fall season'
5. [gez] 'travel'

Modern Greek:

1. [kano] 'do'   2. [kori] 'daughter'   3. [xano] 'lose'
4. [xori] 'dances' 5. [kali] 'charms'   6. [xrima] 'money'
7. [xali] 'plight' 8. [krima] 'shame'   9. [çeli] 'eel'
10. [xufta] 'handful' 11. [ceri] 'candle' 12. [oçi] 'no'
13. [kufeta] 'bonbons' 14. [oci] '2.82 pounds' 15. [çeri] 'hand'

a. Examine the phones [x, k, ç, c] in the data above. Which of the sounds are suspicious pairs (i.e., phonetically similar)? Which of the sounds are in contrastive distribution? Which are in complementary distribution? Explain your answer.

b. Of the sounds in complementary distribution, which ones should be grouped together as allophones of the same phoneme? That is, there is more than one way to group allophones into phonemes here. You should defend one solution as the best.

c. What English words would you expect a Greek speaker to mispronounce? Give five examples, and explain why you expect them to cause problems.

Exercise 5.4: Morphophonemic analysis

Consider the following pairs of words from Indonesian.

Simple form	Prefixed form	English gloss
[lempar]	[məlempar]	'throw'
[rasa]	[mərasa]	'feel'
[masak]	[məmasak]	'cook'
[nikah]	[mənikah]	'marry'
[ŋatso]	[məŋatso]	'chat'
[ambil]	[məambil]	'take'
[isi]	[məɲisi]	'fill-up'
[undaŋ]	[məŋundaŋ]	'invite'
[gambar]	[məŋgambar]	'draw a picture'
[kirim]	[məɲirim]	'send'
[dəŋar]	[məndəŋar]	'hear'
[bantu]	[məmbantu]	'help'

(Halle & Clements, 1983)

a. Identify all alternants of the Indonesian prefix.

b. Identify the contexts/conditions under which each alternant appears.

c. Choose the allomorph that is the basic or the underlying morpheme, and then write out the morphophonemic rule(s) to account for the occurrence of all the allomorphs.

References and Further Reading

Cohn, Abigail C. (1992). The consequences of dissimilation in Sundanese. *Phonology*, 9, 199–220.

Grijzenhout, J., & Krämer, M. (2000). Final devoicing and voicing assimilation in Dutch. *Lexicon in Focus*, 45, 55.

Halle, M., & Clements, G. N. (1983). *Problem Book in Phonology: A Workbook for Introductory Courses in Linguistics and in Modern Phonology*. Cambridge, MA: MIT Press.

Ham, P. (1961). *Apinayé Phonemic Statement*. Summer Institute of Linguistics.

Kennedy, R. (2016). *Phonology: A Coursebook*. Cambridge: Cambridge University Press.

Odden, D. (2005). *Introducing Phonology*. Cambridge: Cambridge University Press.

O'Neill, T. (2015). *The Phonology of Betsimisaraka Malagasy*. Newark, DE: University of Delaware.

Roca, I., & Johnson, W. (1999). *A Workbook in Phonology*. Oxford: Wiley-Blackwell.

Sapir, E. (2008). *The Collected Work of Edward Sapir, Vol.1, General Linguistics,* Pierre Swiggers (ed.), Berlin: Mouton de Gruyter.

6

Basic Acoustics

Learning Objectives

By the end of this chapter, you will be able to:

- Describe and identify different types of sounds, including:
  - Simple periodic sounds
  - Complex periodic sounds
  - Aperiodic sounds
- Identify key concepts involved in describing the acoustic properties of speech sounds, such as:
  - Resonance
  - Source–filter theory
  - Standing wave
- Calculate formant values of a neutral vocal tract: Tube Modeling
- Predict changes in resonance properties of a neutral tube due to local constriction: Perturbation Theory

Introduction

In Chapter 1, speech sounds were described according to how they are produced by the human vocal tract. Movements of the articulators dilate and compress the air inside the vocal tract before it is released and travels as sound waves from the speaker's mouth to the listener's ears. In this and the following chapter, speech sounds are described in terms of their basic acoustic properties, including frequency, intensity, and duration. We begin the chapter with a brief discussion of what sound is in general and how it is generated.

Sounds

Sound is a form of energy. Similar to other forms of energy such as electricity and light, sound has the potential to do work. It can vibrate the eardrums, a wine glass, or a window. Sound energy can be transported from one place to another through a medium such as air, water, or wood, by causing particles of the medium to bump into each other and move in a pattern called a wave.

A sound is made when a disturbance occurs. When the tines of a tuning fork vibrate, a sound is heard. Movements of the tuning fork cause surrounding air particles to alternately crowd together (compress) and move further apart (rarefy), creating a pattern of high-pressure areas alternating with low-pressure areas in the air. This pattern of pressure variation, or wave, travels over a distance at a speed determined by the medium. In general, sound travels faster in a denser medium. At sea level, sound travels through air at approximately 340 meters per second.

A wave pattern of a sound produced by a tuning fork is illustrated in Figure 6.1. At Time 1, the tuning fork is in its resting position and air particles surrounding it are at their normal or preferred distance from each other, so air pressure is at zero, or atmospheric level. At Time 2, a force is applied to the tuning fork, causing its tines to move. As the tines move outward, air particles adjacent to them are crowded together (compression) and air pressure increases. As the tines move the other way, toward each other in Time 3, a vacuum is created, allowing air particles to decompress (rarefaction) and return to their original positions. But because of inertia and elasticity, they go beyond their original positions and are spread further apart, thus lowering air pressure before returning back to normal once the tines come back to their original positions. As the tuning fork continues to vibrate, this pattern of compression and rarefaction of medium particles creates a sound wave with a repeating pattern of high-pressure alternating with low-pressure areas that moves through the medium over a distance.

It is important to note that as the sound wave propagates, individual medium particles simply oscillate in place (see link www.acs.psu.edu/drussell/Demos/rad2/mdq.html for animation). In addition, sound waves radiate in a spherical manner from their source rather than in one direction only as implied in Figure 6.1.

Sound waves also lose energy as they travel through the medium. This is because it takes energy to move medium particles and the number of particles to be moved increases as the wave expands from the source. As a result, the size of particle movements reduces proportionally to the distance the wave moves from the source.

A sound is heard when sustained movements of high pressure alternating with low pressure (i.e., oscillations) reach the listener's ears, causing the eardrum to move. However, the sensation of hearing occurs only when the rate of pressure fluctuation is sufficiently rapid (at least twenty times per second). This is why

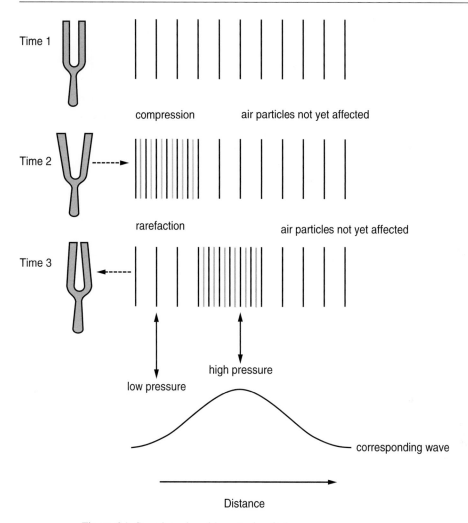

Figure 6.1 Sound produced by a tuning fork

slow hand waving does not produce a sound but the flapping of a bumble bee's wings does. On the other hand, pressure variation at a rate over 20,000 times per second is too high for our hearing range.

As discussed below, a sound can also be heard when there is a sudden change in pressure (an impulse) that is not sustained, such as bursts, taps, clicks, pops, or clanks (see Aperiodic Sounds below).

Types of Sounds

Sounds come in two types: periodic and aperiodic. Periodic sounds are characterized by their repeated pattern that occurs at regular intervals. Periodic sounds can be either simple or complex.

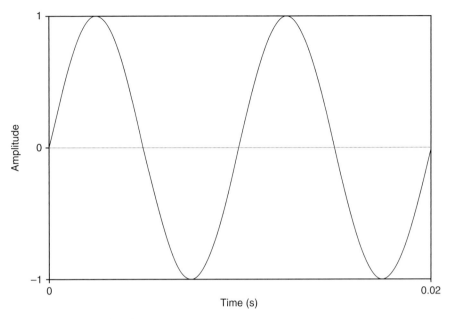

Figure 6.2 Sine wave

Simple Periodic Sounds

Simple periodic sounds are known as sine waves and heard as pure tones. They result from a simple harmonic movement such as a vibrating tuning fork. This is illustrated in Figure 6.2. Notice the repeated pattern of pressure fluctuation that occurs at roughly the same time intervals.

Three properties that define a sine wave are frequency, amplitude (pressure), and phase.

In a sine wave, each repetition of a sinusoidal pattern is called a **cycle** (Figure 6.3a) and the duration of a cycle is called a **period**, as shown in Figure 6.3b.

The **frequency** of a sine wave is usually expressed in hertz (Hz). It corresponds to the number of cycles that occur in one second. To obtain the frequency of a sine wave, one simply divides 1 second by the period, or $1/T$, where T is duration of the period in seconds. For example, if the period of a sine wave is 0.01 seconds, then its frequency equals 1/.01 or 100 Hz. Figure 6.4 shows a 100 Hz (a), a 200 Hz (b) and 400 Hz (c) sine wave.

The **amplitude** of a sine wave is its vertical height. It represents the amount of pressure fluctuation from the normal atmospheric or zero pressure level. Peak amplitude is measured from atmospheric (zero) pressure to either pressure maxima or pressure minima. Peak-to-peak amplitude is measured from pressure minima to pressure minima. This is illustrated in Figure 6.5.

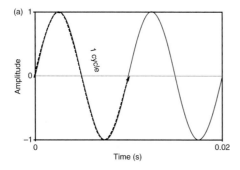

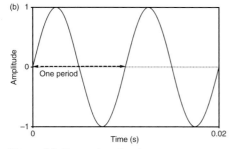

Figure 6.3 Properties of a sine wave
a Cycle of a sine wave
b Period of a sine wave

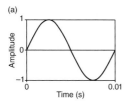
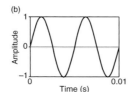
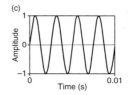

Figure 6.4 Sine wave frequencies
a 100 Hz (1 cycle in .01 sec)
b 200 Hz (2 cycles in .01 sec)
c 400 Hz (4 cycles in .01 sec)

Phase provides information about a specific point in time within a cycle or a period of a sine wave, or the relative positions of two separate sine waves. The location of this point is expressed in geometric degrees (°).

To understand the relationship between phase and period, think of a period as a graphical representation of a point traveling at a constant rate around a circle, and a wave is essentially a sequence of repeating periods. The number of periods per second is its frequency. In geometric terms, one period is equal to 360°. The position within a period can be indicated with a value between 0° and 360° called a phase angle. This is illustrated in Figure 6.6.

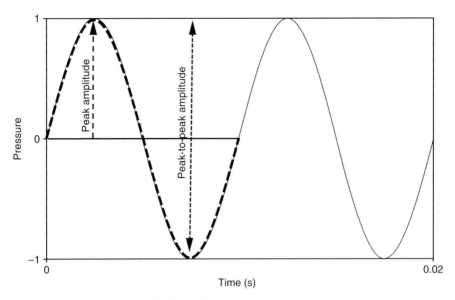

Figure 6.5 Amplitude of a sine wave

Phase angles can also be used to compare the relative positions of two sine waves. A phase shift between two waves can be of any value greater than 0° and less than 360°. When both waveforms are at 0° or 360°, they are in phase with each other.

Figure 6.7(a) shows two sine waves with the same frequency and amplitude. Notice that both waveforms rise and fall at the same time. They are said to be in phase with one another. If these two signals are mixed, the resultant amplitude is the sum of their individual amplitudes. The two waveforms in Figure 6.7(b), on the other hand, are out of phase. When the top wave rises, the bottom wave falls. They are 180 degrees out of phase. In other words, the bottom wave lags behind the top one by half a period. This happens, for example, when a second tuning fork is struck half a period after the first one of equal size was struck. When these two signals are mixed, their amplitudes cancel each other out completely and the resultant amplitude is equal to zero, at atmospheric level. As discussed below, phase relations between two or more sine waves play an important role in the formation of standing waves and the resonant characteristics of the vocal tract of different shapes.

Complex Periodic Sounds

According to the nineteenth-century French mathematician Jean-Baptiste Joseph Fourier, a periodic complex sound wave is composed of a number of sinusoidal components of certain amplitude and phase. This is known as the Fourier

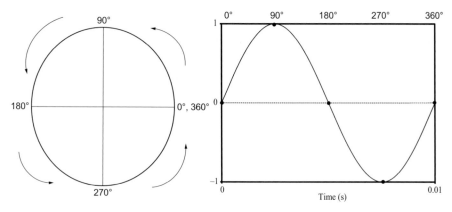

Figure 6.6 Phase angles in a sine wave

theorem. **Fourier analysis** is the process of decomposing a complex wave into its sinusoidal components. Fourier synthesis is the process of combining sinusoidal waves into a periodic complex wave.

Similar to simple periodic waves, **complex periodic waves** exhibit regularly recurring patterns of air-pressure variation. However, unlike simple periodic waves, they are composed of at least two sine waves. An example of a complex periodic wave is shown in Figure 6.8.

This complex periodic wave is composed of two sine waves: 100 Hz and 500 Hz. Its complex pattern (cycle) repeats every 10 milliseconds or .01 seconds. Additionally, there are five small peaks in one cycle, one for each cycle of the additional frequency component (i.e., 500 Hz). The rate at which the complex pattern repeats is called the **fundamental frequency** or F0. It is the greatest common denominator of the frequencies of the sine wave components. This complex periodic wave has a 100 Hz and a 500 Hz sine wave component and a fundamental frequency of 100 Hz.

The frequencies and amplitudes of the simple periodic components of the complex periodic wave shown in Figure 6.8 are represented in a graphic format or power (line) spectrum in Figure 6.9.

Aperiodic Sounds

In contrast to periodic waves, aperiodic waves show no discernible regular patterns of pressure variation, as illustrated in Figure 6.10.

Sounds with aperiodic wave characteristics are perceived as **white noise** similar to radio static. Unlike complex periodic sounds, white noise contains all possible frequencies with equal amplitudes. Fourier analysis performed on white noise will result in a flat power spectrum as shown in Figure 6.11.

Transients are another type of aperiodic sound. They are produced by a sudden change in pressure that is not sustained, such as bursts, taps, clicks, pops,

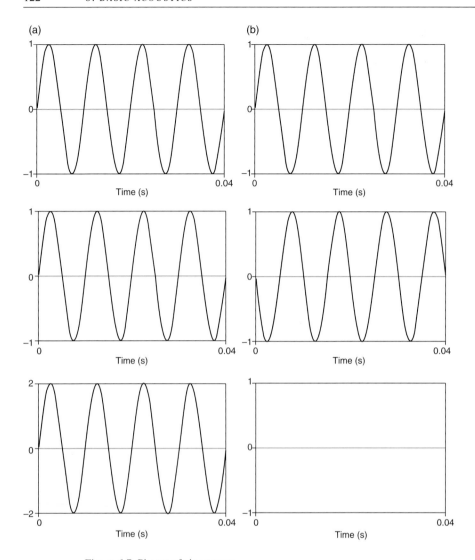

Figure 6.7 Phases of sine waves

or clanks. An example of a natural and idealized acoustic waveform of a transient sound, also known as an impulse, is shown in Figure 6.12a and b. The idealized waveform is characterized by the presence of acoustic energy at only one point in time, and a zero pressure level at all other times. A plosive release is an example of a transient in speech as shown in Figure 6.12c.

Fourier analysis on an impulse will return a flat spectrum similar to the one shown in Figure 6.11 for white noise. The difference between white noise and an impulse is that white noise is continuous, but an impulse is transient.

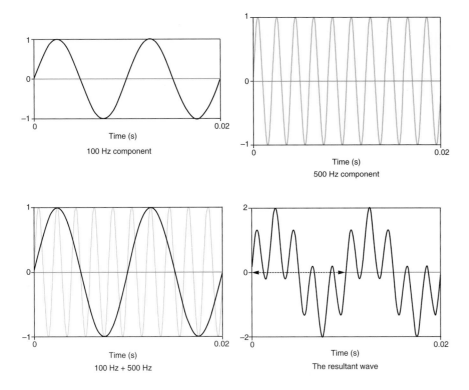

Figure 6.8 A 100 Hz + 500 Hz complex periodic wave

In sum, the two major types of sounds are periodic and aperiodic sounds. Periodic sounds have regular, repeated waveform patterns while aperiodic sounds don't. Periodic sounds can be simple or complex. Simple periodic sounds contain one sine wave component, whereas complex periodic sounds comprise at least two sine waves. Aperiodic sounds are complex and can be either continuous or transient. These are illustrated in Figure 6.13.

Speech Sounds

During speech production, the outbound flow of air from the mouth changes the pressure of the surrounding air from its normal atmospheric level hundreds or thousands of times per second. A sound wave as an acoustic signal is represented as an oscillogram similar to the one shown in Figure 6.14. The zero line represents the atmospheric pressure level while the peak and trough represent points of highest pressure (pressure maxima) and lowest pressure level (pressure minima). Positive and negative zero-line crossing points are the time points where the pressure becomes higher or lower than that of the atmospheric level. Since an oscillogram of a speech sound represents pressure variation over time, it's also referred to as a pressure wave.

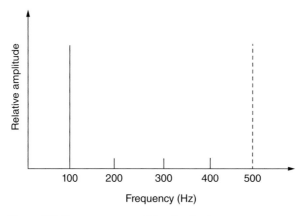

Figure 6.9 Power spectrum of the simple sine wave components of the complex periodic wave shown in Figure 6.8

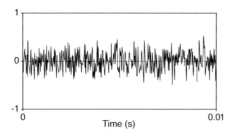

Figure 6.10 Aperiodic wave

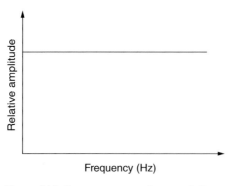

Figure 6.11 Power spectrum of an aperiodic wave

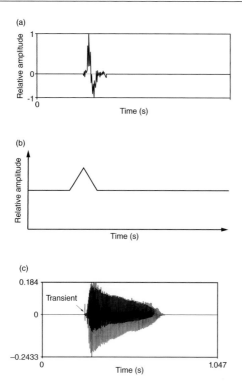

Figure 6.12 A natural (a) and an idealized waveform (b) of a transient and a plosive release (c) as an example of a transient waveform in speech signal

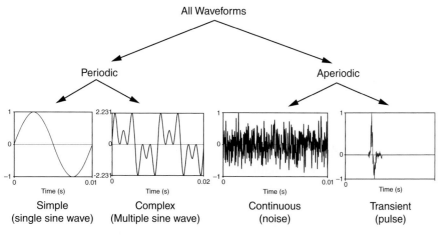

Figure 6.13 Types of sound wave

Acoustics of Speech Sounds

In the next chapter, we will describe the acoustic characteristics of vowels and consonants. To understand the acoustic properties of both types of sounds, it is important to introduce a few relevant concepts. These include the phenomenon

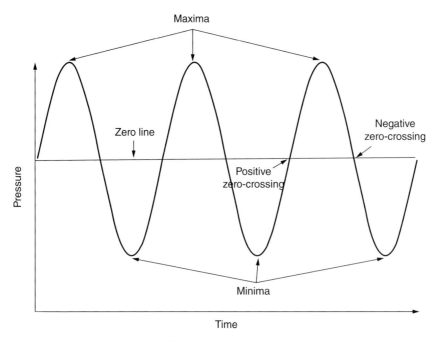

Figure 6.14 An oscillogram of a speech sound

called resonance, and the idea that a speech signal comprises one or more source signals modified by a filter, known as the source–filter theory of speech production.

Resonance

When disturbed, every object can be set into vibration at a particular frequency known as its natural, or resonant, frequency. An object's resonant frequency is determined by its physical properties, including its size and elasticity. For example, a tuning fork will vibrate at the same frequency every time it is struck. A swing will go highest at its natural intervals (its resonant frequency), determined in part by its length. A push at a rate higher or lower than its natural tempo will result in a lower swinging height. Everything else being equal, the bigger the object, the lower its resonant frequency. Depending on their elastic properties, some objects have more resonant frequencies than others.

An object can be set into vibration not only by tapping or striking it but also by the vibration of another object. For instance, a vibrating tuning fork can set another tuning fork of equal size, and thus of the same resonant frequency, into vibration (sympathetic vibration). As shown in Figure 6.15, when the first tuning fork (A) is struck, it vibrates at its natural frequency. The vibration

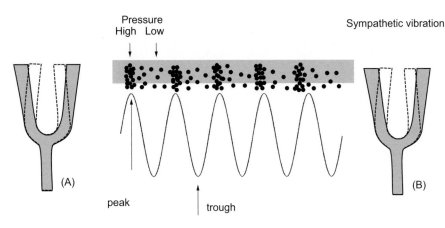

Figure 6.15 Sympathetic vibration

creates a wave of high pressure alternating with low-pressure areas in the surrounding air. This pattern of pressure variation occurs at a rate equal to the resonant frequency of the tuning fork. Similar to a small push on the swing, this pressure variation acts like a tap or a strike on the second tuning fork (B), eventually causing it to vibrate on its own at its maximum amplitude. This sympathetic vibration continues as long as the first tuning fork remains vibrating.

Similar to an object, a column of air has a resonant frequency and can be made to vibrate when excited by a tap, or by other vibrations. Like the sympathetic vibration of the tuning forks discussed above, the vibration of air molecules across the lip of a bottle from a blow can set air molecules confined inside the bottle vibrating at their resonant frequency, producing an audible tone once the amplitude of the vibration builds up to a certain level. The size of the air column determines its resonant frequency and thus the perceived pitch of the tone produced. Blowing harder or softer only makes the tone louder or softer. Its pitch level remains the same.

In short, resonance is the condition of starting or amplifying the vibrations of a physical body such as an object or an air column at its natural frequency by an outside force of the same natural frequency (sympathetic vibration). When exposed to a complex vibration (i.e., with multiple frequencies) an object will pick up and respond most effectively at its natural frequency and tune out other frequencies. Resonance occurs when the resonant frequencies of the two objects are the same, or when the resonant frequency of one is a multiple of the other.

Resonance of the Vocal Tract
As depicted in Figure 6.16, in speech production, air columns inside the oral and nasal cavities have multiple resonant frequencies depending on their shape and

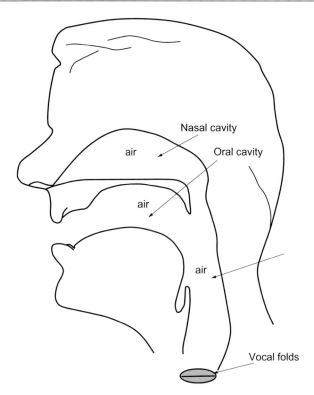

Figure 6.16 Resonance of the vocal tract

length. Voicing, or vibration of the vocal folds, acts as the external force setting and amplifying these air columns into vibration at the resonant frequencies of the vocal tract.

Damping

There is an inverse relation between the number of resonant frequencies and how soon the vibration of an object fades away, a phenomenon known as damping. When a tuning fork is tapped, the energy from the tap is converted into the vibration of the tuning fork. But, due to its elasticity, the tuning fork only vibrates at one frequency. The vibration will continue until all energy from the tap is converted into acoustic energy. On the other hand, a guitar string will vibrate at multiple frequencies. The energy from a pluck, for example, is distributed across these frequencies, causing the vibration to die down quickly. Figure 6.17a shows an undamped, and Figure 6.17b a damped signal.

In sum, it's easier to get an object to vibrate at its resonant frequency. Most objects, including an air column, have more than one resonant frequency. The more rigid the object is, the fewer its resonant frequencies. The vibration of an object with more resonant frequencies fades away faster than that of an object with a lower number of resonant frequencies. Finally, when exposed to a force of

(a)

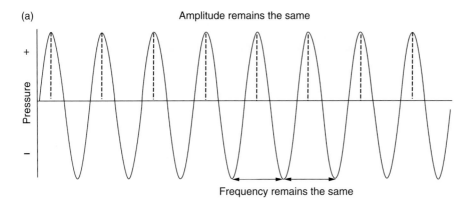

(b)

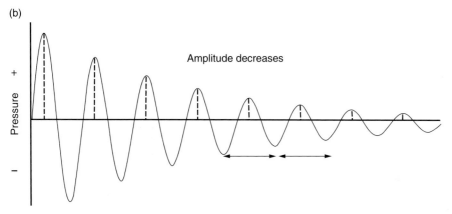

Figure 6.17 Damping

multiple-frequency vibration, an object will respond most effectively at its resonant frequency and tune out other frequencies.

Source–Filter Theory

The source–filter theory describes the acoustic output of speech production as a combination of a source energy modulated by the transfer function of a filter, as schematically shown in Figure 6.18.

Source

The source can be the periodic vibration (voicing) of the vocal folds (glottal source) generated at the larynx, noise generated elsewhere in the vocal tract (supra-glottal source), or the combination of both. For voiced sounds like vowels, vibration of the vocal folds is their main source of energy. When the vocal folds open and close, pulses of energy are generated. The rate of these

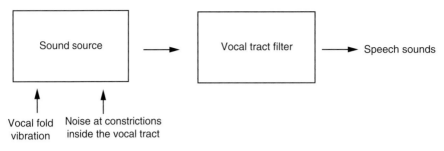

Figure 6.18 Source–filter theory

pulses corresponds to the frequency of vocal fold opening and closing, and determines the fundamental frequency (F0) of the sound source perceived as pitch. On average, the fundamental frequency of a male voice (~120 Hz) is lower than that of a female voice (~225 Hz) and a young child (~300 Hz). Therefore, a male's voice is typically perceived as having a lower pitch than a female's or a child's voice. Tension of the laryngeal muscles and sub-glottal pressure may cause the rate of vocal fold opening and closing to vary during voicing or phonation. In addition, the elastic properties of the vocal folds allow them to vibrate at other rates. These faster modes of vibration add higher frequency components to the source. Frequency components of the source are known as its harmonics. The first harmonic is the source's fundamental frequency. It determines the perceived pitch of the sound produced. Frequencies of the higher harmonics are whole-number multiples of the first. For example, if the first harmonic or H1 is at 100 Hz, the frequency of H2 will be 200 Hz, H3 300 Hz, H4 400 Hz etc. Additionally, with H1 as its strongest component, acoustic energy in the source declines at a rate of 12 dB/octave. Figure 6.19a shows modes of vocal fold vibration, and their corresponding spectrum is shown in Figure 6.19b. Figure 6.20a shows glottal spectrum as input in the source–filter theory of speech production.

Vocal Tract Filter

The vocal tract (the oral, pharyngeal, and nasal cavities) is a resonator. Its resonant frequencies are determined by its shape and length. When excited by a complex excitation source like the vibrating vocal folds, the air body inside it will vibrate maximally at its resonant frequencies, shown as peaks in its transfer function (frequency response curve), as shown in Figure 6.20b. This function shows acoustic energy peaks at 500 Hz, 1,000 Hz, and 1,500 Hz. Viewed as an acoustic filter, the vocal tract allows acoustic energy to pass through effectively at certain frequencies while blocking it at others. Frequencies where acoustic energy is concentrated in the vocal tract transfer function are called formant frequencies.

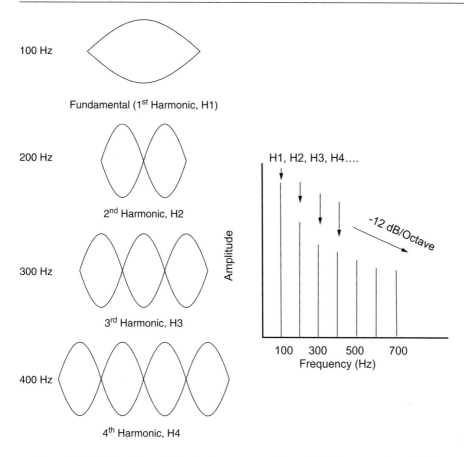

100 Hz

Fundamental (1ˢᵗ Harmonic, H1)

200 Hz

2ⁿᵈ Harmonic, H2

300 Hz

3ʳᵈ Harmonic, H3

400 Hz

4ᵗʰ Harmonic, H4

Figure 6.19a Modes of vocal fold vibration

Figure 6.19b Corresponding glottal spectrum

Figure 6.19 Modes of vocal fold vibration and corresponding glottal spectrum

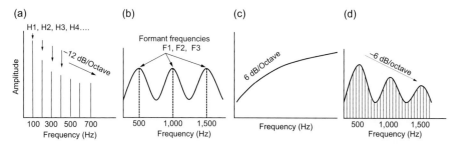

Figure 6.20 Source (a), filter (b), lip radiation factor (c), and output (d)

It's important to note that the frequency response or transfer function of a vocal tract is represented as a continuous curve as it appropriately captures the fact that air inside the vocal tract will respond to various frequencies in the excitation with varying degrees of amplitude, but it responds best to frequencies at or near its resonant frequencies.

Radiation Factor

Leaving the vocal tract and facing a mass of immobile air outside at the lips or the nostrils, some air particles reflect back inside the vocal tract (see Standing Wave section below) while others propagate outward. With a shorter wavelength, air molecules vibrating at a higher frequency (high-frequency components) are at an advantage. They are able to move with greater amplitude relative to those vibrating at a lower frequency by approximately 6 dB/octave, and thus producing a rightward spectral tilt of roughly 6 dB/octave. Consequently, the output spectrum shown in Figure 6.20c – which reflects the combined effect of the source (e.g., vocal fold vibration), the filtering action of the vocal tract, and the radiation factor at the lips – shows a spectral slope of 6 dB/octave rather than the 12 dB/octave from the source (Figure 6.20d).

Standing Wave

Two different waves traveling in the opposite direction interfere with each other. Interference also occurs between a wave and its own reflection. If the two waves are out of phase, their power cancels each other out (destructive interference). On the other hand, if they are in phase, an increase in amplitude will result (constructive interference). In Figure 6.21a, the incidental wave is completely cancelled out by its reflected wave (dotted line) since the two are 180 degrees out of phase. Figure 6.21b, on the other hand, shows that when the incidental wave and the reflected wave are in phase, an increase in amplitude is observed in the resultant wave.

A standing wave is a wave pattern formed as a result of a perfectly timed interference between two waves of the same frequency and amplitude traveling in opposite directions in the same medium. It is characterized by a lack of vibration at certain points (pressure nodes) and maximum vibration (pressure antinodes) at others. Figure 6.22 shows four standing wave patterns corresponding to the first four modes of vibration of a string fixed at both ends.

Pressure antinodes (A) correspond to areas where the string is vibrating maximally up and down (due to constructive interference), and pressure nodes (N) are locations where there is no movement (due to destructive interference). In other words, maximum variation in amplitude occurs in the pressure antinode areas, and minimal to no amplitude variation is observed in the pressure node areas. In this example, besides both ends, pressure nodes alternate with pressure antinodes along the length of the string.

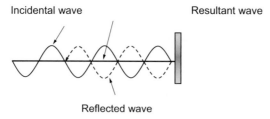

Figure 6.21a Destructive interference

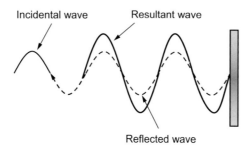

Figure 6.21b Constructive interference
Figure 6.21 Interference of two waves

The standing wave pattern does not occur at just any frequency. Notice that in the first mode, there is only one-half of a wave stretching across the string. That is, the length of the string is equal to one-half the wavelength. For the second, third, and fourth modes, the length of the string is equal to two-halves, three-halves and four-halves of a wavelength, and so on. Frequencies that produce standing wave patterns for this string are its resonant/formant frequencies and can be calculated using the following formula:

$$F\,(n) = \frac{(n-1) \times \text{Sound speed}}{2 \times L}$$

where n is an integer and L is the length of the string.

The formant frequencies of an air column in a tube closed at both ends can also be calculated using the same formula. This type of tube is called a **half-wave-length resonator**.

The vocal tract, on the other hand, is a tube considered closed at one end (the glottis) and open at the other (the lips). Formant frequencies of an air column in the vocal tract, therefore, necessarily differ from those of a closed-closed tube. Standing wave patterns and resonance properties of the vocal tract are discussed in the next section.

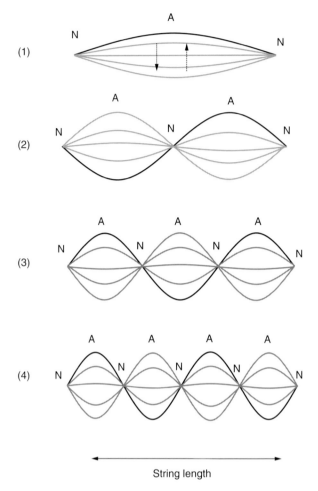

Figure 6.22 Four modes of standing waves of a string fixed at both ends

Standing Waves During Vocal Tract Resonance

Standing wave patterns are also formed during resonance of the vocal tract. As the wave traveling inside the vocal tract reaches the open air at the lips, part of it reflects back inside, creating standing wave patterns at the vocal tract resonant frequencies. Figure 6.23 shows standing wave patterns of the first three resonances of a neutral vocal tract.

As a closed-open tube, the vocal tract is **an (odd) quarter-wavelength resonator**. That is, frequencies whose wavelengths are 4 times, 4/3 times, 4/5 times, 4/7 times, etc. in length will fit well (i.e., resonate) with maximum amplitude. For all three resonances, a low-pressure area (pressure antinode) is at the open end (the lips), and a high-pressure area (pressure node) is near the

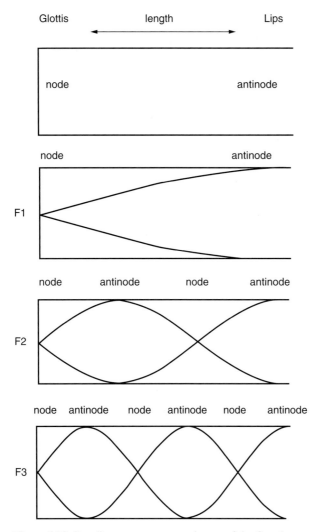

Figure 6.23 Standing wave correspondences of the first three resonant frequencies of a closed-open, neutral tube

closed end (the glottis) (see In Focus for a relationship between pressure and velocity). Second and third resonances have two and three nodes and antinodes, respectively.

Tube Modeling of a Neutral Vowel

Resonance of the neutral vocal tract resembles that during the production of a schwa [ə] vowel and can be modeled using a cylindrical tube closed at one end and open at the other. This type of tube is referred to as a quarter-wavelength resonator (see Standing Wave section above) and its formant frequencies can be calculated using the following formula:

$$F(n) = \frac{c^* (2n-1)}{4L}$$

where F stands for formant frequency, n = an integer, c = the speed of sound, and L = the length of the tube.

Assuming a tube length of 17.5 cm and speed of sound of 350 m/s, the values of the first three formants of this tube will be as follows:

$$F1 = \frac{350 \times 1}{4 \times 17.5} = 500 \text{ Hz}$$

$$F2 = \frac{350 \times 3}{4 \times 17.5} = 1500 \text{ Hz}$$

$$F2 = \frac{350 \times 5}{4 \times 17.5} = 2500 \text{ Hz}$$

Note that as the value of L becomes smaller, the formant value of any particular formant increases. Conversely, as L becomes larger, the formant value increases. In other words, formant frequencies vary with the length of the vocal tract, and therefore with such speaker characteristics as age and sex. The length of the vocal tract may also vary within a given speaker because of lip protrusion and larynx lowering, articulatory attributes of some speech sounds, resulting in an extension of the vocal tract length. Lip protrusion/lip rounding is a common phonetic attribute of most back vowels in American English, and rounded vowels are generally produced with the larynx in a lower position in comparison to unrounded vowels.

The simple tube model of a neutral vowel just discussed above has to be modified in order to apply to different vowels. Specifically, the model has to take into account cross-sectional areas which vary in both size and location along the vocal tract length for different vowels. Tube modeling of non-neutral vowels is beyond the scope of this book. (See Fact box below for how helium affects the resonances of the vocal tract.)

Fact: What Does Helium Do to Speech?

Contrary to popular opinion, inhaling helium doesn't change voice pitch. Because helium is denser than oxygen, sound travels faster in helium than in air. Inhaling helium increases the speed of sound propagation (i.e., the c in our formula above), resulting in higher resonant frequencies of the filter (thus a change in timbre or sound quality), while rates of vocal fold vibration (fundamental frequency, perceived as pitch) remain unaffected.

Perturbation Theory

Besides tube modeling, resonance of the vocal tract can also be discussed in terms of the stationary distribution of particle velocity or its inverse, pressure. (See In Focus for the relationship between pressure and particle velocity below.)

In Focus: Pressure and Particle Velocity

There is an inverse relation between particle velocity and pressure in sound waves (see also the Bernoulli effects in Chapter 1). As depicted in the picture below, when particle velocity (solid curve) is at either a positive or a negative maximum, pressure (dash curve) equals zero, and when pressure is at either a positive or a negative maximum, velocity equals zero.

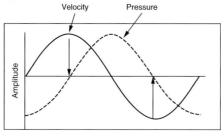

To visualize how this works, imagine an air particle traveling back and forth between its two neighbors. Its speed increases and reaches the maximum when it is at a distance midway between its neighbors, but decreases to the minimum as it approaches the neighbors and is about to turn back (Johnson, 2011). Therefore, the locations of maximum pressure displacement (pressure antinodes) are locations of minimum velocity (velocity nodes) and vice versa as depicted in the picture.

As discussed in the previous section on standing waves, distinct regions of pressure maxima (pressure node) and pressure minima (pressure antinode) occur in the tube due to the interactions of two waves. The stationary distribution of pressure (or particle velocity) is the basis of the perturbation theory. This articulation-to-acoustic theory proposes that a perturbation (i.e., a narrowing or

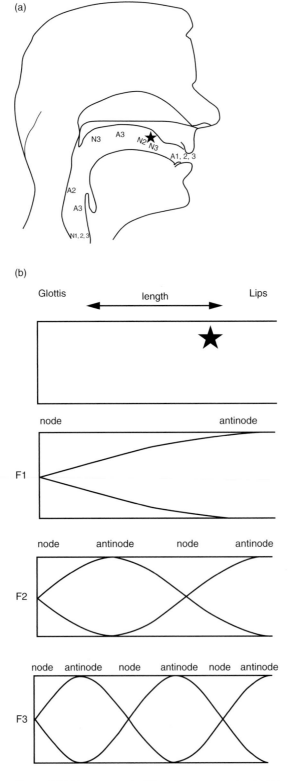

Figure 6.24 Pressure node (N) and pressure antinode (A) areas inside a neutral vocal tract configuration and its corresponding standing wave patterns. 1–3 = first-third formants

a constriction) in the configuration of the neutral vocal tract will produce predictable change in the formant frequency values, depending on the proximity of the narrowing to pressure maxima or minima. Specifically, a perturbation near a pressure minimum (pressure antinode) will cause the frequency of that formant to decrease, whereas a perturbation near a pressure maximum (pressure node) will cause the frequency of that formant to increase.

In other words (see Figure 6.23 above for reference), for the first formant (F1), perturbation theory predicts that its value will be lower (relative to that of a schwa vowel) if the constriction occurs in the front half of the vocal tract (e.g., for [i] and [u]), but will be raised by a constriction in the back of the vocal tract (e.g., for [ɑ]). For the second formant, it is lowered with a constriction near the lips or above the pharynx as in [u], but raised if the constriction is near the palate region as in [i]. Finally, the third formant is lowered with a constriction at the lips, above the pharynx or in the back of the vocal tract as in [ɹ].

To visualize the prediction of the theory, let's take the vowel [i] as an example. Figure 6.24a shows pressure node (N) and pressure antinode (A) areas inside the vocal tract in neutral configuration and Figure 6.24b shows its corresponding standing wave patterns. For the vowel [i] in *beat* the narrowing occurs near N2 and N3 regions (marked with star), suggesting that F1 would be lowered whereas F2 and F3 would be raised from the values expected for a neutral, schwa vowel. As we will see in Chapter 8, these predictions are all borne out. Average F1, F2, and F3 values for men are 270 Hz, 2,300 Hz, and 3,000 Hz, respectively.

Before describing acoustic characteristics of consonants and vowels (Chapter 8), familiarity with how speech signals are digitally processed by the computer is a necessary step. We take up this topic in the next chapter.

Chapter Summary

- Sound is a form of energy.
- Sound needs a medium to travel in.
- Properties of a (sound) wave are cycle, period, frequency, amplitude, wave length, and phase.
- The Fourier theorem states that a complex wave is composed of a series of sinusoidal waves of certain amplitude and phase.
- According to the source–filter theory, a speech output signal results from the filtering action of the vocal tract on the source signal.
- Resonance is the condition of setting and amplifying vibration of a physical object or an air column at its natural frequency.
- Resonant frequencies of the vocal tract vary with its shape and length.

- Perturbation Theory predicts a change in formant frequencies of a uniform tube resonator according to local perturbation along different portions of the tube.

Review Exercises

Exercise 6.1: Match the following terms to their definitions.

Terms	Definitions
1. Waveform ___	a. degrees of variation in air pressure from neutral atmospheric to higher or lower
2. Period ___	b. graphical representation of pressure changes over time
3. Amplitude___	c. simple periodic oscillation with amplitude at each point proportional to the sine of the phase angle of the displacement
4. Fundamental frequency ___	d. the time needed to complete one cycle of vibration
	e. distance traveled by one cycle of vibration
5. Formant Frequency___	f. made of two or more sine waves
	g. an increase in the amplitude of a vibration when force is applied at a natural frequency of an object or medium
6. Resonance___	h. lowest frequency component of a complex sound
7. Sine wave___	i. frequencies that resonate the loudest/peaks in a spectrum
8. Wavelength___	
9. Complex sound___	

Exercise 6.2: What is the frequency in Hz if the period of a sine wave is: 0.25 sec., 0.05 sec., 20 ms, and 25 ms?

Exercise 6.3: What is the wavelength (in meters or centimeters) if the frequency of a sine wave is: (assuming sound speed of 350 meters or 35,000 centimeters per second)?

      a. 500 Hz   wavelength   = _____
      b. 1,500 Hz   wavelength   = _____
      c. 4,500 Hz   wavelength   = _____

Exercise 6.4: The figure below shows two simple periodic (sine) waves, A and B, and a complex periodic wave, A+B, which is the sum of A and B waves. Answer the following questions.
      a. What is the frequency in Hz of wave A (thin solid line)?
      b. What is the frequency in Hz of wave B? (thin dash line)?
      c. What is the fundamental frequency of wave A+B? (thick solid line)?

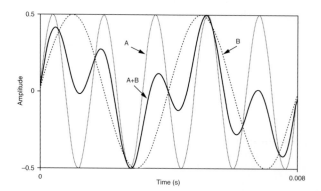

Exercise 6.5: Using the formula $F(n) = c*(2n-1)/4L$, where $c = 35,000$cm/s, what are the first three formants for the schwa vowel [ə] produced by a speaker whose vocal tract length is 10 cm long?

Exercise 6.6. Using the same formula, calculate the first three resonances of a speaker whose vocal tract is 15 cm long. Are the differences in formant values between the two speakers the same for all three formants?

Exercise 6.7: The formant frequencies (F1, F2, F3) of an adult male's voice are as follows: [i] 270, 2,200, and 3,100 Hz; [ɑ] 700, 1,100, and 2,800 Hz; [u] 300, 900, and 2,700 Hz. If the first formant frequency (or F1) of [ɑ] changes from 700 Hz to 350 Hz, will [ɑ] shift in phonetic quality toward [u] or [i]? Why?

Exercise 6.8: The formant frequencies (F1, F2, F3) of an adult male's voice are as follows: [i] 270, 2,200, and 3,100 Hz; [ɑ] 700, 1,100, and 2,800 Hz; [u] 300, 900, and 2,700 Hz. If the fundamental frequency (or F0) of [ɑ] changes from 200 Hz to 300 Hz, will [ɑ] shift in phonetic quality toward [u] or [i]? Why?

Exercise 6.9: From the standing wave pattern of the first three resonances of the vocal tract, where N= pressure node, and A= pressure anti-node, shown in the figure below, explain why [u] has a lower F2 than [i].

	Glottis					Lips
F1	N					
F2	N	A		N		A
F3	N	A	N	A	N	A

Exercise 6.10: Look at the waveform below and determine if the sound has a falling or rising pitch. Explain your answer.

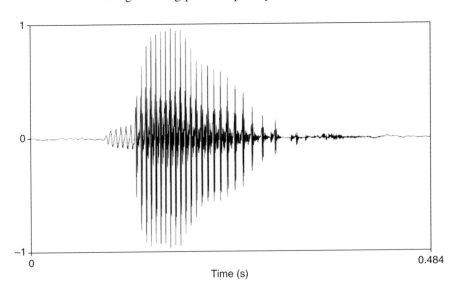

References and Further Reading

Johnson, K. (2011). *Acoustic and Auditory Phonetics*. Oxford: John Wiley & Sons.

Ladefoged, P., & Johnson, K. (2014). *A Course in Phonetics*. Toronto: Nelson Education.

Reetz, H., & Jongman, A. (2009). *Phonetics: Transcription, Production, Acoustics and Perception*. West Sussex: Wiley-Blackwell.

Zsiga, E. C. (2012). *The Sounds of Language: An Introduction to Phonetics and Phonology*. Oxford: John Wiley & Sons.

Stevens, K. N. (2000). *Acoustic Phonetics*. Cambridge, MA: MIT Press.

7
Digital Signal Processing

Learning Objectives

By the end of this chapter, you will be able to:

- Explain how speech sounds are acquired: recording
- Describe how recorded sounds are transformed for further processing by computers: digitization
- Explain spectral representation of speech: spectrum of speech
- Interpret a sound's narrow-band and broad-band spectrogram
- Explicate differences between Fourier and linear predictive coding analyses
- Recognize types of acoustic filters, including:
  - Low-pass filter
  - High-pass filter
  - Band-pass filter

Introduction

We just saw in the last chapter that during speech production, our vocal tract produces sounds with different acoustic characteristics. Computers and computer programs are used to analyze the acoustic properties of speech. Thus, it is important to understand how computers handle acoustic signals. In this chapter, we will discuss how speech signals are transferred to computers for further processing as well as the mathematical computations performed on the speech signals to unveil their spectral (frequency and amplitude) and temporal characteristics. We begin our discussion with recording.

Recording

A speech pressure waveform is a continuous signal, commonly known as an **analog** signal. It represents air-pressure change from instant to instant, and as it goes from one value to the next, it passes through all intermediate values. This means that there are infinite values of air pressure at an infinite number of points in time. This is illustrated in Figure 7.1 below.

Recording is the process of capturing air-pressure variation and converting it to corresponding electrical voltage. During recording, the membrane (diaphragm) of a microphone moves with the air pressure of the sound wave and generates a corresponding electrical signal that is analogous to the air pressure, as shown in Figure 7.2.

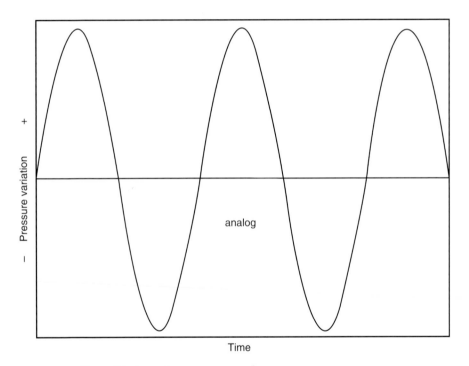

Figure 7.1 An analog pressure waveform

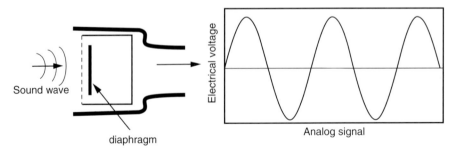

Figure 7.2 An analog electrical signal

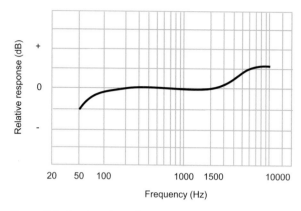

Figure 7.3 A microphone frequency response function

An important consideration in the recording process is the **frequency response** of the microphone used in recording. The frequency response of a microphone refers to the output level at different frequency ranges. It tells us how a particular microphone captures the pressure level of the input signal at different frequencies, usually from 20 Hz to 20 kHz, which corresponds to the human hearing range. A microphone may boost or reduce a particular frequency depending on how it was designed.

Figure 7.3 shows a frequency response of a microphone. The horizontal numbers are the frequency values and the vertical numbers are the pressure or amplitude response values in dB. The solid line shows the microphone output level at different frequencies. An output level at 0 dB means that the input and output levels are the same (a flat response). An output level below or above 0 dB indicates a reduction or a boost from the input to output level, respectively. From this figure, we see that this microphone faithfully transfers the amplitude of the input signal between approximately 200 Hz and 1,500 Hz. However, amplitude input level is reduced for frequencies below 200 Hz but increased for frequencies above 1,500 Hz.

Digitization

As shown in Figure 7.1, a sound pressure waveform is a continuous, analog signal with infinite numbers of pressure values at infinite points in time. A computer is a digital device. Thus, information to be manipulated by the computer must be converted to numbers or digital values. However, since computers cannot represent all possible values, air-pressure values from the analog input signal have to be converted into discrete and finite values. The process of converting an analog signal into a digital form is called an analog-to-digital converter. Figure 7.4 contrasts continuous, analog signal, and a discrete signal.

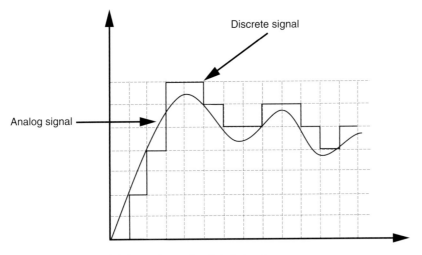

Figure 7.4 An analog and a digital signal

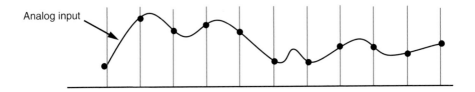

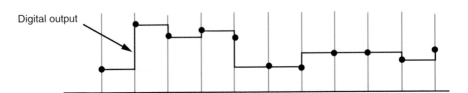

Figure 7.5 Sampling and quantization

Digitization involves two processes: **sampling** and **quantization**. Sampling is the recording of the air pressure at equally spaced time points, and quantization is the process of converting air-pressure values at the sampling points into discrete numbers, as shown in Figure 7.5. To improve the quality of the digitization, and thus produce a faithful transformation of the original analog signal, air-pressure measurement should be as accurate and as often as possible.

Sampling Rate

To prevent any loss in the frequency domain during digitization, at least two air-pressure values should be recorded for each cycle (Figure 7.6). In other words,

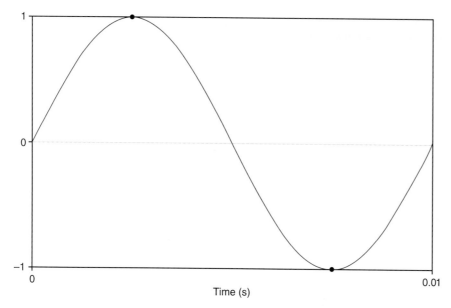

Figure 7.6 Sampling theorem: the original signal can be reconstructed without any loss in information if its sampling rate is twice as high as the highest frequency in the signal

the sampling rate (measured in Hz or number of samples per second) should be at least twice the (highest) frequency present in the signal. For example, if the signal contains frequencies up to 5,000 Hz, the sampling rate should be at least 10,000 Hz. This is known as the **sampling theorem**.

A phenomenon called *aliasing* occurs when the sampling rate is too low. An illustration of aliasing in analog-to-digital conversion is shown in Figure 7.7. The analog signal (darker line) oscillates too quickly to be accurately represented by the samples (dots) in the digital signal. Therefore, the digital signal contains a low-frequency signal (lighter line), rather than an accurate representation of the high-frequency input signal.

Nyquist Frequency
Frequency that is half of the sampling rate is known as the Nyquist frequency. For instance, the Nyquist frequency of a signal sampled at 10,000 Hz is 5,000 Hz.

Quantization Rate

The quantization rate is the number of values available to record air-pressure levels, and is expressed in bits (binary digits). To ensure that air-pressure values are recorded as accurately as possible, a higher quantization rate should be used. Table 7.1 shows the quantization rate in bits, their corresponding number of levels, and the amplitude dynamic range (the difference between the smallest and the largest amplitudes) in dB. For example, a quantization rate of 3 bits means

Table 7.1 *Quantization rate in bits and their corresponding number of amplitude representation levels and dynamic range in dB*

Number of bits	Representation level	Amplitude dynamic range (dB)
$1 = 2^1$	2	6.02
$2 = 2^2$	4	12.04
$3 = 2^3$	8	18.06
$4 = 2^4$	16	24.08
$5 = 2^5$	32	30.10
$6 = 2^6$	64	36.12
$7 = 2^7$	128	42.14
$8 = 2^8$	256	48.16
$9 = 2^9$	512	54.19
$10 = 2^{10}$	1,024	60.21
$11 = 2^{11}$	2,048	66.23
$12 = 2^{12}$	4,096	72.25
$13 = 2^{13}$	8,192	78.27
$14 = 2^{14}$	16,384	84.29
$15 = 2^{15}$	32,768	90.31
$16 = 2^{16}$	65,536	96.34

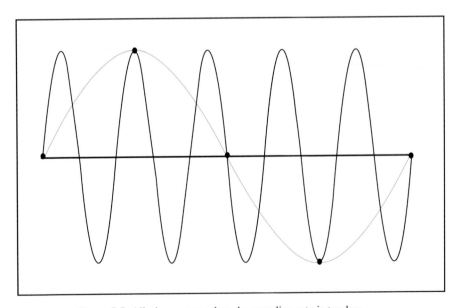

Figure 7.7 Aliasing occurs when the sampling rate is too low

that 8 (2^3) discrete air-pressure levels can be recorded. To accurately represent a wide dynamic range of air pressure in a speech signal, a 16-bit quantization (or resolution) rate is preferred. This gives a total amplitude range of 96 dB, as shown in the formula below.

$$20 \times \log_{10}(65,536/1) = 20 \times 4.816 = 96.3 \text{ dB}$$

Quantization Error

The main issue we need to consider in quantization is the accuracy of the amplitude measurements. The more amplitude representation levels, the more accurate the amplitude values of the original signal that can be recorded. The difference in amplitude between the actual analog amplitude value of the continuous signal and the values represented in the digital signal is called the **quantization error** and is heard as noise (see In Focus for a simplified explanation of sampling and quantization).

In Focus: Sampling and Quantization

Converting an analog signal to a digital signal (A-to-D conversion) is similar to converting a sine wave into a set of numbers by putting equal-interval vertical and horizontal gridlines over it. Then, at each vertical line, the value of the horizontal line is recorded. Placing equal-interval vertical lines corresponds to sampling, and the number of vertical lines placed corresponds to the sampling rate (in Hz). Recording the values of horizontal lines corresponds to quantization, and the number of horizontal lines placed corresponds to quantization precision (in bits).

Speech Spectrum

A speech frequency spectrum shows the frequency components and their amplitudes in the signal. For a sine signal, only a single line appears in the spectrum, representing its sole frequency component. This type of spectrum is also known a line spectrum. Spectra of two sine signals of the same frequency (100 Hz), but with different amplitudes are shown in Figure 7.8.

Spectra of two complex periodic signals made up of different frequencies and amplitudes are shown in Figure 7.9. The spectrum of each signal shows its first harmonic as well as its higher sinusoidal components with decreasing amplitude toward higher frequencies. The first signal contains three sinusoidal components (100 Hz, 300 Hz and 500 Hz), and the second signal comprises two sinusoidal components (200 Hz and 400 Hz). The fundamental frequency of the first signal is 100 Hz, and that of the second signal is 200 Hz.

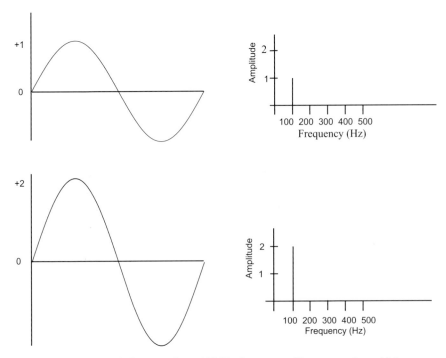

Figure 7.8 Spectra of two 100 Hz sine waves. The top one has a higher amplitude than the bottom one

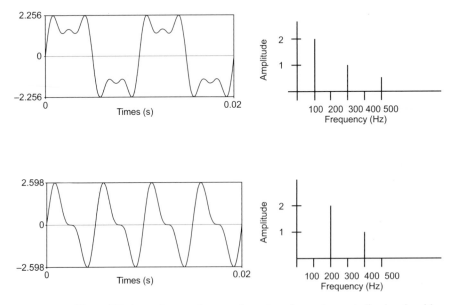

Figure 7.9 Acoustic waveforms and spectra of complex periodic signals with three (top) and two (bottom) sine wave components

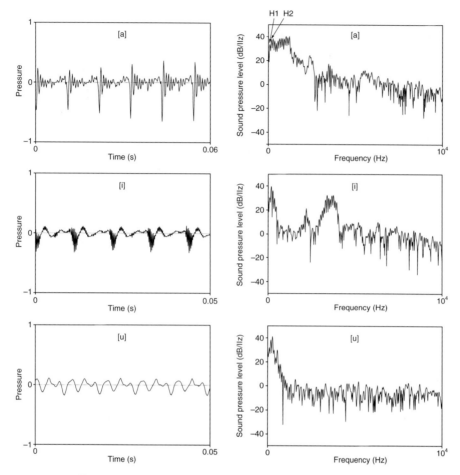

Figure 7.10 Acoustic waveforms of quasi-periodic signals from vowels /a, i, u/ and their corresponding spectra. H1 and H2 are the first and second harmonic respectively

The waveforms and the line spectra of quasi-periodic signals from the vowels /a, i, u/ are shown in Figure 7.10. Since the signals are quasi-periodic, their spectra are continuous, but with visible harmonic components.

On the other hand, no harmonic structure is present in the spectrum of a non-periodic, white noise signal (similar to the frication noise of an /s/ sound) since it is non-periodic. Its spectrum appears continuous and may be idealized as a solid line. This is illustrated in Figures 7.11a and b.

Similar to a non-periodic signal, the spectrum of an impulse signal, such as the release of a plosive /p, t, k/, appears continuous. However, unlike non-periodic noise signals, all the frequency components of an impulse are in phase with one another, with their maximum amplitudes occurring at the same point in time (Reetz & Jongman, 2009). The phase relationship between the frequency

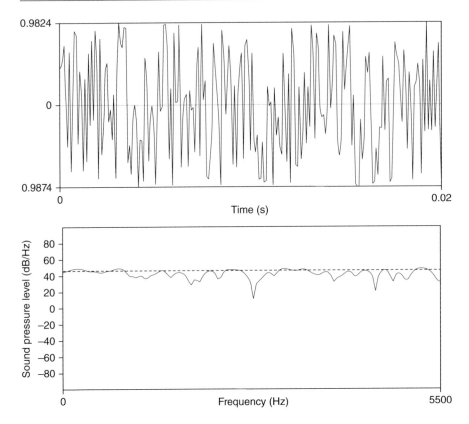

Figure 7.11 Waveform of a white noise (top) and its corresponding spectrum
(bottom)

components of a signal do not appear in a frequency spectrum, and therefore the
spectrum of an impulse looks the same as that of noise. This is illustrated in
Figure 7.12 (bottom).

Sound Spectrograms

In the 1940s, a machine known as the sound spectrograph was invented, allowing
for a display of the spectrum of a speech sound wave as it varies from instant to
instant. Initial models displayed the sound's spectral patterns directly on a
luminous moving belt. The second model printed the spectral patterns on paper
for later examination. The print-out of this type of spectrograph, which took a few
minutes to produce, is called a sound spectrogram. The second model was in
operation at the Cornell University's Phonetic laboratory during my graduate
training there in the 1990s.

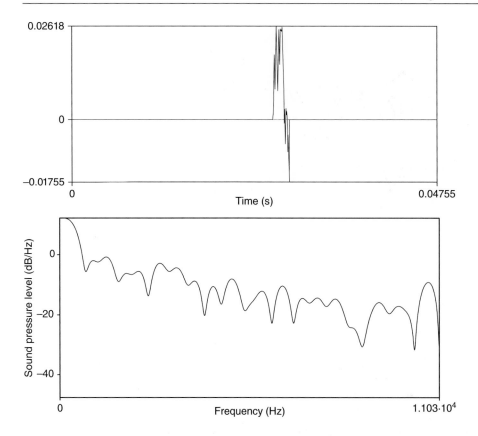

Figure 7.12 Acoustic waveform of an impulse signal in speech (top) and its corresponding spectrum (bottom)

With the advent of computers and fast digital computing methods during the 1970s and 80s, computer-generated sound spectrograms are now freely and commercially available. Sound spectrograms provide a quick overview of the frequency, time, and intensity characteristics of an utterance.

There are two types of spectrogram: wide-band (Figure 7.13 top) and narrow-band spectrograms (Figure 7.13 bottom). For both types of spectrogram, time is displayed along the horizontal axis, and frequency along the vertical axis. The darkness of the traces indicates the intensity level of the frequency components. For example, a formant produces a dark band along the horizontal axis. The first (lowest) dark band corresponds to the first formant (F1), the second band to the second formant (F2), the third band to the third formant (F3), and so on.

In a narrow-band spectrogram, the individual harmonics (labeled H1, H2 in Figure 7.13 bottom) are visible as dark horizontal lines, while individual glottal pulses show up as vertical striations in the wide-band spectrogram. This is

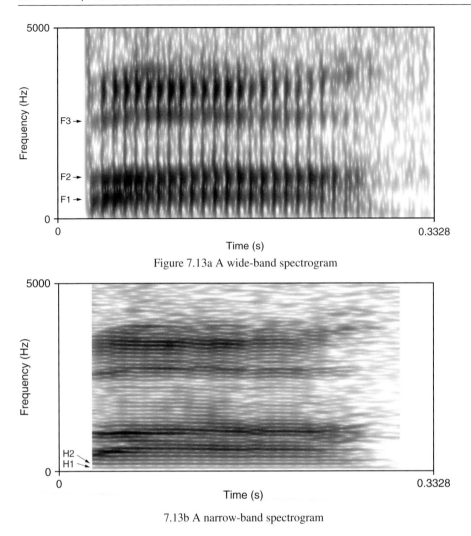

Figure 7.13a A wide-band spectrogram

7.13b A narrow-band spectrogram

Figure 7.13 A wide- and a narrow-band spectrogram

because a narrow-band spectrogram has better frequency resolution than a wide-band spectrogram, as illustrated in Figure 7.14.

A wide-band spectrogram has better temporal resolution (Figure 7.15a) than a narrow-band spectrogram (Figure 7.15b). Therefore, a short and transient acoustic event, such as a plosive's release burst, is clearly visible in a wide-band spectrogram, but not in a narrow-band spectrogram.

From this figure, we can see that the release burst of the [pʰ] in *pick* is clearly marked on the wide-band spectrogram, but appears as a blurred transition in the narrow-band spectrogram.

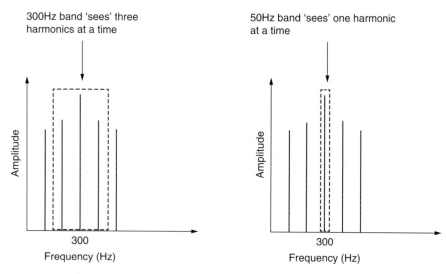

Figure 7.14 Frequency resolution in a wide-band and a narrow-band spectrogram

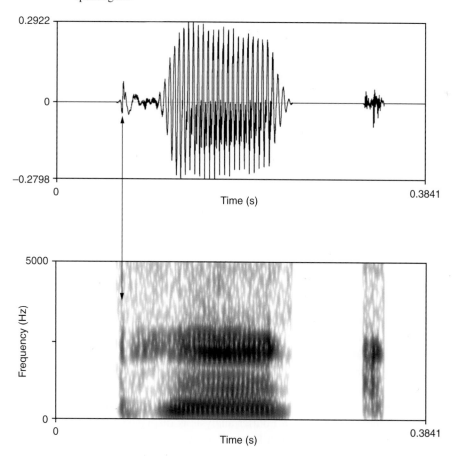

Figure 7.15a Waveform (top) and wide-band spectrogram (bottom) of English word *pick*.

Figure 7.15 Waveform, wide-band and narrow-band spectrograms of English voiceless aspirated bilabial plosive [pʰ] in *pick*. The arrows mark the release burst

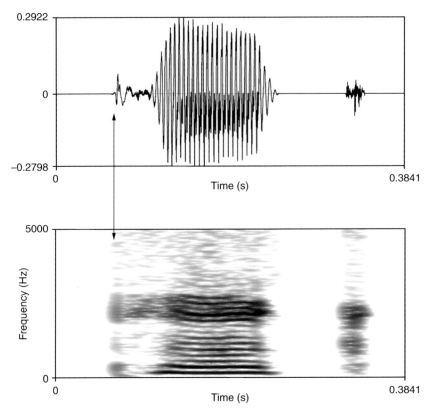

Figure 7.15b Waveform (top) and narrow-band spectrogram (bottom) of English word *pick*

Figure 7.15 (*cont.*) Waveform (top) and narrow-band spectrogram (bottom) of English word *pick*

Fourier Analysis

In 1822, the French mathematician Fourier proved that any complex periodic signal may be decomposed into its sine wave components of different frequencies, amplitudes, and phases. In other words, any complex periodic signal is constructed from a unique set of sine waves of certain frequencies, amplitudes, and phases. Figure 7.16 shows how complex periodic signals (column C) are built from a combination of two (100 Hz and 300 Hz), three (100 Hz, 300 Hz, and 500 Hz), and four (100 Hz, 300 Hz, 500 Hz, and 700 Hz) sine waves (rows 2, 3, 4 respectively). Their corresponding line spectra are shown in column D.

Fourier analysis is performed to find the unique combination of sine waves of a complex periodic signal. The output of a Fourier analysis is displayed in a frequency spectrum, as shown in column D in Figure 7.16, with frequency on the x-axis and amplitude on the y-axis. Each line on the graph represents each sine

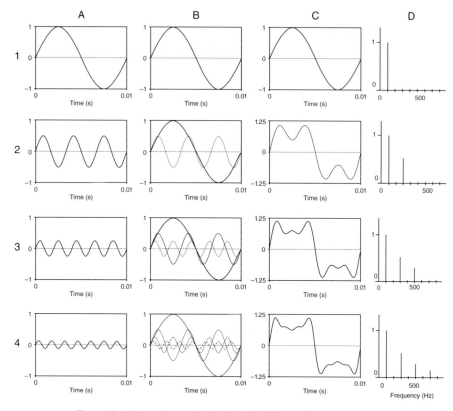

Figure 7.16 Complex periodic signals with two, three, and four
sine wave components and their corresponding line spectra

wave component of the complex periodic signal. The height of the line corresponds
to its amplitude. Phase information is not represented in a frequency spectrum.

Note that the frequencies in a frequency spectrum are always multiples of the
lowest frequency or the first harmonic (H1). For example, a complex signal with
a fundamental frequency of 100 Hz contains only sine components of 100 Hz,
200 Hz, 300 Hz, etc. This is because the signal is periodic.

However, as already mentioned, a speech signal is quasi-periodic at best, even
for a vowel. Therefore, its frequency spectrum is continuous, but with clearly
visible harmonic structure, as shown in Figure 7.10. (see Fact box below for
other applications of Fourier analysis).

Fact: Applications of Fourier Transformation

Fourier analysis has many applications including image processing (image
analysis, compression, reconstruction, recognition, etc.). For instance, the
Joint Photographic Experts Group (JPEG), a commonly used method to
compress digital images, uses discrete cosine transformation, a kind of
discrete Fourier transformation (DFT).

(Marcus, M. (2014) Jpeg image compression. In M. W. Marcellin, M. Gormish, A. Bilgin, M. P. Boliek (eds.), An Overview of JPEG2000, Proc. of the Data Compression Conference (pp. 523–544). Snowbird, Utah, March 2000.)

Windowing

In Fourier analysis, a spectrum is calculated from a small portion of the signal. That is, a short stretch of the signal is windowed or chunked out for analysis to yield a short time spectrum. The size of the window is taken to be the duration of one period, from which the amplitude and phase of the first harmonic (of the window size) are computed. The computation is then repeated for two, three, four, etc. periods, giving amplitude and phase information for the respective harmonics. Since period is inversely related to frequency, the spectral resolution, or the spacing between the frequency values, is inversely related to the window size (in ms or sample numbers): the larger the window size, the closer the spacing. For instance, for a signal sampled at 10 kHz, a 10 ms window yields a spectral resolution of 100 Hz (1,000 samples per 100 msec/10 ms), a 50 ms window gives one of 20 Hz (1,000/50), etc. Finer spectral resolution increases the accuracy of approximating the frequency components of the original signal. Figure 7.17 shows output spectra of large (top) and small (bottom) analysis windows of a vowel signal sampled at 10 kHz.

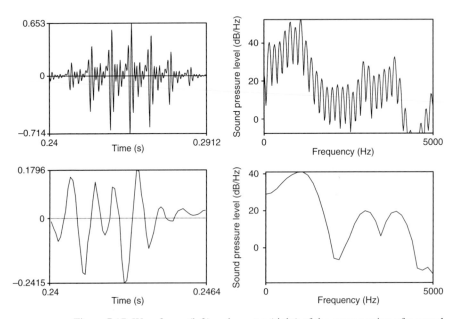

Figure 7.17 Waveforms (left) and spectra (right) of the same portion of a vowel analyzed with a 51.2 ms analysis window (top) and a 6.4 ms analysis window (bottom)

Table 7.2 *Relation between sample rate, FFT analysis window size, and spectral resolution in FFT analysis*

Sample rate (Hz)	Nyquist frequency (Hz)	Window size		Frequency interval between component (Hz)
		(Points)	(Ms)	
10,000	5,000	2,048	204.8	4.88
		1,024	102.4	9.76
		512	51.2	19.53
		256	25.6	39.06
		128	12.8	78.12
		64	6.4	156.25
		32	3.2	312.5

As we can see, individual peaks corresponding to the harmonics of the analyzed portion of the vowel are clearly separated with a larger analysis window (top right), but appear as broad peaks when analyzed with a smaller analysis window (bottom right).

There are two types of Fourier analysis: a discrete Fourier transformation (DFT) and a fast Fourier transformation (FFT). Both are performed by a computer using discrete time values, but DFT takes longer to compute than FFT. Computation time is reduced in FFT because the number of sample points (analysis window size) included in the analysis is limited to those with a power of 2 (32, 64, 128, 256, 512, 1,024, 2048, etc.). However, even with the higher processing capacity of the new generation of computers, FFT is still preferred over DFT.

Table 7.2 shows the relation between FFT analysis window size and interval between frequency components (spectral resolution) for a signal sampled at 10 kHz, thus a Nyquist frequency of 5,000 Hz.

Window Type

Besides window size, the type of window used to cut out the signal to be analyzed is another important consideration in speech analysis. Some of the most common window types are Hann, Hamming, Blackman, and Kaiser windows, named after their shapes or their inventors. Figure 7.18a shows the shapes of a Hamming windows, and Figure 7.18b a Blackman window.

Simply put, windows are mathematical functions applied to the windowed signal such that the amplitudes along the edges are zero, or as close to zero as possible, while amplitudes in the remaining portion of the signal remain intact. Windowing helps reduce the distortion of both the frequency components and their amplitudes in the output spectrum resulting from abrupt amplitude discontinuity along the edges. Figure 7.19 shows output spectra of the same portion of a

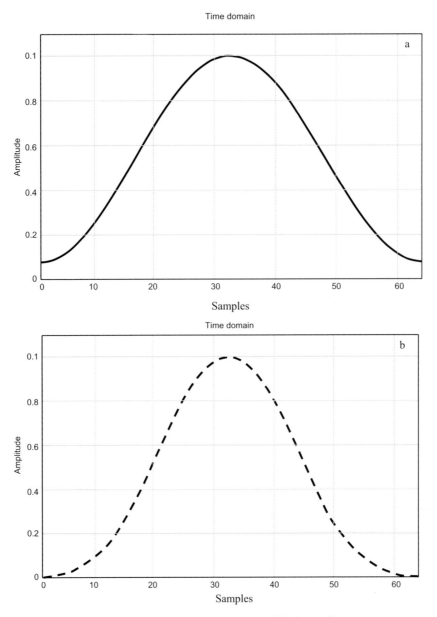

Figure 7.18 Window types: Hamming (a), Blackman (b)

vowel signal extracted with a rectangular shape window (right) and a Hamming window (left).

From this figure, we can see that the frequency components of the signal are better defined when a Hamming window is applied to the signal before analysis. Amplitude discontinuity introduces frequency components that are not part of the original signal.

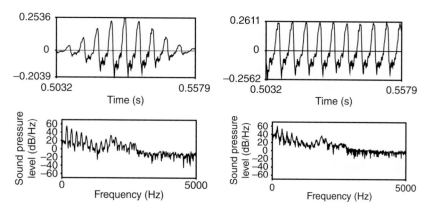

Figure 7.19 FFT spectra of an abruptly excised signal (right) and a Hamming-windowed signal (left)

Zero Padding

Windowing also offers an additional benefit, particularly in FFT. As we can see from Table 7.2 above, the larger the window size, the better the spectral/frequency resolution. However, since the acoustic speech signal changes rapidly, a bigger window size may also include parts of the signal that we don't want to analyze. For example, if we want to get the spectrum of a stop burst, which typically lasts for only a few milliseconds, a larger window size may also include part of the following vowel, resulting in a spectrum that is averaged across both parts. In order to maximize spectral resolution for a small window size, zero samples can be added to the signal after it is windowed.

Zero padding is possible because after windowing, the signal amplitude at its edges is reduced to zero, or to a near-zero level, thus allowing for any number of additional zero samples to be added in order to obtain a desirable FFT analysis window size and spectral resolution level.

Fourier Analysis of Non-Periodic Signals

With quasi or non-periodic signals, the assumption that the signal to be analyzed is periodic is violated. However, one can argue that every signal is periodic with an infinitely low fundamental frequency. For example, if 100 Hz and 100.5 Hz sine signals are added together, the fundamental of the output signal is 0.5 Hz even though this 0.5 Hz signal is not one of the sine components of the sum signal. Theoretically, the fundamental frequency of a complex signal can be infinitely low, such that *any* frequency may be present in the spectrum as a multiple of an infinitely small fundamental frequency. This mathematical trick justifies the use of Fourier analysis on quasi-periodic signals, non-periodic noise, and impulses. As already shown in Figure 7.9, the spectrum of a quasi-periodic signal is more structured, with visible harmonics, than non-periodic noise

(Figure 7.11). Spectra of non-periodic noise and impulses have no harmonic structure (Figures 7.10, 7.12). The difference between these two types of signals lies in their phase characteristics. All frequency components of an impulse are in phase with one another at a single point in time, while those of a non-periodic noise are out of phase with one another, thus appearing as a random sequence of displacement on its waveform (Reetz & Jongman, 2009).

Linear Predictive Coding (LPC) Analysis

Besides FFT, another analysis that is widely performed on speech signals is linear predictive coding or LPC. LPC is a mathematical procedure originally developed to reduce the amount of data needed to transmit telephone conversations. Due to its quasi-periodic nature, it is relatively easy to predict the characteristic of the next part of a speech signal from its previous parts. Mathematically, this can be modeled as a system of linear equations. Thus, instead of transmitting the entire signal itself, it is sufficient to only transmit the encoded mathematical parameters used to solve the equations.

Besides type and size of window discussed earlier, another parameter that needs to be specified in LPC analysis is the number of poles, or coefficients. This parameter determines the number of spectral peaks or formants to be computed. Two coefficients, or poles, are needed for each formant, so a 10-pole LPC analysis will display five spectral peaks. These five peaks are spread across the Nyquist frequency of the signal. For instance, the five peaks will be distributed from 0 to 5,000 Hz for a signal that was sampled at 10 kHz. If the sampling is 44.1 kHz, then the five peaks will be located between 0 and 22,050 Hz. Consequently, fewer peaks (or no peak) may appear in a given frequency range. Since the important frequency range for vowels is below 5 kHz, this means that some vowel formant frequencies may not be present in the spectrum. To avoid this problem, one can either increase the number of poles or low-pass filter the signal before the analysis is performed (see Acoustic Filters below). It is recommended that the number of poles should equal the sampling rate in kHz plus 2, but no more than 24. Too many poles may result in spurious peaks being introduced in the spectrum.

Unlike an FFT spectrum, which reflects the influence of both the source (the larynx) and the filter (the vocal tract), an LPC spectrum attempts to remove the effect of the source and displays only the effect of the filter. Consequently, an LPC spectrum shows only broad frequency peaks, rather than individual harmonic frequency components. These peaks correspond to the resonances of the vocal tract. Each peak is characterized by its center frequency (frequency of highest point) and bandwidth (broadness) (see band-pass filter below). Figure 7.20 shows an example of an LPC spectrum with five peaks corresponding to the first five formants in the signal: F1 has the lowest center frequency and F5 has the highest. F2 shows the narrowest bandwidth, F4 the widest.

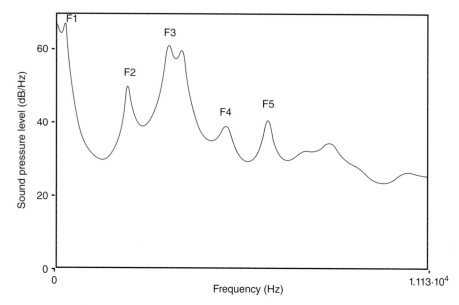

Figure 7.20 An LPC spectrum of a portion of a vowel. F1–F5 are marked

In our discussion of the source–filter theory in Chapter 6, we learned that as an acoustic filter, the vocal tract allows some frequencies of the complex signal produced by vocal fold vibration to pass through relatively unimpeded while blocking other frequencies. Which frequencies are passed through and which are blocked vary as a function of the vocal tract shape and length. The filtering action of the vocal tract turns the same laryngeal input signal to different sounds, such as /a/, /i/, and /u/. In short, filters allow some frequencies to pass through easily, while blocking out others.

Acoustic Filters

In acoustic theories, three types of filter are often discussed: a low-pass, a high-pass, and a band-pass filter. Each filter is characterized by its cut-off frequency and its steepness. **Cut-off frequency** is the frequency above which the acoustic energy is dampened or attenuated, and **steepness** is the rate of the attenuation of the frequencies above the cut-off frequency.

Low-Pass Filter

A low-pass filter allows frequencies lower than the cut-off frequency to pass. However, it is physically impossible for a low-pass filter to let all frequency components up to the cut-off frequency through to their fullest extent, and

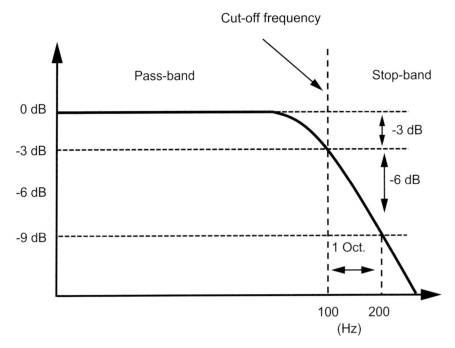

Figure 7.21 A low-pass filter with a cut-off frequency of 100 Hz and a slope of 6 decibels per octave

completely block all frequencies above it. As shown in Figure 7.21, the pass-band, where the frequencies pass through relatively unhindered, and the stop-band or the reject-band, where the frequencies are attenuated, are gradual rather than abrupt. For this reason, the cut-off frequency is usually defined as the frequency where a filter attenuates the intensity of frequency components by 3 dB (see Chapter 10 for a discussion on intensity vs. amplitude, and the dB scale). Additionally, since intensity attenuation usually occurs with every doubling or halving in frequency, the steepness of the slope is measured in decibels (dB) per octave. The low-pass filter shown in Figure 7.21 has a cut-off frequency of 100 Hz, and a steepness of 6 dB/octave. That is, every time the frequency is doubled (e.g., from 100 Hz to 200 Hz), the amplitude is dampened by 6 dB.

High-Pass Filter

A **high-pass** filter allows frequencies above the cut-off frequency to go through relatively freely while dampening those frequencies below it. Figure 7.22 shows a high-pass filter with a cut-off frequency of 1,000 Hz and a slope of 6 dB/octave.

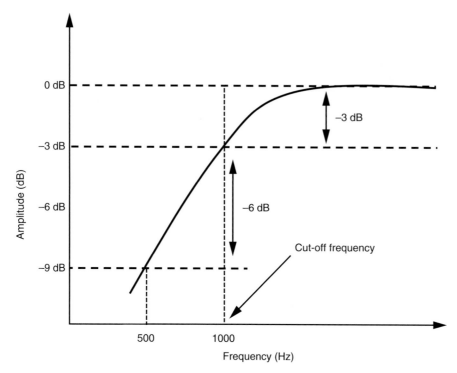

Figure 7.22 A high-pass filter with a cut-off frequency of 1,000 Hz and a slope of 6 decibels per octave

Band-Pass Filter

A band-pass filter is a combination of a low-pass and a high-pass filter, with the cut-off frequency of the high-pass filter being lower than that of the low-pass filter. Frequencies between these two cut-off frequencies are passed through, while those above and below are attenuated. Therefore, a band-pass filter is characterized by its **bandwidth**: the range (in Hz) where the two filters overlap, and center frequency: the frequency at the center of the bandwidth where the intensity is the least attenuated. Since the filter attenuates the amplitude by 3 dB, it is called a 3-dB bandwidth. A large bandwidth allows a wider frequency range to pass through, while a small bandwidth allows a narrower frequency range. Figure 7.23 shows a band-pass filter made from overlapping a low-pass filter with a cut-off frequency of 600 Hz and a high-pass filter with a cut-off frequency of 200 Hz. Its 3-dB bandwidth is therefore 400 Hz.

The filtering action of the vocal tract can be described as a system of band-pass filters, with their center frequencies corresponding to formant frequencies and 3 dB bandwidths.

Having learned how computers process, analyze, and display speech, we are now ready to appreciate the acoustic characteristics that differentiate vowels and consonants presented in the next chapter.

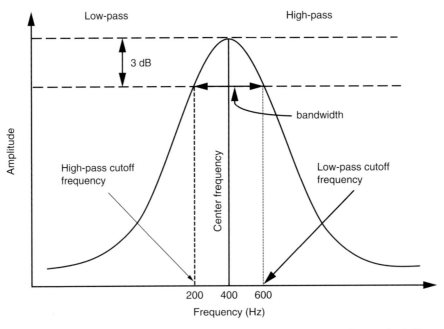

Figure 7.23 A band-pass filter with a center frequency at 400 Hz and a 3 dB bandwidth of 400 Hz (200 Hz–600 Hz)

Chapter Summary

- Digitization involves two processes: sampling and quantization.
- The sampling theorem states that the original signal can be reconstructed without any loss of information if its sampling rate is twice as high as the highest frequency in the signal.
- The Nyquist frequency is the frequency at half the sampling rate.
- Aliasing occurs when the sampling rate is too low.
- A low quantization rate results in quantization errors and introduces "noise" into the output digital signal.
- The Fourier theorem states that all complex periodic signals can be decomposed into their sine wave components.
- Fourier analysis is performed to discover frequency components and their amplitudes.
- The linear predictive coding (LPC) spectrum shows frequency peaks corresponding to resonances of the vocal tract.
- Acoustic filters allow certain frequencies to pass through relatively freely while blocking others.
- Three types of acoustic filters are low-pass, high-pass, and band-pass filters.

- Resonances of the vocal tract (formant frequencies) can be described as a system of band-pass filters with their corresponding center frequencies and bandwidths.

Review Exercises

Exercise 7.1: To prevent aliasing, how frequently (what sampling rate) should signals with the following frequencies be sampled in the analog-to-digital conversion process?
   a. 250 Hz
   b. 5,400 Hz
   c. 11,025 Hz
   d. 20,000 Hz

Exercise 7.2: What is the Nyquist frequency of a signal sampled at 22,250 Hz?

Exercise 7.3: What type of spectrogram (narrow-band or wide-band) is produced using an analysis method that emphasizes temporal changes in the signal? Explain.

Exercise 7.4: What type of spectrogram (narrow-band or wide-band) is produced using an analysis method that emphasizes frequency changes in the signal? Explain.

Exercise 7.5: If you want frequencies lower than a certain value to pass through a filter, what type of filter would you use?

Exercise 7.6: If you want frequencies between 500 Hz and 2,000 Hz to pass through a filter, what type of filter would you use? What are the high and low cut-off frequencies of this filter?

Exercise 7.7: If the vocal tract shape changes, does it affect the fundamental frequency? Does it affect the formant frequencies? Explain your answer.

Exercise 7.8: What is the spectral resolution (frequency interval between components) of a signal sampled at 22,050 Hz with FFT analysis window sizes of 10 ms, 20 ms and 50 ms?

References and Further Reading

Fry, D. B. (1979). *The Physics of Speech*. Cambridge: Cambridge University Press.

Johnson, K. (2011). *Acoustic and Auditory Phonetics*. Oxford: Wiley-Blackwell.

Ladefoged, P., & Johnson, K. (2015). *A Course in Phonetics*, 7th edn. Boston, MA: Cengage Learning.

Marcus, M. (2014). Jpeg image compression. In M. W. Marcellin, M. Gormish, A. Bilgin, & M. P. Boliek (eds.), *An Overview of JPEG2000, Proc. of the Data Compression Conference* (pp. 523–544). Snowbird, Utah, March 2000.

Reetz, H., & Jongman, A. (2009). *Phonetics: Transcription, Production, Acoustic, and Perception*. Oxford: Wiley-Blackwell.

Rosen, S., & Howell, P. (1991). *Signals and Systems for Speech and Hearing*. San Diego, CA: Academic Press.

Stevens, K. N. (1999). *Acoustic Phonetics*. Cambridge, MA: MIT Press.

8

Acoustic Properties of Vowels and Consonants

Learning Objectives

By the end of this chapter, you will be able to:

- Differentiate vowels based on their acoustic properties, such as:
  - Formant frequency
  - Intensity
  - Duration
  - Fundamental frequency
  - Nasalization
- Recognize acoustic properties of consonants according to their place, manner, and phonation type, including:
  - Plosives
  - Fricatives
  - Affricates
  - Nasals
  - Approximants: central and lateral

Introduction

In Chapter 7, the general acoustic properties of speech sounds were described. In this chapter, we will focus on the acoustic characteristics of vowels and consonants. We begin with the main acoustic cue to vowel quality: formant frequencies. Other acoustic attributes that also help differentiate vowels, including duration, intensity, and fundamental frequency, are also discussed. Finally, the acoustic characteristics of oral and nasalized vowels are explored.

For consonants, acoustic cues to plosives, fricatives, affricates, approximants, liquids, glides, and nasals are examined.

Acoustic Properties of Vowel Sounds

As already discussed in Chapter 1, vowels are produced with a more open vocal tract than consonants. They are louder than consonants because the airstream is less severely obstructed. They are also typically produced with vocal fold vibration. Vowel quality changes with the shape of the vocal tract. Since the resonant properties of the vocal tract change with its shape, formant frequencies are the main acoustic correlates of vowels.

Formant Frequency

Figure 8.1 illustrates vocal tract shapes during the production of the vowels [i], [ɑ], and [u] and their corresponding output spectra. As we can see, the first formant (F1) inversely correlates with tongue height, and the second formant (F2) with tongue backness. Low F1 values are associated with high vowels [i, u] and low F2 values are associated with back vowels [ɑ, u].

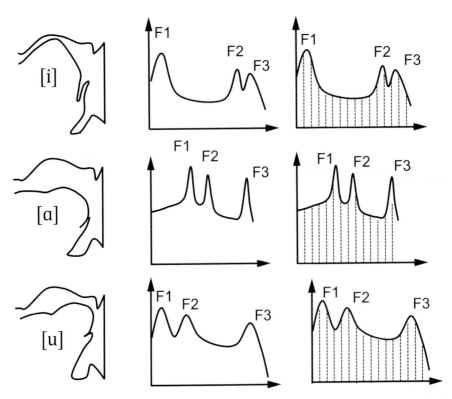

Figure 8.1 Vocal tract shapes during vowel [i], [ɑ] and [u] production and their corresponding output spectra

Monophthongs

Spectrograms of four front [i, ɪ, ɛ, æ] and four back [ɑ, ɔ, ʊ, u] monophthongs in English produced by a female speaker are shown in Figure 8.2. The front vowels are in descending order of height, from high [i] to low [æ]. The back vowels are in

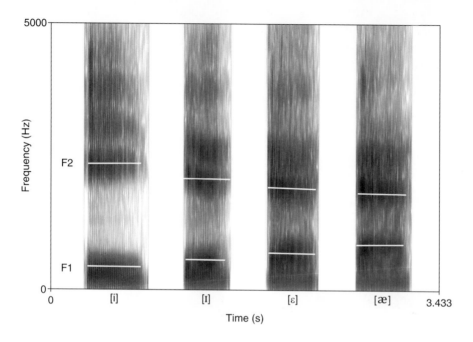

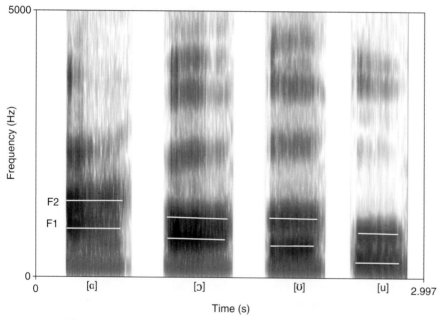

Figure 8.2 Spectrograms and F1–F3 formant values for four front and four back American English vowels produced in isolation

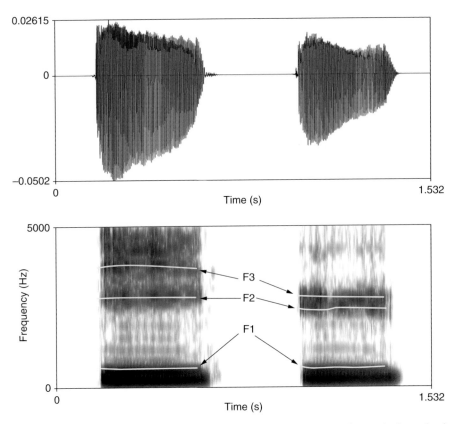

Figure 8.3 Waveforms (top) and wide-band spectrograms (bottom) of sustained vowels [i] and [y] showing a lower F2 and F3 for [y]

ascending order of height from low [ɑ] to high [u]. The F2s of the front vowels are higher than the F2s of back vowels and the F1s of high vowels are lower than those of low vowels. The distance between F2 and F1 is greater for front than for back vowels.

The third formant (F3) does not change as much as F1 and F2, so it is not very useful as an acoustic cue to vowel quality in English. However, it's an important cue in languages such as French, German, and Dutch, where an unrounded vowel is contrasted with a rounded vowel. Lip rounding lengthens the vocal tract and lower all formants, resulting in a reduced distance between F3 and F2, an important cue to distinguish a front unrounded [i] vowel from a front rounded [y] vowel, as illustrated in Figure 8.3.

Diphthongs

Vocal tract configuration changes in a diphthong, causing the formant pattern to change. Spectrograms of three English diphthongs [aɪ, aʊ, ɔɪ], as in *buy*, *bow* and *boy*, are shown in Figure 8.4. The formant pattern changes from that of a low front vowel [a] to a high front [ɪ]; from [a] to [ʊ], and from [ɔ] to [ɪ] in [aɪ], [aʊ], and [ɔɪ], respectively.

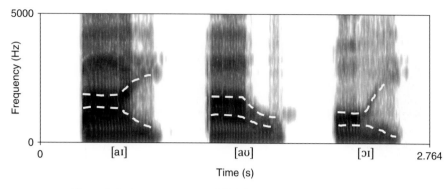

Figure 8.4 Formant patterns of diphthongs [aɪ, aʊ, ɔɪ] in English

In Chapters 3 and 4, we saw that vowel intensity, duration, and fundamental frequency (F0) may be manipulated to signal prominence or contrast at word and sentence level (e.g., stress, tone, intonation). In the following section, inherent differences in intensity, duration, and F0 will be discussed.

Intensity

Vowels may also inherently differ in their intensity level. Typically, vowel intensity correlates with its height, or openness of the vocal tract, with lower vowels being more intense than higher vowels. Variation in vowel intensity may also result from a phonological process such as lexical stress. For example, the vowel of the first syllable in *nature* is more intense than that of the second because the first vowel is stressed while the second is not.

Duration

Besides formant frequencies, the durations of different vowels may also be inherently different. In general, lower vowels are longer than higher vowels. This has been explained in terms of the distance between the roof of the mouth and the articulatory excursion of the tongue made for the vowel such that the greater this distance is, the longer the vowel is. Furthermore, tense vowels are usually longer than lax vowels.

As discussed previously in Chapter 4, vowel duration may also vary depending on the consonant context it appears in. The [æ] vowel in *bad* is longer than that in *bat*. That is, the same vowel is longer when followed by a voiced consonant than by a voiceless one. This is illustrated in Figure 8.5.

Fundamental Frequency (F0)

Fundamental frequency also inherently varies across vowels. High vowels are produced with a higher F0 than low vowels by approximately 4–25 Hz. Several

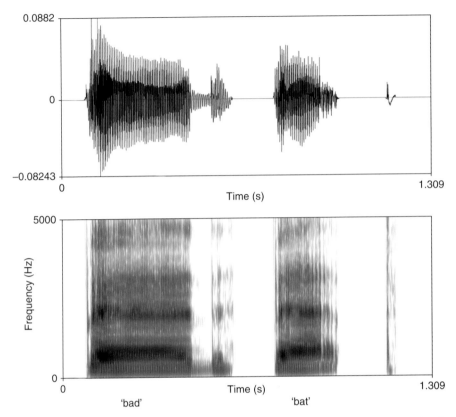

Figure 8.5 Waveforms (top) and wide-band spectrograms (bottom) of *bad* and *bat*. Duration of the vowel /æ/ in English *bad* (left) is longer than that in *bat* (right)

explanations have been proposed to account for this so-called "vowel intrinsic pitch" effect. According to one hypothesis, a tongue raising gesture pulls on the larynx, and thus increases the tension of the vocal folds. Everything being equal, taut vocal folds vibrate faster than lax ones, resulting acoustically in an increase in F0.

Table 8.1 shows average durations, F0, and F1–F4 values for twelve American English vowels spoken by forty-five men, forty-eight women, and forty-six children. As expected, formant frequency values are lower for men than for women and children due to vocal tract length differences. F0 values are also lower for men than women and children due to differences in vocal fold size. Interestingly, men's vowels are shorter than women's and children's.

Oral Versus Nasal and Nasalized Vowels

When nasality in the vowel distinguishes word meaning, as in French [sa] 'his or her' versus [sã] 'without', it is referred to as a nasal vowel. On the other hand,

Table 8.1 *Average durations (in ms), F0, and F1–F4 (in Hz) values for twelve American English vowels produced by 45 males, 48 females, and 46 children*

		/i/	/ɪ/	/e/	/ɛ/	/æ/	/a/	/ɔ/	/o/	/ʊ/	/u/	/ʌ/	/ɝ/
Dur	M	243	192	267	189	278	267	283	265	192	237	188	263
	W	306	237	320	254	332	323	353	326	249	303	226	321
	C	297	248	314	235	322	311	319	310	247	278	234	307
F0	M	138	133	129	127	123	123	121	129	133	143	133	130
	W	227	224	219	214	215	215	210	217	230	235	218	217
	C	246	241	237	230	228	229	225	236	243	249	236	237
F1	M	342	427	476	580	588	768	652	497	469	378	623	474
	W	437	483	536	731	669	936	781	555	519	459	753	523
	C	452	511	564	749	717	1002	803	597	568	494	749	586
F2	M	2322	2034	2089	1799	1952	1333	997	910	1122	997	1200	1379
	W	2761	2365	2530	2058	2349	1551	1136	1035	1225	1105	1426	1588
	C	3081	2552	2656	2267	2501	1688	1210	1137	1490	1345	1546	1719
F3	M	3000	2684	2691	2605	2601	2522	2538	2459	2434	2343	2550	1710
	W	3372	3053	3047	2979	2972	2815	2824	2828	2827	2735	2933	1929
	C	3702	3403	3323	3310	3289	2950	2982	2987	3072	2988	3145	2143
F4	M	3657	3618	3649	3677	3624	3687	3486	3384	3400	3357	3557	3334
	W	4352	4334	4319	4294	4290	4299	3923	3927	4052	4115	4092	3914
	C	4572	4575	4422	4671	4409	4307	3919	4167	4328	4276	4320	3788

(Reproduced from Hillenbrand, J., Getty, L. A., Clark, M. J., & Wheeler, K. (1995). Acoustic characteristics of American English vowels. *The Journal of the Acoustical Society of America, 97*(5), 3099–3111, with permission from the Acoustical Society of America.)

if vowel nasality is acquired in the context of a nasal consonant and its presence or absence doesn't affect the word's meaning, as in English [kʰæ̃n] *can*, then the term nasalized vowel is often used.

Both oral and nasal cavities are involved in nasal and nasalized vowel production. Due to the coupling of the two cavities and severe damping because of a greater total vocal tract area, including the pharynx, the oral cavity, the nasal cavity, and its side cavities, nasalized vowels exhibit anti-formants (see also: Nasals), overall lower amplitude, wider formant bandwidths, and a low-frequency nasal formant. Figures 8.6a and b show waveforms and spectrograms of oral [ɑ] and nasalized [ɑ̃] and their spectra produced by a female speaker. The overall lower amplitude of nasalized [ɑ̃] can be seen on the spectrogram. There is also an increase in acoustic energy in the second harmonic (H2) around 300 Hz, and a dip around 500 Hz (in the third harmonic region) in the spectrum of the nasalized [ɑ̃] due to the presence of the nasal formant and the anti-formant respectively.

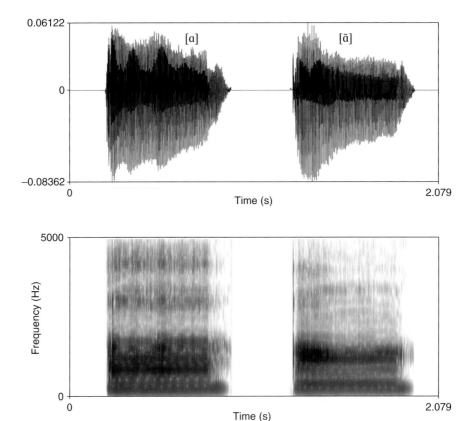

Figure 8.6a Waveforms (top) and wide-band spectrograms (bottom), oral [ɑ] and nasal [ɑ̃]

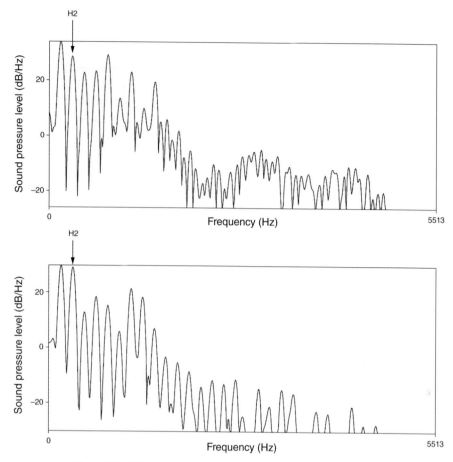

Figure 8.6b FFT spectra of oral [ɑ] and nasal [ɑ̃]

Figure 8.6 Waveforms, wide-band spectrograms, and FFT spectra of oral [ɑ] and nasal [ɑ̃] produced in isolation. Amplitude of the second harmonic (H2) is higher for nasal [ɑ̃] than oral [ɑ].

In Focus: Nasalization and Vowel Height

The effects of nasalization on vowel spectra have been shown to be similar to those of tongue and jaw movements that alter vowel height in that they mainly alter F1 frequencies. Perceptual findings have shown that nasalization lowers the perceived height of high vowels and some mid vowels, but raises the perceived height of low vowels and other mid vowels (Wright, 1975, 1980). The F1 frequency of a nasal vowel is higher relative to that of an oral vowel. This upward shift in F1 (Ohala, 1986) or a higher nasal formant (FN) frequency relative to the F1 frequency in the corresponding oral vowel may explain a vowel-lowering effect of nasalization (Krakow et al., 1988). On the other hand, a raising effect of nasalization on vowel height may result when the FN frequency in the nasal vowel is lower than the F1 frequency of the corresponding oral vowel (Krakow et al., 1988).

Acoustic Properties of Consonants

Consonants are produced with the airstream being more severely obstructed than it is in vowels. The degree of airflow obstruction ranges from the most severe, in the case of plosives, to the least, in approximants. Consonants can be produced with or without vocal fold vibration. We will discuss the acoustic properties of consonants in order of their degree of airflow obstruction, or manner of articulation.

Plosives

The production of plosives involves a momentary blockage of the airstream in the oral cavity. Air pressure is built up behind the closure, and airflow abruptly rushes out upon release of the constriction. The acoustic dimensions differentiating the place and voicing are discussed below.

Place of Articulation

Two main acoustic characteristics of the place of articulation of plosives are the frequency of the **release burst** and the **formant transitions** to the following vowel. Figure 8.7 shows waveforms and spectrograms for voiceless plosives /p/,

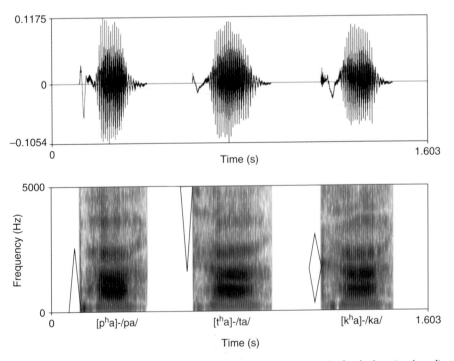

Figure 8.7 Waveforms (top) and spectrograms (bottom) of voiceless (aspirated) plosive /pa/-[pʰa], /ta/-[tʰa] and /ka/-[kʰa]. The arrows indicate the locations of areas with the strongest bursts

/t/, and /k/. The areas indicated by the arrows are where the acoustic energy of the release burst is concentrated. Burst frequency varies as a function of the length of the vocal tract in front of the constriction. Because there is no appreciable vocal tract length in front of a bilabial constriction, and because bilabial constriction lowers formant frequencies, the acoustic energy of a bilabial burst is concentrated in a relatively lower frequency region (500–1,500 Hz). An alveolar burst energy is concentrated in a higher frequency region (2,500–4,000 Hz) because of the relatively short vocal tract length in front of the alveolar constriction. The burst frequency of a velar plosive (1,500–2,500 Hz) is concentrated in a frequency range that is intermediate between that of a bilabial and an alveolar plosive.

Formant transitions reflect articulatory movement from a plosive to an adjacent vowel, or vice versa, which typically takes 50 ms or less. Particularly useful as cues to place of articulation are second and third formant transitions. These are illustrated in Figure 8.8 for [b, d, g].

As seen in this figure, all three plosives exhibit a rising F1 transition. This is because F1 stays relatively low (around 200 Hz) during plosive constriction, then rises into the following vowel. On the other hand, F2 and F3 transitions vary according to place of articulation. For bilabial plosives, F2 and F3 rise from the low-frequency burst to the F2 and F3 of the following vowel [ɑ], and F2 and F3 transitions from the vowel fall toward the closure gap. For alveolar plosives, F2 and F3 fall from the typically high-frequency burst toward the following vowel, and vowel formants rise into the closure gap. For velar plosives, F2 falls but F3 rises from the mid-frequency burst toward the formants of the following vowel, and F2 of the preceding vowel rises while F3 falls toward the closure gap. The close proximity between F2 and F3 of velar plosives is known as the **velar pinch**.

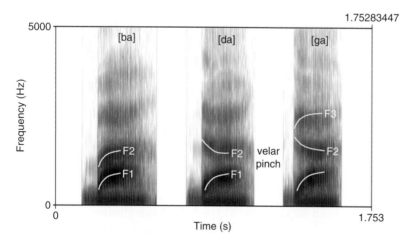

Figure 8.8 Wide-band spectrograms showing format transitions from [b, d, g] to the following vowel [a]. A velar pinch is clearly visible in [ga]

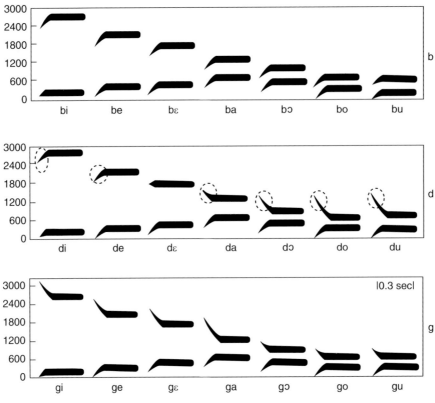

Figure 8.9 Formant transitions from /b, d, g/ to different following vowels. F2 transitions, particularly for /d/, rise when followed by a front vowel, and fall when followed by a back vowel

(Reused from Delattre, P. C., Liberman, A. M., & Cooper, F. S. (1955). Acoustic loci and transitional cues for consonants. The Journal of the Acoustical Society of America, 27(4), 769–773, with permission from the Acoustical Society of America.)

It is important to note that formant transition patterns, particularly F2 transitions of an alveolar, vary as a function of the following vowel. This is illustrated in Figure 8.9.

From this figure, we see that from [d], F2 rises toward F2 of front vowels /i, e/ because of their high F2, but falls toward back vowels /a, ɔ, o, u/ because of their low F2s.

Voicing

In *syllable-initial* position, the main acoustic cue to voicing among plosives is voice onset time (VOT), defined as the time lapse between constriction release and onset of vocal fold vibration and burst amplitude, which is stronger for voiceless than voiced plosives. Types of VOTs are negative or lead VOT, zero

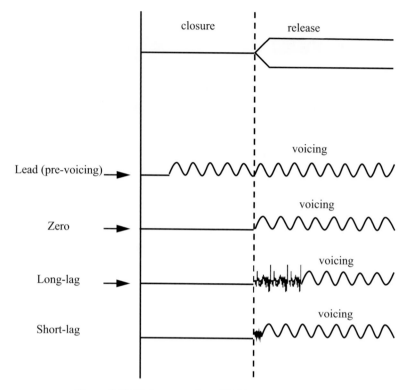

Figure 8.10 Voice onset time (VOT)

VOT, and positive or lag VOT. Lag VOT can be either short or long. These are schematically illustrated in Figure 8.10.

Lead VOT is also known as pre-voicing because voicing begins during plosive closure before the constriction release. Lead VOT is measured from the onset of voicing to constriction release. For lag VOTs, voicing lags behind the constriction release. Zero VOT occurs when voicing begins at the constriction release. Plosives produced with a lag VOT are aspirated, whereas those produced with a zero VOT are unaspirated.

In English, voiced plosives are produced with either a lead or a short-lag VOT whereas voiceless plosives are always produced with a long-lag VOT as shown in Figure 8.11.

On the other hand, voiced and voiceless plosives in Dutch are produced with lead and short-lag VOT respectively, as shown in Figure 8.12.

On yet another hand, Thai differentiates among three types of stops: pre-voiced, voiceless aspirated, and voiceless unaspirated – produced with lead, zero or short-lag and long-lag VOT, respectively. These are illustrated in Figure 8.13.

In *intervocalic* (between vowels) position, the voice-bar and closure duration distinguish voiced and voiceless plosives. A voice-bar is present during the

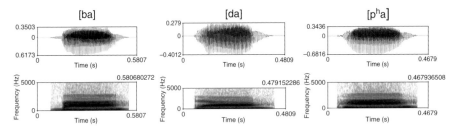

Figure 8.11 Waveforms (top) and wide-band spectrograms (bottom) showing lead-, short-lag, and long-lag VOT for voiced [b], [d], and voiceless (aspirated) [pʰ] plosives in English

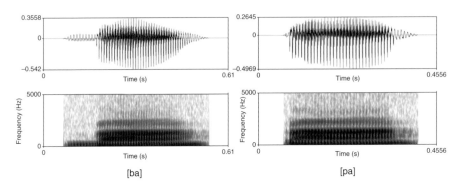

Figure 8.12 VOT of voiced [ba] (left) and voiceless (unaspirated) [pa] (right) in Dutch

closure of a voiced plosive, but absent during a voiceless plosive. Closure duration is typically longer for voiceless than for voiced plosives. Figure 8.14 shows waveforms and spectrograms of *a pie* and *a buy* with a voiceless /p/ and voiced /b/ bilabial plosives, respectively.

In *syllable-* or *word-final* position, vowel duration, closure duration, and voice-bar are acoustic cues to the voicing of plosives. The duration of the preceding vowel is longer for a final voiced plosive than for a voiceless plosive, as previously discussed. On the other hand, the closure duration of a final voiced plosive is shorter than that of a voiceless one. Finally, a voice-bar is present during the closure of a voiced plosive, but absent during the closure of a voiceless plosive. In Figure 8.15 are waveforms and spectrograms of English *bead* and *beat*, illustrating cues to final /d/ and /t/, respectively.

In sum, acoustic markers of plosives are oral closure, constriction release burst, and formant transitions. F2 formant transition and burst frequency are the main cues to plosive place of articulation, while VOT, burst amplitude, oral closure duration, duration of preceding vowel, and the presence or absence of a voice-bar during closure differentiate voiced and voiceless plosives. (See Fact box below on VOT and gender differences).

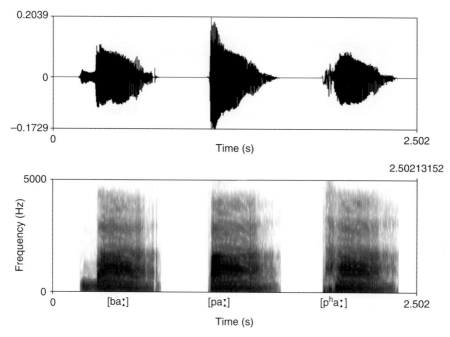

Figure 8.13 Waveforms (top) and wide-band spectrograms (bottom) showing VOTs of Thai voiced [b]-[baː], voiceless unaspirated [p]-[paː], and voiceless aspirated [pʰ]-[pʰaː]

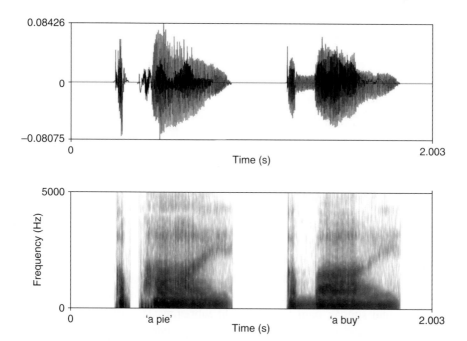

Figure 8.14 Waveforms (top) and wide-band spectrograms (bottom) of voiceless /p/ (left) and voiced /b/ (right) in syllable or word-medial position

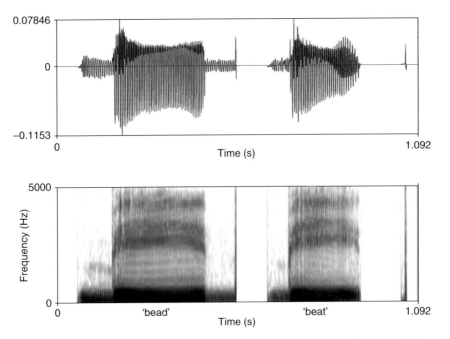

Figure 8.15 Waveforms (top) and wide-band spectrograms (bottom) of [d] and [t] in word-final position, as in *bead* (left) and *beat* (right)

Fact: VOT and Gender Differences

VOT has been shown to vary according to phonetic context, native language, age, etc. In addition, a number of investigations revealed sex differences in VOT values. For example, analysis of VOTs of stressed English plosives in both word-initial and prevocalic positions were on average longer among adult females than adult males (Whiteside & Irving, 1997). Similar findings were reported in Swartz (1992), Ryalls et al. (1997) for adults, and Whiteside and Marshall (2001) for pre-adolescents (7–11 years old).

Fricatives

The production of fricatives involves passing a jet of air through a narrow constriction inside the oral cavity generating turbulent noise – the main sound source for both voiced and voiceless fricatives. However, voiced fricatives have an additional sound source, namely vocal fold vibration. The acoustic characteristics of fricatives are spectral peak frequency, amplitude, duration of the friction noise, and the spectral properties of the transition into and out of the vowel.

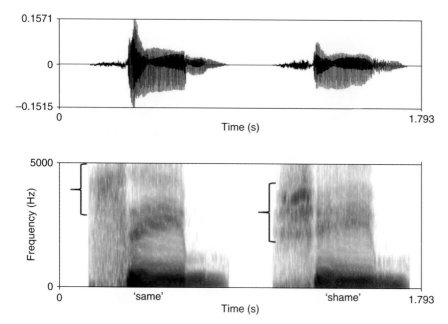

Figure 8.16 Waveforms (top) and wide-band spectrograms (bottom) of /s/ and /ʃ/ in English *same* (left) and *shame* (right). The frequency ranges where most acoustic energy is concentrated are indicated by the brackets

Place of Articulation

Fricative place of articulation is cued by the spectral peak frequency, the frequency range where most acoustic energy is concentrated. Similar to white noise, air molecules move in an irregular pattern in turbulent airflow, leading to a random pattern of air-pressure fluctuation. Unlike white noise, however, the spectrum of turbulent noise is not flat. Instead, it contains a spectral peak or location of concentrated acoustic energy. The location of the spectral peak depends on the length of the oral cavity anterior to the constriction, the resonating chamber for the frication noise. In general, the more posterior the constriction is, the lower the spectral peak frequency. Alveolar fricatives [s, z] are produced with a shorter anterior cavity, and their spectral peak is located in a higher (~ 4–7 kHz) frequency region than that of post-alveolar [ʃ, ʒ] (~ 2.5–3.5 kHz), as illustrated in Figure 8.16.

The absence of an anterior oral cavity to filter the frication noise in labio-dental [f, v] and (inter-)dental [θ, ð] fricatives causes the acoustic energy to spread across a broad range of frequencies. Therefore, their spectra show no peaks. This can be seen in Figure 8.17.

Manner of Articulation

There are two types of fricatives: sibilants [s, z, ʃ, ʒ] and non-sibilants [f, v, θ, ð]. Sibilants are produced when a jet of air passes through a narrow constriction and

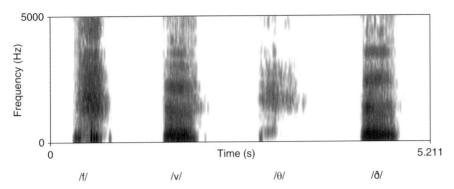

Figure 8.17 Wide-band spectrograms of [f], [v], [θ], and [ð] showing acoustic energy spread across a broad range of frequencies due to the absence of an anterior oral cavity filter

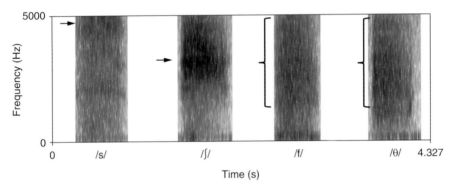

Figure 8.18 Wide-band spectrograms of [s], [ʃ], [f], and [θ]. The arrows indicate the frequency range where most acoustic energy is concentrated. Acoustic energy is spread over a wider frequency range for [f], [θ] than for [s] and [ʃ]

hits an obstacle downstream (upper teeth for [s, z] and lower teeth for [ʃ, ʒ]), causing the amplitude of the frication noise generated to be higher than that of non-sibilant fricatives. Because of a longer anterior cavity, the spectra of sibilants are also better defined than those of non-sibilants. This is illustrated in Figure 8.18.

Noise duration may also distinguish sibilants from non-sibilants, with sibilants being longer than non-sibilants.

Voicing

The acoustic energy in voiced fricatives comes from both turbulent noise generated at the constriction and the vibration of the vocal folds. As illustrated in Figure 8.19, spectrograms of voiced fricatives are similar to those of their voiceless counterparts, except for the vertical striations which correspond to glottal pulses. The amplitude of frication noise, especially in the higher frequency region, may be

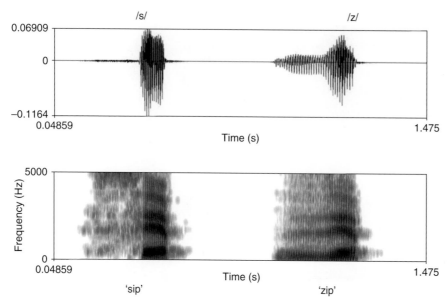

Figure 8.19 Waveforms (top) and wide-band spectrograms (bottom) of [s] in *sip* and [z] in *zip*. Vertical striations corresponding to voicing are clearly visible in [z] but not [s]

weaker in voiced than in voiceless fricatives because vocal fold vibration or voicing during voiced fricative production results in a reduced amount of airflow through the glottis relative to when the glottis remains open in voiceless fricatives. Frication noise duration is also relatively shorter in voiced compared to voiceless fricatives.

Affricates

Affricates are produced with an oral closure similar to that of a plosive, but with the more gradual release of a fricative. An affricate waveform thus shows a release burst followed by a frication. The main acoustic difference between a fricative and an affricate is the frication amplitude rise-time, as illustrated in Figure 8.20.

Nasals

Production of a nasal consonant involves two resonators: the oral and the nasal cavities. There is a closure inside the oral cavity, but the velum is in a lowered position so that the airflow escapes only through the nasal cavity, producing the sound called a **nasal murmur**. Total cavity length, which includes the pharyngeal, the oral, and the nasal cavities, is longer for a nasal consonant than for an oral consonant. Therefore, nasal murmur consists of a **very low F1** (around 200–300 Hz), sometimes known as the **nasal formant**. A reduction of airflow

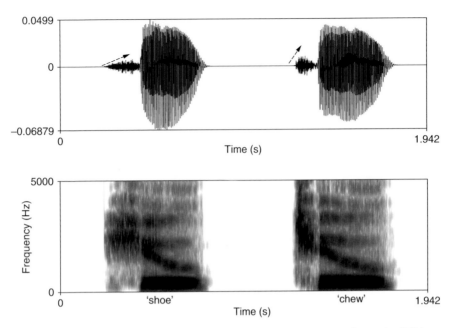

Figure 8.20 Waveforms (top) and wide-band spectrograms (bottom) of [ʃ] in *shoe* (left) and [tʃ] in *chew* (right). Amplitude rise times are indicated by the arrows

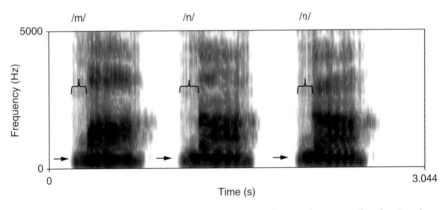

Figure 8.21 Wide-band spectrograms showing nasal murmur (brackets) and nasal formant (arrows) in [m], [n], and [ŋ]

into the narrower opening of the nasal cavity causes nasals to have **lower formant amplitude**, particularly in comparison to neighboring vowels. Moreover, sound energy absorption by the walls of both the oral and the nasal cavities **increases formant bandwidths**. Figure 8.21 shows nasal murmur, nasal formant (low F1), and formant amplitude of bilabial [m], alveolar [n], and velar [ŋ] nasals in [ma], [na], and [ŋa] syllables, respectively.

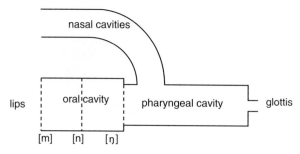

Figure 8.22 Length of oral cavity for bilabial [m], alveolar [n], and velar [ŋ] nasals

Anti-Formants

During the production of a nasal consonant, the obstructed oral chamber is considered a side branch, or a shunt resonator, since the sound energy from the source that excites the oral cavity cannot radiate out into the atmosphere. Therefore, the resonances of the oral cavity are not directly evident in a nasal spectrum. Instead, unusually low valleys, known as anti-formants, appear in the spectrum.

These anti-formants are the result of the interaction between the oral and the nasal cavities: resonant frequencies near the resonances of the oral cavity are removed or subtracted from the output spectrum. If there are no formants nearby, anti-formants may appear as a white band on the spectrogram (also see Figure 8.23 below). The frequency of an anti-formant is the same as that of a formant, but its amplitude (formant peak) will be reduced.

The locations of anti-formants vary as a function of the length of the oral cavity, or the nasal place of articulation (Figure 8.22). The longer the oral cavity, or the more anterior the place of articulation, the lower the anti-formant values in the output spectrum. Figure 8.23 shows anti-formants (indicated by arrows) of the bilabial [m], the alveolar [n], and the velar [ŋ] nasals produced by a native Thai female speaker taken from nasal murmur at the locations marked on the spectrograms. As shown in this figure, the anti-formants are in the lower frequency range (622 Hz) for bilabial [m], higher for alveolar [n] (1,250 Hz), and highest for velar [ŋ] (2,608 Hz).

Central Approximants

Approximants are produced with the most open vocal tract of all the consonants. Thus, they are the most sonorant or loudest consonants. Their production involves two articulators coming toward each other, but not close enough to substantially impede the airflow. For this reason, they exhibit acoustic properties similar to those of vowels produced at similar locations in the vocal tract. For example, the palatal approximant [j] is produced when the tongue blade rises toward the palate, similar to that of the vowel [i]. The formant patterns of [j] and

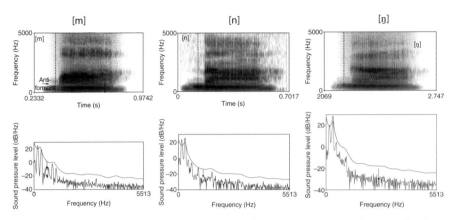

Figure 8.23 Wide-band spectrograms (top) and FFT spectra (bottom) showing anti-formants (arrows) for bilabial [m], alveolar [n], and velar [ŋ] nasals

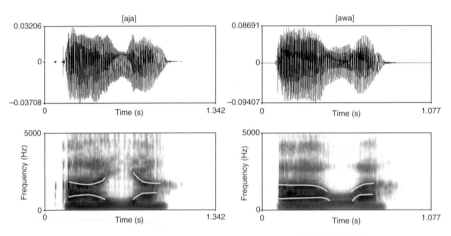

Figure 8.24 Waveforms (top) and wide-band spectrograms (bottom) of [j] in [aja] (left) and [w] in [awa] (right). White lines are formant traces. Both [j] and [w] are shorter and weaker than their neighboring vowels

[i] are, therefore, similar, with low F1 and high F2 values. However, the proximity between the tongue and the palate is closer for [j] than for [i], thus having a greater degree of airflow impedance and a weaker or lower amplitude spectrum.

The labio-velar approximant [w] shares acoustic properties with the vowel [u], since both are produced with lip rounding and an approximation between the back of the tongue and the velum. Figure 8.24 shows waveforms and wide-band spectrograms of [aja], and [awa]. Note that both [j] and [w] are relatively shorter and weaker than their neighboring vowels.

The alveolar approximant [ɹ] is characterized by a very low F3. Its production involves three articulatory gestures: lip rounding, close proximity between the

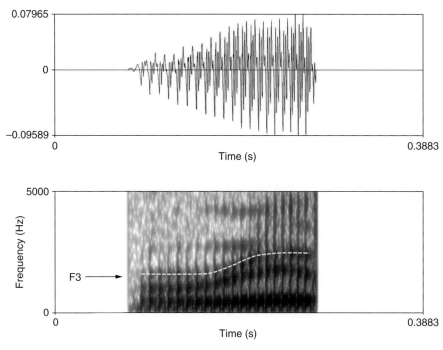

Figure 8.25 Waveform (top) and wide-band spectrogram (bottom) of English [ɹ] in rip

tongue tip and the alveolar ridge, and between the tongue root and the pharyngeal wall, narrowing the pharyngeal cavity. Consistent with Perturbation Theory (Chapter 6), constrictions at these three locations lower the F3 value. This is shown in Figure 8.25.

This figure clearly shows a much lower F3 (white line) for [ɹ] than for the following vowel [ɪ]

Lateral Approximants

Lateral approximants share some of the acoustic characteristics of nasals. The sound [l], for example, is produced with the tongue tip touching the alveolar ridge while one or both sides of the tongue are lowered, letting the air escape through. A small air pocket is present on top of the tongue, constituting a short side branch, and contributes to the total cavity length, introducing anti-formants and relatively low amplitude formants in the output spectrum. Figure 8.26 shows linear predictive coding (LPC) and FFT spectra for [l] (see Chapter 7 for a discussion on LPC and FFT analyses). Anti-formants appear at approximately 850 Hz, 2,000 Hz, and 3,400 Hz, attenuating F2 and F4 relative to F1 and F3.

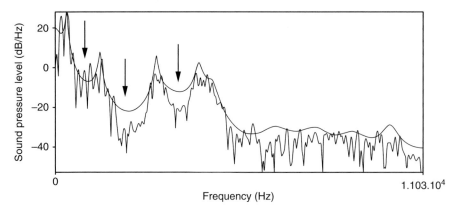

Figure 8.26 LPC and FFT spectra of alveolar lateral approximant [l] with anti-resonances at about 850 Hz, 2,000 Hz and 3,400 Hz indicated by arrows

The similar acoustic properties of [l] and [n] are likely responsible for these two sounds being allophones of the same phoneme in some Chinese dialects. For these speakers, a distinction between the English words *night* and *light* is not easily perceptible.

Despite the importance of its acoustic characteristics, comprehension of speech ultimately depends on how the signals are processed in the ears and interpreted by the brain. In the next chapter, we discuss the auditory system and how it transforms the speech signals.

Chapter Summary

- The main acoustic marker for vowels is formant frequency.
- Intensity, duration, and F0 may aid vowel identification.
- Acoustic cues for consonants are more diverse than those for vowels.
- Acoustic markers for plosive consonant place of articulation are release bursts and formant transitions.
- Manner and voicing of plosives are cued mainly by their voice onset time (VOT).
- Sibilant and non-sibilant fricatives are differentiated by the amplitude and duration of their fricative noise.
- The presence of vertical striations on the spectrogram distinguishes voiced from voiceless fricatives.
- Fricatives' places of articulation are cued by frequency of concentrated frication noise.
- The presence of a release burst and frication noise amplitude rise-time separate affricates from fricatives.

- Acoustic markers for the place of articulation of nasal consonants are formant transition shape and locations of anti-resonances.
- Approximants share acoustic properties of vowels, but are shorter and weaker than vowels.
- The lateral approximant [l] shows similar acoustic properties to the nasal [n].

Review Exercises

Spectrogram Reading

Exercise 8.1: *She Shoe* or *Shoe She*?

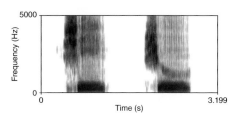

Exercise 8.2: *Hid Heed* or *Heed Hid*?

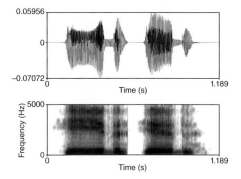

Exercise 8.3: *How High* or *High How*?

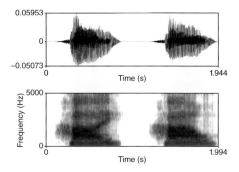

Exercise 8.4. *Lay Ray* or *Ray Lay*?

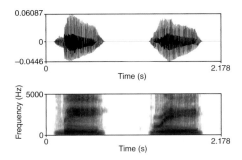

Exercise 8.5: *Way Ray* or *Ray Way*?

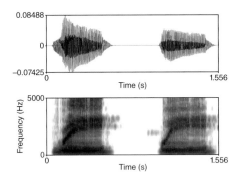

Exercise 8.6: *Shoe Sue* or *Sue Shoe*?

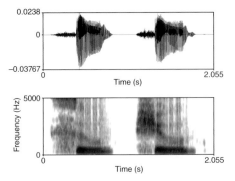

Exercise 8.7: *Cash Catch* or *Catch Cash*?

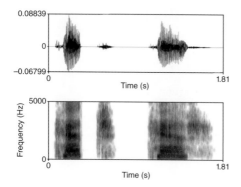

Exercise 8.8: *Duck Dug* or *Dug Duck*?

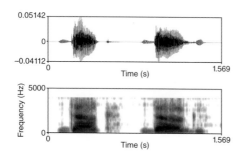

Exercise 8.9: Examine the FFT and LPC spectra below and label the following:

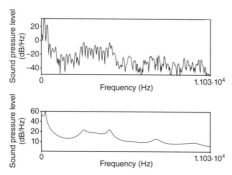

first harmonic (H1), first formant (F1), second formant (F2), and third formant (F3).

Exercise 8.10: Match [i], [y] and [u] to their corresponding LPC spectrum. Justify your choice.

a. Vowel

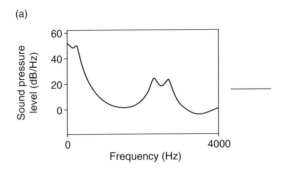

b. Vowel _____

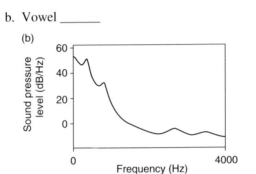

c. Vowel _____

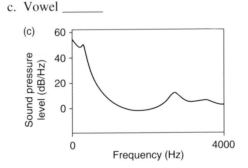

References and Further Reading

Delattre, P. C., Liberman, A. M., & Cooper, F. S. (1955). Acoustic loci and transitional cues for consonants. *The Journal of the Acoustical Society of America*, 27(4), 769–773.

Hillenbrand, J., Getty, L. A., Clark, M. J., & Wheeler, K. (1995). Acoustic characteristics of American English vowels. *The Journal of the Acoustical Society of America*, 97(5), 3099–3111.

Krakow, R. A., Beddor, P. S., Goldstein, L. M., & Fowler, C. A. (1988). Coarticulatory influences on the perceived height of nasal vowels. *The Journal of the Acoustical Society of America*, 83(3), 1146–1158.

Ohala, J. J. (1986). Phonological evidence for top-down processing in speech perception. In J. S. Perkell & D. H. Klatt (eds.), *Invariance and Variability of Speech Processes* (pp. 386–401). Hillsdale, NJ: Lawrence Erlbaum Associates.

Pickett J. M. (1980). *The Sounds of Speech Communication*, Baltimore, MD: University Park Press.

Reetz, H., & Jongman, A. (2009). *Phonetics: Transcription, Production, Acoustics, and Perception* (Vol. 34). Oxford: John Wiley & Sons.

Ryalls, J., Zipprer, A., & Baldauff, P. (1997). A preliminary investigation of the effects of gender and race on voice onset time. *Journal of Speech, Language, and Hearing Research*, 40(3), 642–645.

Swartz, B. L. (1992). Gender difference in voice onset time. *Perceptual and Motor Skills*, 75(3), 983–992.

Whiteside, S. P., & Irving, C. J. (1997). Speakers' sex differences in voice onset time: some preliminary findings. *Perceptual and Motor Skills*, 85(2), 459–463E.

Whiteside, S. P., & Marshall, J. (2001). Developmental trends in voice onset time: Some evidence for sex differences. *Phonetica*, 58(3), 196–210.

Wright, J. T. (1975). Effects of vowel nasalization on the perception of vowel height. In *Nasalfest: Papers from a Symposium on Nasals and Nasalization*. Stanford University: *Language Universals Project* (p. 373).

Wright, J. (1980). The behavior of nasalized vowels in the perceptual vowel space. *Report of the Phonology Laboratory Berkeley, Cal.*, 5, 127–163.

9

Hearing

Learning Objectives

By the end of this chapter, you will be able to:

- Describe the anatomy of the auditory system and how it transforms speech signals, including:
  - The outer ear
  - The middle ear
  - The inner ear
- Differentiate physical properties: pressure and intensity, their corresponding subjective sensation of loudness, and the scales used to quantify them, including:
  - The decibel scales
  - The phon scale
  - The sone scale
- Recognize the difference between frequency and its auditory impression of pitch, and the scales used to quantify them, including:
  - The mel scale
  - The bark scale
  - The equivalent rectangular bandwidth (ERB) scale
- Characterize the auditory system's sensitivity to duration changes in the signal

Introduction

Speech sounds are traditionally described in terms of how they are made by the vocal apparatus, as we saw in Chapter 1. However, we know that the same sound can be produced by different articulatory gestures. For example, /u/ may be produced with or without lip rounding, or /i/ may be produced with different degrees of tongue height, frontness, and even lip rounding (try to see if you can produce an /i/ vowel with lip rounding!). This suggests the perception of a sound goes beyond its articulatory characteristics, and its auditory properties also play a role in its perception.

In this chapter, we will begin with a quick tour of the anatomy and physiology of the hearing organs, and a discussion of how speech signals are transformed by the auditory system. We will conclude the chapter with an examination of our subjective auditory experience of different physical properties of sound stimuli, including frequency and intensity.

The Auditory System

The hearing or auditory system comprise the outer ear, the middle ear, and the inner ear, as shown in Figure 9.1.

The Outer Ear

The outer ear consists of three parts: the pinna (auricle), the ear canal (meatus), and the ear drum (tympanic membrane).

Visible from the outside, the **pinna** gathers the signal and funnels it to the ear canal. It also helps locate the direction of the sound.

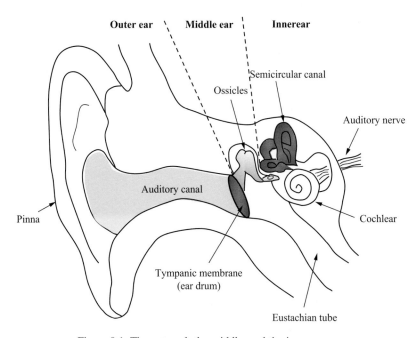

Figure 9.1 The external, the middle, and the inner ear

The **ear canal** is about 2.5 cm long and 0.8 mm wide. It is open at one end near the pinna and closed at the other end by the eardrum. As a quarter-wavelength resonator, the eardrum amplifies frequencies around 3,400 Hz, which is its first resonating frequency (34,000/4*2.5). It is estimated that the amplitudes of frequencies between 2 kHz and 5 kHz are amplified approximately 15 dB greater than other frequencies by the ear canal. This allows us to hear frequencies that would otherwise be undetectable.

The **eardrum** is a thin elastic membrane (tympanic membrane) that closes one end of the ear canal and forms an airtight divider between the outer ear and the middle ear. It moves inward and outward, following the pattern of pressure variations of the sound wave. The movement is then transferred to the middle ear. Being inside the head, the eardrum is protected from physical damage and from external temperature and humidity levels.

The Middle Ear

The middle ear is an air-filled chamber inside the skull. It contains three small bones, or ossicles, namely the **malleus** (hammer), the **incus** (anvil), and the **stapes** (stirrup) (Figure 9.2). These bones are the smallest in the human body, with the hammer being the largest and longest of the three, and the stapes the smallest. They are suspended within the middle ear by ligaments attached to the wall of the chamber. The handle of the malleus is attached to the eardrum, and covers more than half of its surface area. The footplate of the stapes covers the oval window, the entrance to the inner ear.

Movements of the eardrum are transferred to the malleus, the incus, and then to the stapes. Together, they form a lever system (Figure 9.3) and work to

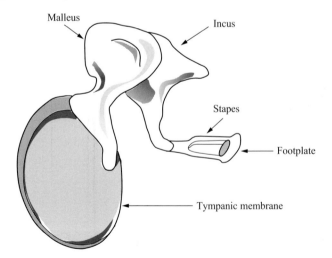

Figure 9.2 Three small bones (malleus, incus, and stapes) in the middle ear

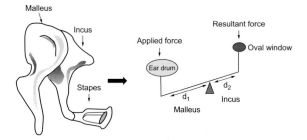

Figure 9.3 A lever system formed by the malleus, the incus, and the stapes

transmit and amplify the sound vibrations. In this figure, the length of the malleus corresponds to d_1, the distance between the applied force (at the eardrum) and the fulcrum. The length of the incus corresponds to d_2, the distance between the fulcrum and the resultant force (at the stapes). If d_2 is less than d_1, then the resultant force will be greater than the applied force. Relative to those of the malleus, the displacement of the stapes' footplate decreases while the force increases by a factor of approximately 1.15 (Reetz & Jongman, 2009) (see animation of middle ear mechanics here https://sites.stanford.edu/otobiome chanics/middle-ear-mechanics). In addition, the vibrating portion of the tympanic membrane (the eardrum) is larger than the area of the oval window. Therefore, if the force exerted on the vibrating portion of the eardrum is transferred to the oval window (via the stapes footplate), then the pressure (force per unit area) has to be greater at the oval window. These two mechanical advantages, the lever effect and the difference in surface area between the eardrum and the oval window, together cause the amplitude of the pressure variations that are transmitted from the external ear to the internal ear to increase approximately 25-fold, or 27 dB (Reetz & Jongman, 2009). This pressure gain is largely compensating for the potential loss during sound transmission. Depending on the frequency, only about 60 percent of sound energy is transmitted from the eardrum to the oval window (Bell & Rhoades, 2012).

The increase in pressure performed by the middle ear allows pressure waves from the middle ear to penetrate the inner ear more effectively.

Besides increasing the amount of acoustic energy entering the inner ear, the middle ear also helps protect the inner ear from the adverse effects of loud sounds. In response to loud noise, the stapedius muscle, connected to the stapes, draws the stapes away from the oval window leading to an increase in the stiffness of the chain of the middle ear's bones, and thus its ability to amplify acoustic energy to the inner ear is temporarily decreased.

The Inner Ear

The inner ear is a system of fluid-filled cavities. It contains the **vestibular system**, which helps us maintain equilibrium and balance, and the **cochlea**, which helps us hear sounds.

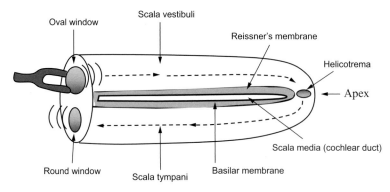

Figure 9.4 The cochlea when uncoiled

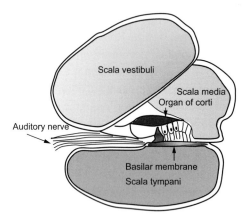

Figure 9.5 Cross-sectional view of the unrolled cochlea

The **cochlea** is a snail-shaped bony structure that would be about 3.5 cm if uncoiled (Figure 9.4). It is thicker and narrower at its base near the oval window, but thinner and wider at its tip or apex. It is partitioned into three fluid-filled chambers by membranous structures: the scala vestibuli, the scala media or the cochlear duct, and the scala tympani. Reissner's membrane separates the cochlear duct from the scala vestibuli, and the basilar membrane separates the duct from the scala tympani. Fluids from the scala vestibule and the scala tympani can pass freely through the helicotrema, an opening at the far (apical) end of the cochlea. The oval window and the round window lie at the basal end of the cochlea. The oval window, covered by the footplate of the stapes, is the opening between the scala vestibuli and the middle ear. The round window is a membrane-covered opening between the scala tympani and the middle ear.

Lying on the basilar membrane are a collection of cells called the **Organ of Corti** (Figures 9.5, 9.6), which contain hair cells, and the tectorial membrane, which can move in response to the movement of the fluid in the vestibuli and the tympani. The Organ of Corti is linked to the auditory nerves.

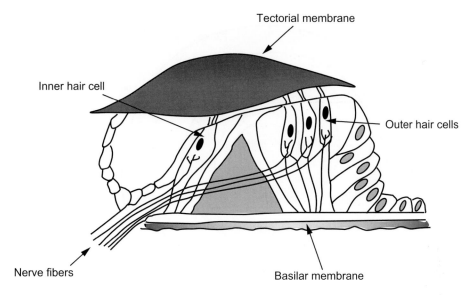

Figure 9.6 The Organ of Corti

During hearing, mechanical movements of the stapes in the middle ear are transmitted to the fluid inside the cochlea through the oval window, causing the basilar membrane to oscillate. The oscillations of the basilar membrane are then converted to neural impulses by the inner hair cells and transmitted to the brain by the auditory nerves.

Due to variation in the stiffness and the width of the basilar membrane along its length, its deformation in response to input frequencies (from the displacement of the stapes through the oval window) form a "traveling wave" with maximum amplitude at a position along its length corresponding to the particularly frequency of the input. For high frequencies, the vibration amplitude of the basilar membrane is highest at its basal end, near the oval window where it is lightest and stiffest. For low frequencies, areas of strongest vibration occur near the apex where it is wider and more elastic. Figure 9.7 shows areas along the basilar membrane and its response to different frequencies.

The frequency tuning effect of the basilar membrane means that only hair cells located at a particular place along the membrane are maximally stimulated by a given frequency or pitch. This frequency localization is the basis of a pitch discrimination theory known as the **place theory**, and the mapping of specific pitches (or tone) to specific areas along the basilar membrane is called **tonotopic organization**. The tonotopic organization is partially preserved as the signals from the cochlea travel through the complex pathways of the auditory system in the brain, so pitch can be spatially localized throughout the system (Bell & Rhoades, 2012).

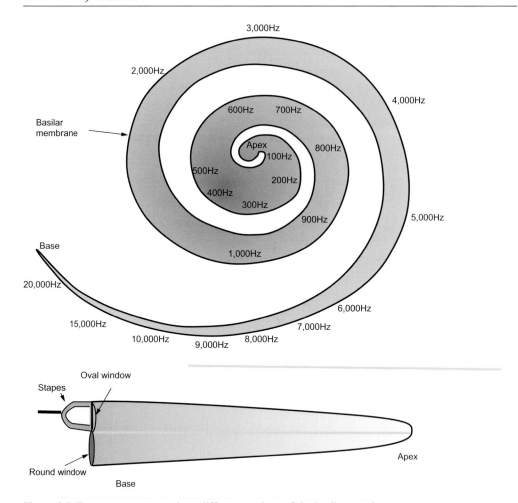

Figure 9.7 Frequency response along different portions of the basilar membrane

Hearing Sounds

From our discussion on the auditory system above, we learn that hearing is a complex phenomenon. The physical properties of the signals, including frequency and amplitude, are transformed in many ways by the auditory system. As such, the firing patterns of the auditory nerve cells and our corresponding hearing sensation can be very different from the acoustic properties of the input signals. Therefore, besides linear scales measuring the physical properties of the input signals, we also need auditory scales approximating our subjective sensation of different physical properties of the signals for a better understanding of sound perception.

Sound Pressure, Intensity, and Loudness

We experience sounds when air particles are moved from their resting positions by an external force, the vibrating prongs of a tuning fork, for example. In turn, each air particle transfers the force to its neighboring particles. Two measures of the force or the magnitude of a sound are pressure and intensity. A sound's **pressure** is the amount of force the sound exerted over a unit area of surface. It is measured in **dynes per square centimeter** (dyne/cm^2). Normal atmospheric pressure is approximately one million dynes per square centimeter. A pressure variation of about 0.0002 dynes per square centimeter would produce an audible sound (threshold of hearing), while a sound pressure of 200 dynes per square centimeter can produce sound waves that could damage the ear.

In speech, a sound's pressure level is reflected in its amplitude on the waveform, and the unit of sound pressure value is expressed in pascals (Pa) instead of dyne/cm^2 ($P_{Pa} = P_{dyne/cm^2} \times 0.01$).

The softest sound that the human ear can detect has a pressure variation of 20 μPa (micro pascals) or 20×10^{-6} Pa (20 millionths of a pascal), whereas a sound with a pressure variation of 20 Pa, or 20×10^{-7} (20,000,000) μPa, can damage our ears. Normal conversational speech has a pressure variation of about 0.02 Pa, or 20×10^{-4} (20,000) μPa.

Intensity is the amount of energy transmitted along the wave through an area of one centimeter at right angles to the direction of wave propagation. As the number of the air particles to be moved by the vibrating tuning fork increases with the distance from the source, less and less energy is available to move a particle. This is the reason why sound becomes fainter over a distance (see also damping in Chapter 6). The intensity or power of a sound wave corresponds to the amount of available energy over a small area where the measurement is taken, not the total energy produced by the vibrating tuning fork. The unit of intensity is watts per square centimeter. A sound intensity of 10^{-16} watts per square centimeter produces a just-audible sound, while a sound intensity of ten thousandths of a watt per square centimeter can damage the ear.

In general, the pressure (amplitude) of a sound wave is easier to measure than its intensity. In addition, intensity can be inferred from the pressure value since sound intensity is proportional to the square of the corresponding pressure variations of the wave. That is:

$$I(ntensity) = P(ressure)^2$$

The Decibel Scales

Because the human ear is sensitive to a large range of intensity and pressure, and our perceived loudness of a sound depends on its pressure or intensity relative to that of another (reference) sound, it is more practical to measure them using a decibel (dB) scale.

Recall that the pressure amplitude, the vertical distance between the zero line and the pressure maxima or minima, of a sound wave reflects the extent to which molecules of the medium are displaced from their resting position. The higher the amplitude – that is, the greater the distance over which the molecules oscillate – the greater the change in air pressure from the atmospheric level (zero amplitude), and the louder the sound is perceived. During speech, pressure level changes constantly and covers a wide range. As mentioned above, the smallest sound pressure level detectable by the human ears is 20 µPa, and the largest at the threshold of pain is 20 Pa, or one million times the smallest value. Interestingly, human ears are more sensitive to pressure or amplitude differences between two relatively quiet sounds than between two loud sounds. In other words, a small difference at a low amplitude is more perceptible than the same difference at a higher amplitude. To deal with the large range of sound pressure detectable by the human ear and to capture the seemingly logarithmic nature in our sense of hearing, amplitude values are measured in decibels (dB).

The dB scale is a logarithmic scale. In a log scale, equal ratios are spaced equally. For example, the log difference between 10 and a 100 is the same as between 100 and 1,000, namely 1. This is illustrated below:

$$\mathrm{Log}_{10}\ 10 = 1$$
$$\mathrm{Log}_{10}\ 100 = 2$$
Distance on the log scale = 2–1 = 1, and;
$$\mathrm{Log}_{10}\ \text{of}\ 100 = 2$$
$$\mathrm{Log}_{10}\ \text{of}\ 1,000 = 3$$
Distance on the log scale = 3–2 = 1

Or

Absolute value	Log equivalent value
1,000	3
100	2
10	1

When used with pressure values, we see that the log scale compresses the range of absolute pressure values and better captures our ears' response to pressure changes.

In speech, dB expresses the relationship between two amplitude values, namely amplitude of the sound being measured and that of a reference sound, as shown in the formula below:

$$\left[\mathrm{Log}_{10}\ \frac{\text{measured amplitude}}{\text{reference amplitude}} \right]$$

This formula yields a measure called the bel in honor of Alexander Graham Bell, the inventor of the telephone. It is important to note that the bel is a method of calculation – a way to describe a ratio which could be pressure, intensity, power, voltage, or anything including the numbers. However, the bel scale is too compressed to capture our sensitivity to amplitude differences between sounds, and so they are multiplied by 10. In other words, one bel equals 10 decibels. The formula now looks as follows:

$$\left[10 \times \log_{10} \frac{\text{measured amplitude}}{\text{reference amplitude}} \; [\text{dB}] \right]$$

A higher amplitude means air molecules travel a greater distance than a lower amplitude. If the frequencies of the two signals are the same, this means that, in the same amount of time, the air molecules cover a greater distance in the higher-amplitude signal than in the lower-amplitude signal. It also means that the speed at which air molecules travel is faster in higher-amplitude signals. Since the energy of air molecules increases with the square of their speed, energy in the higher-amplitude signal is greater than that of the lower-amplitude signal. Furthermore, our perception of loudness depends on the amount of energy (intensity or power) in the signal. In order to approximate or infer the amount of energy in the signal, and thus its relation to perceived loudness, the amplitude values are squared in the dB calculation, as shown below:

$$\left[10 \times \log_{10} \frac{\text{measured amplitude}^2}{\text{reference amplitude}^2} \; [\text{dB}] \right]$$

$$\downarrow$$

$$\left[20 \times \log_{10} \frac{\text{measured amplitude}}{\text{reference amplitude}} \; [\text{dB}] \right]$$

If we use P_0 to represent measured amplitude in μPa and P_1 to refer to a reference amplitude, then the formula can be shortened to:

$$dB = 20 \times \log_{10} \frac{P_0}{P_1}$$

Here are two examples of dB calculations.

Example 1

$P_0 = 1{,}000 \, \mu\text{Pa}$ and $P_1 = 100 \, \mu\text{Pa}$

$dB = 20 \, x \, \log_{10} 1{,}000/100$

$P_0/P_1 = 100$

$\text{Log } P_0/P_1 = 2$

$dB = 20 \, x \, 2 = 40 \, \text{dB}.$

Example 2

$P_0 = 3000 \, \mu\text{Pa}$ and $P1 = 350 \, \mu\text{Pa}$

$dB = 20 \, x \, \log_{10} 3{,}000/350$

$$P_0/P_1 = 8.57$$

$$\text{Log } P_0/P_1 = 0.93$$

$$dB = 20 \times 0.93 = 18.7 \text{ dB}.$$

Several dB scales exist, but the two most common ones are **dB$_{spl}$** and **dB$_{rms}$**. The former, dB$_{spl}$, is computed by the formula:

$$\left[20 \times \log_{10} \frac{\text{measured amplitude in } \mu \text{ Pa of sound}}{20 \ \mu \text{ Pa}} \left[dB_{spl} \right] \right]$$

It expresses the measured pressure value relative to 20 µPa, the pressure value at hearing threshold. As shown in Examples 3 and 4 below, dB$_{spl}$ values for sounds with pressure amplitude values of 2,000 µPa and 4,600 µPa are 40 and 47.2, respectively.

Example 3

$$P_0 = 2,000 \, \mu Pa$$

$$dBspl = 20 \times \log_{10} 2,000/20$$

$$P_0/P_1 = 100$$

$$\log P_0/P_1 = 2$$

$$dB_{spl} = 20 \times 2 = 40$$

Example 4

$$P_0 = 4,600 \, \mu Pa$$

$$dB_{spl} = 20 \times \log_{10} 4,600/20$$

$$P_0/P_1 = 230$$

$$\log P_0/P_1 = 2.36$$

$$dB_{spl} = 20 \times 2.36 = 47.2$$

Table 9.1 below gives examples of dB values and the corresponding pressure and intensity ratios of common natural sounds.

Table 9.1 *Intensity and pressure ratios and their dB equivalents*

Intensity ratio	dB equivalent	Pressure ratio	dB equivalent
1:1	0	1:1	0
10:1	10	10:1	20
100:1	20	100:1	40
1,000:1	30	1,000:1	60
10,000:1	40	10,000:1	80
100,000:1	50	100,000:1	100

In Focus: Adding Two Identical Sounds?

Adding two identical sounds equates to increasing the intensity or pressure ratio from 1/1 to 2/1, therefore,

the intensity of these two sounds combined equals $10 \log_{10} 2/1 = 10 \times 0.3 = 3\,\text{dB}$

and

the pressure of these two sounds combined equals $20 \log_{10} 2/1 = 20 \times 0.3 = 6\,\text{dB}$

In other words, doubling the sound intensity increases the sound level by 3 dB, and doubling the sound pressure increases the sound level by 6 dB.

Because the sound pressure varies quickly from one instant to the next, a measurement of amplitude at a given point in time is not very useful. In speech research, the most common method used to compute amplitude values is the root mean square (RMS) method. The RMS method calculates amplitude values over a stretch of time, and is believed to roughly approximate the amount of energy in the signal, and thus its perceived loudness, relatively well. In addition, since a calibrated device is rarely used to measure sound pressure to obtain its absolute values, sound pressure level is expressed relative to an arbitrary reference, or to 1. The formula can be rewritten as follows:

$$20 \times \log(\text{amplitude}) \ [\text{dB}]$$

where amplitude is understood to be RMS amplitude, and the units are in plain dB since the reference is arbitrary, or 1.

To sum up, pressure and intensity are two measures of a sound's magnitude or level, the amount of acoustic energy. Because of the large range of intensity and pressure that our ears are sensitive to and the relative nature of how our ears perceive loudness, a logarithmic dB scale is used to quantify the magnitude of a sound. The dB unit expresses ratios between the pressure amplitude or intensity of a sound measured and a reference sound (see Fact box below on what 0 dB means). In speech, the sound pressure amplitude level over a stretch of time, known as the RMS amplitude, is typically measured. RMS amplitude values in dB indicate pressure values of a sound relative to 1 or to an arbitrary reference.

Fact: Does Zero dB Mean No Sound?

No, dB is a relative scale. A number of dB is not a pressure or intensity value of a sound but rather the difference (ratio) in pressure or intensity between two sounds (on a logarithmic scale). The logarithmic of 1 is zero, therefore 0 dB means that the sound pressure or intensity is equal to that of the reference sound (20 μPa or 0.0002 dynes per square centimeter), a very small value, but not zero.

Auditory Scales of Loudness

As mentioned above, our subjective auditory sensation of amplitude is loudness. However, as seen in previous sections, the auditory system selectively transforms the input signal such that high frequencies are attenuated in the ear canal whereas low frequencies are dampened by the middle ear. Consequently, frequencies ranging between 2 kHz and 4 kHz are perceived best by the human auditory system. The dB$_{spl}$ scale discussed above does not take this into account and instead gives equal weight to all frequencies. The two auditory scales, the phon and the sone scales, that we are about to discuss take into account variation in the perceptual salience of different frequencies.

Phon Scale

The phon scale is a psychoacoustic scale derived to reflect the perceived loudness of sine tones. Unlike a dB scale, it takes into account the fact that sine tones at very low and very high frequencies are not perceived as well as those between 2 kHz and 4 kHz. It also takes into account the fact that the damping level for different frequencies varies as a function of the tone's amplitude level. The phon value of a sound is defined as the dB$_{spl}$ value of a

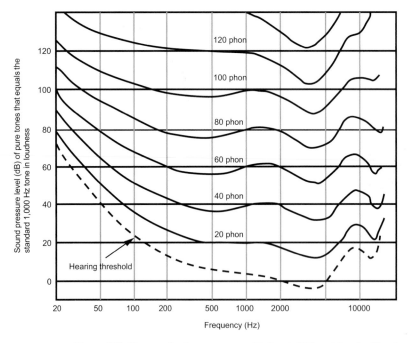

Figure 9.8 Phon scale: frequency sensitivity at different level of loudness *(Reproduced from Robinson, D. W., & Dadson, R. S. (1956). A re-determination of the equal-loudness relations for pure tones. British Journal of Applied Physics, 7(5), 166, with permission from IOP Science.)*

Phons	Sones
100	64
90	32
80	16
70	8
60	4
50	2
40	1

Figure 9.9 Sone scale

1,000 Hz tone that sounds equal in loudness to a given tone (see Figure 9.8). For example, a sound of 40 phons means that it sounds as loud as a 40 dB$_{spl}$, 1 kHz, tone. The numbers on each of the contours are the number of phons corresponding to that contour, and all tones on that contour have equal loudness. Thus, all points on the 40 phon contour are equal in loudness to a 1,000 Hz tone at an intensity level of 40 dB$_{spl}$.

Sone Scale

The phon scale allows us to rank-order the magnitude of loudness of different tones. It tells us, for instance, that a 50 phon tone is louder than a 40 phon tone. But the phon scale does not tell us how much louder a tone is over the other. Another scale, called the sone scale was developed to compare loudness levels between tones. A loudness of one sone has been arbitrarily assigned as equal to the loudness of a 1,000 Hz tone at an intensity level of 40 dB$_{spl}$. As shown in Figure 9.9, the sone value doubles for every increase of 10 phons. That is, 2 sones are equal to 50 phons; 4 sones are equal to 60 phons; 8 sones are equal to 70 phons, etc. Phon is a logarithmic scale whereas sone is a linear scale. Therefore, doubling sone values means doubling perceived loudness.

Frequency and Pitch

The hertz (Hz) scale is a linear scale representing the frequency of the signal. Equal distance on the Hz scale represents equal difference in frequency. For example, the distance between 100 Hz and 105 Hz is the same as that between 500 Hz and 505 Hz. The Hz scale accurately captures our perception of frequency up to 1,000 Hz. The perceived difference between two signals with frequencies of 1,000 Hz or below equals their absolute distance on the scale. That is, a 5 Hz difference between 100 Hz and 105 Hz, 500 and 505 Hz, or 900 Hz and 905 Hz are equally detectable by the human ear.

On the other hand, defined as "that attribute auditory sensation in terms of which sounds may be ordered on a scale extending from high to low" by the American National Standards Institute, **pitch** is an auditory impression of frequency: the higher the frequency, the higher the perceived pitch. A tone of 105 Hz is perceived to have a higher pitch than a tone of 100 Hz. A 200 Hz tone is perceived as having a pitch level that is twice as high as the pitch of the 100 Hz tone. In musical terms, the pitch of the 200 Hz tone is one octave higher than that of the 100 Hz tone. In this case, a difference of 100 Hz results in an octave difference in perceived pitch.

Interestingly, however, to increase the perceived pitch of a 200 Hz tone by an octave requires a difference of 200 Hz rather than 100 Hz. That is, a 400 Hz tone, not a 300 Hz tone is perceived as having a pitch that is one octave higher than that of the 200 Hz tone. Similarly, the pitch of an 800 Hz tone is one octave above that of a 400 Hz tone, a difference of 400 Hz. In other words, in order to double or increase the perceived pitch of a frequency by one octave, the frequency has to double. This relationship between frequency and pitch is better expressed on a logarithmic scale where the perceptual difference between two octaves (e.g., 100 Hz to 200 Hz; and 200 Hz to 400 Hz) is always represented by an equal distance on the scale even though the physical difference (e.g., 100 Hz vs. 200 Hz) is not. In other words, regardless of their place along the scale, equal ratios between two physical values (e.g., 2:1) are represented by equal distances in a logarithmic scale.

Auditory Scales of Pitch

Pitch is a subjective attribute of sounds. Therefore, it cannot be measured by physical means or expressed in physical units (e.g., hertz). For pure tones, its primary objective physical correlate is frequency. However, the intensity and duration of a tone may also affect its perceived pitch.

Mel Scale

The mel, or melodic, scale expresses the relationship between the frequency of sine tones and their perceived pitch based on human subjects' judgments. Using a sine tone of 1,000 Hz as the reference, subjects were asked to listen to sine tones of various frequencies and determine their pitch levels. One mel equals one thousandth of the pitch of the 1,000 Hz tone. Thus, a 500 mel sine tone is a tone whose pitch was determined to be exactly half of that of the 1,000 Hz tone. Similarly, the pitch of a 2,000 mel tone was indicated to be twice as high as that of the 1,000 Hz tone. Figure 9.10 shows the relationship between frequency (Hz) and pitch (mels).

Strictly speaking, the mel scale can only be obtained from actual listeners' impressions, and cannot, therefore, be calculated. There are several mel-scale formulae. The one given below is from Reetz and Jongman (2009).

$$1 \text{ Mel} = 3{,}322 \times (\log_{10}(1{,}000 + f\,[\text{Hz}]) - 3)$$

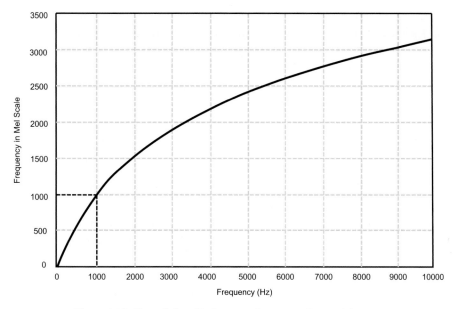

Figure 9.10 The relationship between frequency (Hz) and frequency (mels). Lines indicate arbitrary reference of 1,000 Hz = 1,000 mels

Bark Scale

The bark scale is another auditory scale of pitch perception. Unlike the mel scale, which is derived from subjective impressions of the perception of pure tones, the bark scale is based on human perception of complex tones. It is consistent with the **critical band** theory formulated by Harvey Fletcher in 1940. This theory stipulates that, during pitch perception, frequencies in the input signal are divided into frequency bands with different center frequencies and bandwidths. All frequencies within a band are perceived to have the same pitch. The bandwidth is narrower for low frequencies than for high frequencies, reflecting people's higher sensitivity to a change in pitch in the low-frequency range.

The bark scale is considered a more accurate scale for pitch perception than the mel scale. The relationship between frequencies in Hz and their perceived pitch values in barks can be calculated using the following formula (Reetz & Jongman, 2009):

$$1 \text{ Bark}_{CB} = \frac{26.81 \times f \text{ (Hz)}}{1,960 + f \text{ (Hz}} - 0.53$$

Equivalent Rectangular Bandwidth (ERB) Scale

The ERB scale is derived similarly to the bark scale, but with a more refined process in determining the critical band to realistically reflect perceived frequency values of complex sounds. Hertz values between 100 and 6,500 can be converted into ERB values by the following formula (Reetz & Jongman, 2009):

$$1 \text{ Bark}_{ERB} = 25.72 \times \log_{10} = \frac{312 \text{ f [Hz]} + 43}{14,675 + \text{f [Hz]}}$$

Pitch of Complex Signals

Besides pure tones, we know that sounds with complex waveforms such as musical notes from a piano, a flute, or a clarinet, vowels, or the rumbling of a motorcycle also have relatively distinct pitches. The pitches of these complex periodic sounds depend largely on the frequency of their spectrum's fundamental (lowest) component, namely the first harmonic, even when its acoustic power is weak. For example, the pitch of a complex tone with 100, 200, 300, and 400 Hz components is judged to be that of a 100 Hz tone. When the first harmonic is missing altogether, the pitch of a complex tone can still be detected, and its perceived pitch is that of a tone whose frequency is equal to the common difference of the frequency components. For example, the pitch of a complex tone with 400, 600, and 800 Hz components is that of a 200 Hz tone. This phenomenon has been referred to as periodicity pitch or the problem of the missing pitch (Licklider, 1954), and has been used as an argument against the place theory of pitch perception already discussed above, as it suggests that the main cue for perceived pitch is not a simple frequency place code in the cochlea but the periodicity (repeating pattern of identical waveform) in the signal.

Auditory Temporal Acuity

Research has been conducted to examine how sensitive the human auditory system is to stimulus change in the temporal domain. One line of research tries to determine a threshold for gap duration. Listeners are asked to listen to two identical signals with the gap duration between them gradually increased until they can distinguish between the two signals, or alternatively, until they hear the gap as a discontinuity in the signal. For sine tones, it was found that gap thresholds were approximately constant at 6–8 ms for frequencies from 400 to 2,000 Hz, at 8–10 ms for 200 Hz, and at about 18 ms for 100 Hz.

Another line of research examines whether events with small temporal separations are interpreted as simultaneous or non-simultaneous. One study (Pisoni, 1977) examined listeners' ability to identify and discriminate between a 500 Hz tone and a 1,500 Hz tone that only differed by the onset of the 500 Hz tone relative to the onset of the 1,500 Hz tone. The results obtained led to the conclusion that a minimum of 20 ms difference in onset times is required to identify the temporal order of two different stimuli. In other words, listeners reported hearing two stimuli as successive events when they had onset times greater than 20 ms, but as simultaneous with onset times less than 20 ms.

Complex stimuli such as vowels and consonants may be perceived as short or long, and two-way length contrasts for both vowels and consonants exist among the world's languages (see Chapter 3). The absolute difference between a short and a long vowel, or a short and a long consonant, however, is language dependent. In addition, a short and a long vowel in different positions in a syllable, a word, or a sentence may exhibit variations in their duration. Thus, it appears that the contrastive categorization of short versus long complex signals in languages depends on relative duration rather than absolute duration.

In the next chapter, we will discuss the acoustic properties that the auditory system relies on for vowel and consonant identification as well as the effects of various factors on speech perception and how speech perception develops in infants and evolves among adults.

Chapter Summary

- The auditory system is composed of the outer ear, the middle ear, and the inner ear.
- The ear canal amplifies frequencies between 2 kHz and 5 kHz.
- The middle ear boosts the amplitude of the sound wave from the external ear to the inner ear by 27 dB.
- Different portions of the basilar membrane respond effectively to different frequencies.
- The subjective auditory sensation of sound intensity is loudness.
- The subjective auditory sensation of sound frequency is pitch.
- The dB, phon, and sone are auditory scales of loudness.
- Mel and bark are auditory scales of pitch.
- Languages rely on relative, rather than absolute, duration to categorize long versus short vowels and consonants.

Review Exercises

Exercise 9.1: Discuss how sound transmission from the external ear to the middle ear would be affected if the eardrum were located on the surface of the head instead of inside the skull.

Exercise 9.2: What are the functions of the middle ear?

Exercise 9.3: Describe how transferring sound from the external ear to the inner would be less efficient without the middle ear.

Exercise 9.4: How are the ossicles in the middle ear important to the transmission of sound from the external ear to the inner ear?

Exercise 9.5: Describe how the basilar membrane responds to different input frequencies.

Exercise 9.6: How do mel and bark scales differ from the linear hertz scale?

Exercise 9.7: How does the phon scale differ from the sone scale?

Exercise 9.8: From Figure 9.8, what is the minimum dB$_{spl}$ value for a 50 Hz sound that can be heard by humans?

    a. 20 dB$_{spl}$

    b. 40 dB$_{spl}$

    c. 70 dB$_{spl}$

Exercise 9.9: Which sounds louder?

    a. A 100 Hz tone at 35 dB$_{spl}$

    b. A 1,000 Hz tone at 40 dB$_{spl}$

Exercise 9.10: Which two sounds are equal in loudness?

    a. A 200 Hz tone at 60 dB$_{spl}$ and a 1,000 Hz tone at 80 dB$_{spl}$

    b. A 20 Hz tone at 100 dB$_{spl}$ and a 200 Hz tone at 60 dB$_{spl}$

Exercise 9.11: Sound A is a 1,000 Hz tone; sound B is a 2,000 Hz tone; sound C is 10 kHz (10,000 Hz) tone, and sound D is a 11 kHz tone. If all tones are played at 60 dB$_{spl}$, a greater increase in pitch will be perceived between . . .

    a. Sound A and Sound B

    b. Sound C and Sound D

    c. The pitch increase from Sound A to Sound B is the same as the pitch increase from Sound C to Sound D.

Exercise 9.12: Sound A is a 2,000 Hz tone played with 200,000 μPa (micro pascals); sound B is a 2,000 Hz tone played at 300,000 μPa; sound C is a 2,000 Hz tone played at 1,000,000 μPa, and sound D is a 2,000 Hz tone played at 1,100,000 μPa. A greater increase in loudness will be perceived between . . .

    a. Sound A and Sound B

    b. Sound C and Sound D

    c. The loudness increase from Sound A to Sound B is perceived to be about the same as the loudness increase from Sound C to Sound D.

References and Further Reading

Bell, D. R., & Rhoades, R. A. (2012). Sensory physiology. In R. A. Rhoades & D. R. Bell (eds.), *Medical Physiology: Principles for Clinical Medicine*. Philadelphia, PA: Lippincott Williams & Wilkins.

Green, D. M. (1971). Temporal auditory acuity. *Psychological Review*, 78(6), 540.

Licklider, J. C. R. (1954). "Periodicity" pitch and "place" pitch. *The Journal of the Acoustical Society of America*, 26(5), 945–945.

Moore, B. C. (2012). *An Introduction to the Psychology of Hearing*. Leiden: Brill.

Patterson, R. D. (1976). Auditory filter shapes derived with noise stimuli. *The Journal of the Acoustical Society of America*, 59(3), 640–654.

Pisoni, D. B. (1977). Identification and discrimination of the relative onset time of two component tones: Implications for voicing perception in stops. *The Journal of the Acoustical Society of America*, 61(5), 1352–1361.

Reetz, H., & Jongman, A. (2009). *Phonetics: Transcription, Production, Acoustics and Perception*. Oxford: Wiley-Blackwell.

Robinson, D. W., & Dadson, R. S. (1956). A re-determination of the equal-loudness relations for pure tones. *British Journal of Applied Physics*, 7(5), 166.

10

Speech Perception

Learning Objectives

By the end of this chapter, you will be able to:

- Identify the acoustic properties used in vowel perception
- Distinguish between extrinsic and intrinsic vowel normalization processes
- Recognize the acoustic properties used in consonant perception
- Describe and identify sources of variation in acoustic signals
- Characterize the effects of previously formed categories on speech perception: categorical perception
- Describe the roles of context, visual information, and background knowledge on speech perception
- Differentiate core tenets of different speech perception theories, such as:
  - Motor theory
  - Direct realism
  - General Auditory Approach
- Describe how speech perception develops in infants and evolves in adults
- Express how suprasegmental features, including stress, lexical tones, and intonation, are perceived

Introduction

Speech perception refers to the process whereby the speaker's intended message is recovered from the acoustic information analyzed by the listener's auditory system. The fact that most of us seem to be able to perceive speech with ease under most circumstances disguises the complexity of the process involved in speech perception. To appreciate this complexity, consider your experience with computer speech recognition systems, widely used to provide such services as ticket reservations, banking information, automated bill payment, technical support. It is more than likely that you have been frustrated with the systems' inability to recognize what you said if you speak too fast, have a foreign accent or a regional dialect, or if there is background noise. Despite advances in speech recognition technology in recent years, computers are no match for humans in their ability to recognize and process speech effectively. Unlike computers, humans seem to be able to adapt to the poverty of the speech signal (e.g., slurred speech, dialect and foreign accented) under various adverse listening conditions.

In this chapter, we will first discuss the acoustic parameters used by listeners to perceive vowels and consonants. Other issues related to speech perception, including its basic units, the variable relationship between a perceptual unit and the acoustic signal, categorical perception, and the roles of context, visual, and background knowledge, are discussed next, followed by speech perception theories. We conclude the chapter with speech perception development in infants and the perception of non-native languages.

Vowel Perception

Vowel perception is generally more accurate than consonant perception because vowels are generally more salient acoustically than consonants. They are usually voiced, relatively louder because they are produced with a more open vocal tract configuration, and are usually longer. The main acoustic cue used to differentiate vowels is the location of the **formant frequencies**. Front vowels are characterized by a relatively low F1 and a higher F2 than back vowels. The difference between F2 and F1 (F2-F1) is relatively greater for front than for back vowels.

However, vowel formant values may be affected by several factors, including phonetic context, speaking rate, and the size of the speaker's vocal tract (see Source of Acoustic Variation section below). Figure 10.1 shows variation in vowel formant values for American English vowels produced in /hVd/ syllables by forty-five adult male speakers.

The average durations, F0, and F1–F4 values for twelve American English vowels spoken by forty-five men, forty-eight women, and forty-six children are shown in Table 10.1. As expected, formant frequency values are lower for men than for women and children due to vocal tract length differences. F0 values are also lower for men than women and children due to differences in vocal fold size. Interestingly, however, vowel durations are also shorter for men than for women and children. There is evidence that vowel perception accuracy increases when **duration and F0** cues are included (Hillenbrande et al., 1995). A number of studies have also shown that two simultaneously presented synthesized vowels are better identified when their F0 are different (Assmann & Summerfield, 1990; Chalikia & Bregman, 1989; Zwicker, 1984).

Since formant frequency values depend mainly on vocal tract length, the same vowel produced by different speakers will have different formant values. However, despite this variation, listeners report hearing the same vowel. This occurs

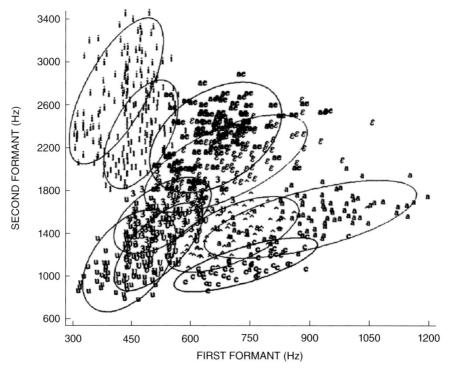

Figure 10.1 Vowel formant values for American English vowels in /hVd/ syllables
(Reproduced from Hillenbrand, J., Getty, L. A., Clark, M. J., & Wheeler, K.
(1995). Acoustic characteristics of American English vowels. The Journal of the
Acoustical Society of America, *97(5), 3099–3111, with permission from the*
Acoustical Society of America.)

because listeners factor out systematic acoustic differences (due to differences in
vocal tract length in this case) to arrive at a stable vowel percept. The process of
tuning out acoustic differences to reduce the overlap among vowels is called
normalization. Besides vocal tract normalization, listeners also normalize for
speaking rate, phonetic context, and dialects.

Vowel Normalization

Despite a large variation in the acoustic patterns (e.g., vowel formants), listeners
rarely have difficulty assigning them to the same phoneme. For example, due to
differences in vocal tract length, the formant frequency values of a vowel /i/
produced by an adult and a child vary considerably. However, they are heard as
the same vowel, suggesting that variation in vocal tract size is compensated for
by the listener, a process known as vocal tract normalization. Since variation in
vocal tract length mostly affects the acoustic properties of vowels, many normalization theories have been proposed to account for vowel perception, particularly
the process whereby listeners estimate the speaker's vowel space.

Table 10.1 *Average durations (in ms), F0 and F1-F4 (in Hz) values for twelve American English vowels produced by 45 males, 48 females, and 46 children.*

		/i/	/ɪ/	/e/	/ɛ/	/æ/	/ɑ/	/ɔ/	/o/	/ʊ/	/u/	/ʌ/	/ɝ/
Dur	M	243	192	267	189	278	267	283	265	192	237	188	263
	W	306	237	320	254	332	323	353	326	249	303	226	321
	C	297	248	235	235	322	311	319	310	247	278	234	307
F0	M	138	135	129	127	123	123	121	129	133	143	133	130
	W	227	224	219	214	215	215	210	217	230	235	218	217
	C	246	241	237	230	228	229	225	236	243	249	236	237
F1	M	342	427	476	580	588	768	652	497	469	378	623	474
	W	437	483	536	731	669	936	781	217	519	459	753	523
	C	452	511	564	749	717	1002	803	236	568	494	749	586
F2	M	2322	2034	2089	1799	1952	1333	997	910	1122	997	1200	1379
	W	2761	2365	2530	2058	2349	1551	1136	1035	1225	1105	1426	1588
	C	3081	2552	2656	2267	2501	1688	1210	1137	1490	1345	1546	1719
F3	M	3000	2984	2691	2605	2601	2522	2538	2459	2434	2343	2550	1710
	W	3372	3053	3047	2979	2979	2815	2824	2828	2827	2735	2933	1929
	C	3702	3403	3323	3310	3289	2950	2982	2987	3072	2988	3145	2143
F4	M	3657	3618	3649	3677	3624	3687	3486	3384	3400	3357	3557	3334
	W	4352	4334	4319	4294	4290	4299	3923	3927	4052	4115	4092	3914
	C	4572	4575	4422	4671	4409	4307	3919	4167	4328	4276	4320	3788

(Reproduced from Hillenbrand, J., Getty, L.A., Clark, M.J., & Wheeler, K. (1995). Acoustic characteristics of American English vowels. *The Journal of the Acoustical Society of America*, 97(5), 3099–3111), with permission from the Acoustical Society of America).

Extrinsic Normalization

Two main approaches to vowel normalization are discussed in the literature. They differ mainly in the purported source of information used by the listener in the normalization process. In the first approach, normalization is made possible by information from the surrounding context. To identify a vowel, listeners place it in the speaker's vowel space calibrated from formant values of surrounding vowels. This approach is known as the **extrinsic normalization** approach. The findings from a classic study by Ladefoged and Broadbent (1957) that a listener's percept of the vowel in a /bVt/ syllable varied as a function of the F1 and F2 values of the vowels in the preceding carrier phrase are consistent with the extrinsic normalization approach. Specifically, the study found that what was perceived as /bɪt/ *bit* when presented in isolation was heard as /bɛt/ *bet* when the F1 values of the precursor vowels were relatively low.

The finding that vowel identification is more accurate under single-voice in comparison to multi-voice listening conditions also supports the extrinsic normalization approach. If vowel identification does not depend on previously heard vowels (produced by other speakers), then the number of voices in a listening session should not matter.

The idea that perception of a vowel is dependent on the vowels preceding it raises the question of how many preceding vowels and which ones are needed for it to be successful. One view suggests that only one vowel is needed, and the most likely candidate is the vowel /i/ since it is located at the extreme point in vowel space with unique and extreme formant patterns, and is less affected by small changes in tongue position. As such, an /i/ produced by any speaker is likely to be accurately identified by a listener, allowing for an estimation of the speaker's vocal tract length, and thus the calibration of his or her vowel space.

Another view suggests that at least two preceding vowels are needed for the calibration. Besides /i/, the likely candidates are two other extreme vowels, namely /a/ and /u/. However, the finding that vowel perception remains highly accurate under mixed-voice conditions weakens the notion of extrinsic normalization.

Intrinsic Normalization

Unlike extrinsic normalization, the **intrinsic normalization** theory posits that information needed for vowel identification resides in the vowel itself, and that vowel categories are better separated if their acoustic properties are appropriately transformed. This approach seeks to reduce the amount of overlap between vowel categories by representing their acoustic properties on an auditory scale (e.g., bark, ERB) rather than on linear scale, to approximate the transformation performed by the human auditory system. Besides the traditional parameters of F1 and F2, other acoustic parameters, including F0 and F3, have also been used to calculate a normalized vowel space.

In summary, vowel normalization is a process by which listeners factor out acoustic variation across speakers in vowel production. Most theories of normalization involve the estimation of the speaker's vowel space. The extrinsic normalization approach posits that listeners rely on information provided by preceding vowels for calibration, whereas the intrinsic normalization approach suggests that the information, when appropriately evaluated, necessarily resides within the vowels themselves. There's evidence for and against both views, and it is likely that both methods of normalization facilitate accurate vowel perception.

Consonant Perception

As already mentioned, consonant perception is generally less accurate than vowel perception. Besides being relatively shorter than vowels, the acoustic attributes of consonants are more complex and more variable due to the effects of several factors, including phonetic context, speaking rate, and vocal tract size. Let's take a look at the acoustic cues to the perception of plosives first.

Plosives

Plosive consonants are produced with a momentary complete blockage of airflow inside the vocal tract before it is released. Their acoustic attributes include articulatory closure, release burst, and formant transition into and out of the vowel. Most research on plosive stop perception focuses on cues to its place of articulation.

Place of Articulation

Research shows that **formant transition patterns** and **release burst frequencies** are important perceptual cues to plosive place of articulation. Figure 10.2 shows wide-band spectrograms for [bæb], [dæd], and [gæg], with closure duration of the final consonants marked and formant frequencies highlighted. Here we see a rising F2 transition for [b] and [d], but a falling transition for [g] at vowel onset. At vowel offset, the F2 transition falls for /b/, /d/, and rises for [g].

However, F2 transition patterns vary as a function of the following and preceding vowels. Nonetheless, research shows that listeners mostly perceive a bilabial plosive when F2 of the following vowel rises, but either an alveolar or a velar when F2 falls, as shown in Figure 10.3.

The frequency of the **plosive release burst** is another cue reported for plosive place of articulation. This cue has been shown to be more robust for voiceless plosives than for voiced ones. Figure 10.4 shows waveforms and wide-band spectrograms for syllables /pɑ/, /tɑ/, and /kɑ/. The width of the line drawings at syllable onsets suggest that the spectral energy of the release burst is in a low-frequency region for /p/, high-frequency for /t/, and mid-frequency for /k/.

A burst perception experiment shows, however, that burst frequency is not a reliable cue to plosive place of articulation. As shown in Figure 10.5, low-frequency bursts are perceived mostly as /p/, and high-frequency bursts are

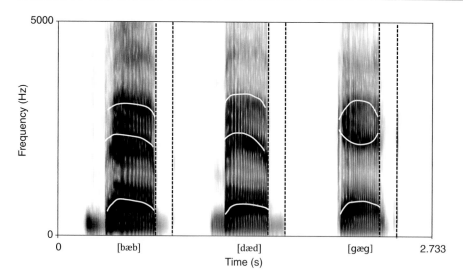

Figure 10.2 Wide-band spectrograms with formant traces of [bæb], [dæd], and [gæg] produced by a male speaker

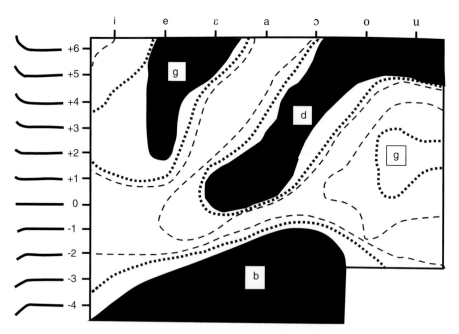

Figure 10.3 Regions where [b], [d], and [g] are heard as a function of F2 transition patterns

(Reproduced from Liberman, A. M., Delattre, P. C., Cooper, F. S., & Gerstman, L. J. (1954). The role of consonant-vowel transitions in the perception of the stop and nasal consonants. Psychological Monographs: General and Applied, 68(8), 1–13, with permission from the American Psychology Association.)

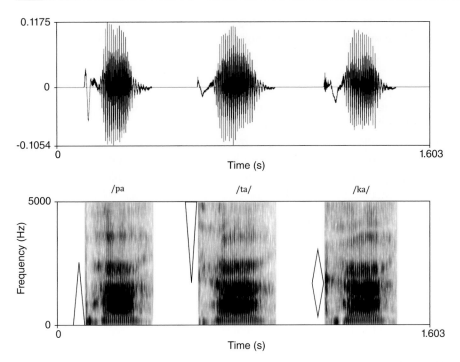

Figure 10.4 Waveforms (top) and wide-band spectrograms (bottom) for English syllables /pa/, /ta/, and /ka/. The location and width of the line drawings at syllable onset indicate the frequency region and amount of spectral energy of the release burst

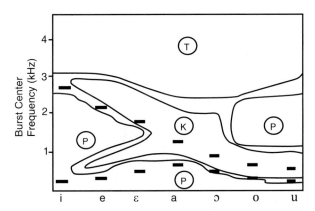

Figure 10.5 Identification of synthetic bursts of different center frequencies (in Hz) followed by two formant frequencies appropriate for /i, e, ɛ, a, ɔ, o, u/. (Adapted from Liberman, A. M., Delattre, P., & Cooper, F. S. (1952). The role of selected stimulus-variables in the perception of the unvoiced stop consonants. The American Journal of Psychology, 65(4), 497–516. with permission from University of Illinois Press.)

consistently heard as /t/. However, mid-frequency bursts were perceived as /k/ when followed by /ɛ, a, ɔ/, but as /p/ when followed by /i, e, o, u/.

Voicing

Voiced and voiceless plosives can be cued by a number of acoustic parameters. As mentioned above, at syllable onset, release bursts for voiceless plosives are stronger than for voiced plosives. F1 onset frequency and F0 are also higher for voiceless than for voiced plosives. However, the most well-known cue to plosive voicing is voice onset time (VOT). In English, a long-lag VOT is perceived as voiceless while a short-lag (or a lead) VOT is associated with voiced plosives (Figure 10.6).

On the other hand, a long-lag VOT is not present in Dutch. Instead, voiced and voiceless plosives are cued by a lead VOT and a short-lag VOT, respectively. Finally, because of the need to differentiate three rather than two categories of plosives, Thai relies on all three types of VOT: lead VOT for voiced, short-lag VOT for voiceless unaspirated, and long-lag VOT for voiceless aspirated plosives (Figure 10.7).

In syllable- or word-final position, the presence or absence of a voice-bar during oral closure could also help distinguish voiced from voiceless plosives. However, the most salient cue to voicing of final plosives is the duration of the vowel preceding the oral closure. Vowels preceding voiced plosives are longer than the same vowels preceding voiceless plosives. On the other hand, the oral closure duration for a final voiced plosive is shorter than that of a final voiceless plosive (Figure 10.8). In addition, a voice-bar is evident during oral closure of final voiced /b/ but not of final voiceless /p/.

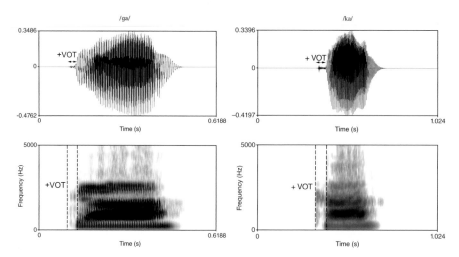

Figure 10.6 Waveforms (top) and wide-band spectrograms (bottom) illustrating short- and long-lag VOT for voiced /ga/ and voiceless /ka/ in English

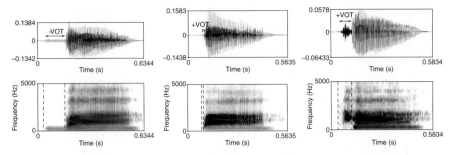

Figure 10.7 Waveforms (top) and wide-band spectrograms (bottom) showing lead [baː], short-lag [paː], and long-lag VOT [pʰaː] for Thai plosives

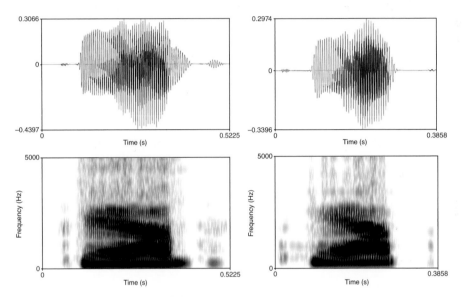

Figure 10.8 Waveforms (top) and wide-band (bottom) spectrograms for English /kæb/-[kʰæb] cab (left), and /kæp/-[kʰæp] cap (right) showing a longer vowel duration but a shorter closure duration for [b] in cab than for [p] in cap

In sum, release bursts and formant transitions are important cues to plosives' place of articulation. Voicing among plosives in syllable-onset position is cued by VOT, burst amplitude, F1, and F0. Vowel duration, closure duration, and the presence or absence of voicing during closure cue plosive voicing in syllable-final position. However, the acoustic properties that cue both place and voicing among plosives are sensitive to phonetic context. This has prompted some researchers to search for global rather than local cues, for example energy distribution in low-frequency regions relative to high-frequency regions, F2 values at vowel onset relative to vowel mid-point, and so on.

Nasals

Nasal murmur contains several acoustic parameters that cue its manner of articulation. This includes weak (low amplitude) formants with wider bandwidths, the presence of a nasal formant (low-frequency formant at around 300 Hz), and anti-formants. Nasal murmur, nasal formant, and anti-formants for the bilabial nasal [m] in a /ma/ syllable are shown in Figure 10.9. In English, nasalization during the last portion of a preceding vowel also cues the upcoming nasal.

The perceptual cues to nasal place of articulation are the anti-formants during nasal murmur and the formant transitions into and out of the vowel. Research shows that although comparable in cuing place of articulation when presented in isolation, the combination of both cues is more effective than each individual cue alone.

Liquids

Similar to what the oral cavity does with nasal consonants, a pocket of air on top of the tongue during the production of /l/ produces anti-formants, causing the higher formants to weaken. In addition, due to a relatively narrower outlet cavity (sides of the tongue), /l/ and other lateral sounds are weaker than vowels. However, formant spacing is greater in laterals than in nasals because the main resonant cavity in laterals is shorter than that in nasals. Figure 10.10 shows waveforms and spectrograms, and spectra of /la/ and /ma/.

Lateral /l/ is different from /ɹ/ in several ways, but the most obvious is the location of the third formant. The F3 of /ɹ/ is substantially lower than that of /l/.

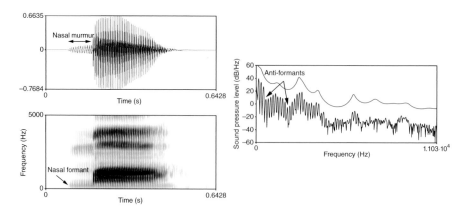

Figure 10.9 Waveform (top left) and wide-band spectrogram (bottom left) of the syllable /ma/, and LPC and FFT spectra of the nasal /m/ murmur (right)

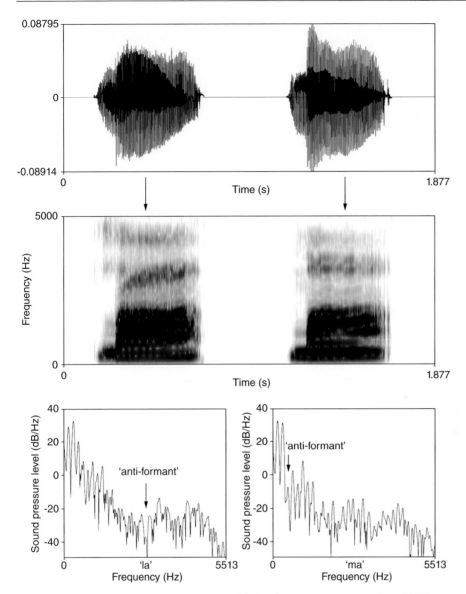

Figure 10.10 Waveforms (top), wide-band spectrograms (center), and FFT spectra (bottom) of /la/ (left) and /ma/ (right). Anti-formants are marked with arrows

In addition, the onset frequency of F2 is lower for /ɹ/ than for /l/, but formant transition duration of F1 is longer for /ɹ/ than for /l/. English /l–ɹ/ distinction is difficult for native speakers of Japanese because they both share similarity with the only liquid phoneme in Japanese, namely the flap /ɾ/. Figure 10.11 shows waveforms and spectrograms of /la/ and /ɹa/.

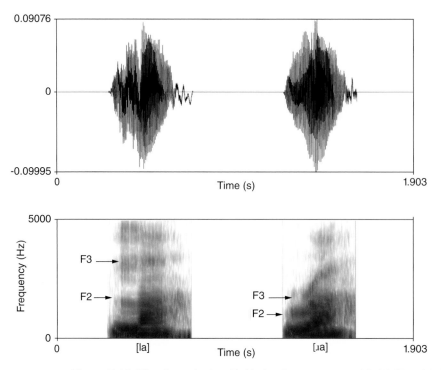

Figure 10.11 Waveforms (top) and wide-band spectrograms of /la/ (left) and /ɹa/ (right) showing F2 and particularly F3 are lower for /ɹ/ than for /l/

Glides

The acoustic properties of the glides /w/ and /j/ are similar to those of vowels since, like vowels, their production involves an approximation between the tongue and the roof of the mouth. The /w–j/ distinction is cued mainly by the onset frequency of the F2 transition. It is lower for /w/ because of lip rounding and higher for /j/ because of the constriction at the palate, thus creating a shorter front cavity.

The distinction between /w/ and /b/ has also been examined, and the duration of the F2 transition has been found to be the primary cue. It is shorter for /b/ and longer for /w/.

Fricatives

Place of Articulation

The primary acoustic attribute that differentiates *place of articulation* among fricatives is spectral peak location. In voiceless fricative production, the frication noise generated in front of the constriction is its sound source and the filtering action of the front cavity determines the location of its spectral peak: the shorter the front cavity, the higher the peak. Research shows that listeners can reliably use spectral peak location to distinguish /s, ʃ/ from /f, θ/ and /s/ from /ʃ/, but not /f/ from /θ/. Other cues for fricative place of articulation reported in the literature are frication noise amplitude relative to vowel onset amplitude, noise amplitude, noise duration, and formant transition.

Voicing
Voicing distinctions among fricatives are cued mainly by the presence or absence of vocal fold vibration during frication. Frication duration also aids the perception of fricative voicing since voiceless fricatives are usually longer than voiced fricatives.

Fricatives vs. Plosives vs. Affricates
To distinguish fricatives from plosives and affricates, amplitude rise-time has been shown to be a reliable cue. Plosives have the shortest rise-time followed by affricates and fricatives.

Variable Relationship between Perceptual Units and Acoustic Signal

Perceiving speech involves segmenting a continuous acoustic signal into discrete perceptual units. However, the size of these units is still under debate. Evidence in support of speech perception units of various sizes, from phonetic features, phonemes, and syllables to words, has been reported in the literature. Even though most speech perception research has been conducted using the phoneme as the basic perception unit, it is likely that these units are all involved at various levels of speech perception.

Linguistic units are processed in a successive and linear fashion during speech perception. For instance, we hear a /p/ followed by an /i/ and then a /k/ in *peak*. However, linearity is rarely observed in the acoustic signal. In other words, the acoustic speech signal cannot be easily segmented to match individual units of speech perception (e.g., phonemes). This is because phonemes (or other perception units) are converted into continuous and overlapping movements of the articulators during speech production, generating non-sequential acoustic events that are only later recovered as linearly ordered strings of perceptual units by the listener. This is known as the **linearity** or **segmentation problem**. As shown in Figure 10.12, distinct, discernible boundaries between phonemes are difficult to locate in the utterance *I owe you a yoyo*.

Besides the lack of linearity in the speech signal, another well-known challenge to theories of speech perception is the lack of a one-to-one mapping between the acoustic properties and the perceptual categories of speech sounds or phonemes. This is known as the **lack of acoustic invariance** problem. That is, the same phoneme can have different acoustic manifestations in different

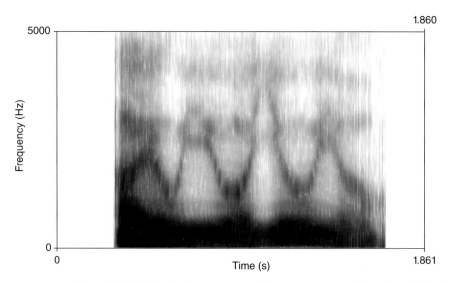

Figure 10.12 Wide-band spectrogram of *I owe you a yoyo* illustrating a lack of clear boundaries between phonemes

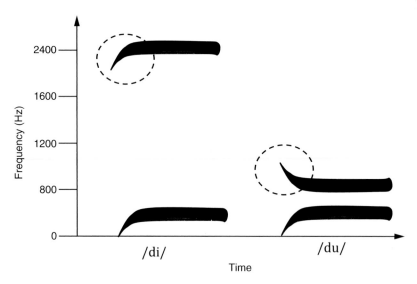

Figure 10.13 Stylized first and second formant frequencies (F1 and F2) of /di/ (left) and /du/ (right)

contexts. As shown in Figure 10.13, for example, the acoustic patterns (F2 formant transition) perceived as the phoneme /d/ vary depending on the following vowel.

Specifically, F2 transition falls in /di/ but rises in /du/. Linearity and the lack of acoustic invariance are two fundamental problems in speech perception, and different solutions have been proposed by various theories (see Speech Perception Theories later in the chapter).

Source of Acoustic Variation

Variation in the acoustic signal stems from several factors, including **speaker**, **speaking rate**, and **phonetic context**. As seen in Figure 10.2, due to differences in vocal tract length, the formants of the vowels produced by an adult male differ from those of an adult female and a child speaker.

The same utterance can be spoken at a slower or a faster tempo, causing variation in both vowel and consonant duration. Segments are shortened when the speaking rate increases and lengthened when the speaking rate decreases. Generally, longer segments are affected to a greater extent by the speaking rate. Therefore, vowel duration varies more than consonant duration when speaking rate changes.

Besides segmental duration, F0 range also varies with speaking rate. In general, a decrease in a speaker's F0 range is observed at a faster speaking rate, whereas a slower speaking rate expands the F0 range.

Finally, the acoustic properties of a vowel or a consonant are also affected by the phonetic context in which it occurs. Due to coarticulation, both the preceding and following segments exert influence on the production of a target vowel or consonant (e.g., Figure 10.2 above).

Categorical Perception

Discovered in 1957 (Liberman et al., 1957), categorical perception (CP) is a phenomenon by which listeners' perception is shown to be influenced by the categories they have previously formed. It is revealed when successive and equally spaced stimuli from a physical continuum are identified by listeners not as a continuum but as members of discrete categories. More importantly, listeners are only able to discriminate two stimuli drawn from separate categories, but not those from the same category. In other words, they are more sensitive to between – rather than within – category differences.

In order to show that perception of a continuum is categorical, both identification and discrimination data are necessary. The identification task shows how the stimuli are labeled into different categories, and the discrimination task reveals how well members of the same or different categories are discriminated. Idealized identification and discrimination functions for categorical perception of an equally spaced, eight-member VOT /ba–pa/ continuum are shown in Figure 10.14. This shows that a bilabial plosive produced with a VOT of 30 ms or less is categorized as a voiced /b/, whereas one with a VOT value greater than 30 ms is heard as a voiceless /p/. More importantly, tokens

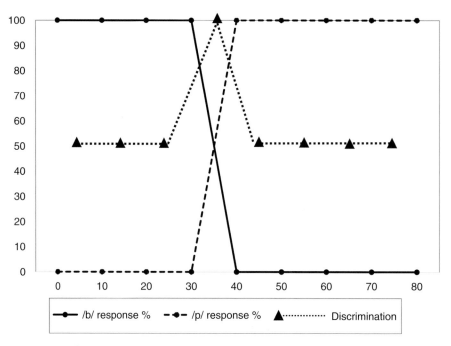

Figure 10.14 Idealized identification and discrimination functions

heard as /b/ or /p/ are not well discriminated, whereas the two that straddle the category are maximally distinct despite having the same acoustic distance (10 ms).

CP has been shown for other acoustic continua, including F2 onset frequency, fricative noise duration, and vowel duration preceding a final fricative or stop consonant.

The strongest version of CP claims that listeners' categorical identification completely predicts their discrimination. However, empirical results rarely support the strong relationship between identification and discrimination. With additional reaction time and goodness ratings measures, listeners can perceive differences between members of the same category. Stimuli near category boundaries are identified more slowly and receive lower goodness ratings. In addition, a stronger relationship between identification and discrimination is found in consonant perception than in vowel perception. That is, in contrast to consonant perception, particularly plosive stops, vowel perception is continuous rather than categorical. Interestingly, however, vowel perception becomes categorical when the sound's duration is shortened to be comparable to that of a plosive. Vowel perception also becomes more categorical with a longer stimulus interval. This suggests that a decay in auditory memory of the stimuli encourages listeners to rely more on phonemic labeling to discriminate between stimuli, thus providing a closer relationship between identification and discrimination.

The CP Debate

The discovery of CP generated quite a debate. The first issue raised is whether CP is innate or learned. The finding that some regions of acoustic continua are more discriminable than others, and that infants as young as four months old show increased sensitivity to the same acoustic regions as adults are consistent with the innate hypothesis. Specifically, using a /ba–pa/ continuum with VOT values increasing from 0 to 80 ms in 20-ms steps, Eimas and colleagues (1971) show that four-month-old American English-speaking infants are able to differentiate between two stimuli, a 20 ms VOT and a 40 ms VOT, that for adults belong to two distinct categories, but they fail to distinguish between two stimuli, a 0 ms VOT and a 20 ms VOT; or a 60 ms VOT and an 80 ms VOT that belong to the same adult categories. Even though we cannot conclude from discrimination results alone that infant perception of the VOT continuum is categorical, the data suggest that categorical perception shown among adults is not due to linguistic experience. Nonetheless, there's evidence that the CP effect may be produced by extensive training.

The finding that categorical boundaries may be present at birth without prior linguistic exposure leads to the second issue in the debate regarding the brain mechanism underlying the processing of speech. Two opposing accounts have been proposed. According to the first account, special neural mechanisms evolved in the human brain specially to process speech. Unlike perception of other auditory stimuli, speech perception is special as it engages speech-specific neural mechanisms. Such dedicated mechanisms make possible, for example, the detection of acoustic features in the auditory stream that are relevant for identification of phonetic segments. The fact that categorical perception is found for speech or speech-like stimuli is taken as evidence in support of the special mechanism view.

On the other hand, the general mechanism account contends that speech perception relies on general auditory and cognitive mechanisms. Research findings that animals such as chinchillas with similar auditory systems to humans show similar categorical boundaries for VOT continua, and that adult listeners show categorical perception for non-speech continua are consistent with the general, non-speech-specific mechanisms (Kuhl & Miller, 1978; Miller et al., 1976).

In sum, CP illustrates that speech sounds in a continuum that varies in equal steps along some physical dimension are assigned to discrete categories. Discrimination between members of the same category is poor whereas that between different categories is enhanced. The presence of CP in infants and its prevalence in speech or speech-like stimuli lead to the hypothesis that CP may be innate, and that speech perception involves speech-specific brain mechanisms. However, CP patterns found in animal perception and perception of non-speech stimuli suggest that general auditory mechanisms are used to process both speech and other auditory stimuli in the environment. The debate will likely continue to fuel speech perception research for decades to come. However, what clearly emerged from research on both sides of the debate is that we are sensitive to the acoustic and auditory properties of speech and are able to process them with ease. Perhaps our sensitivity to acoustic differences that straddle phonemic categories is increased due to a combination of the innate properties of our auditory system and the acoustic properties of speech signals.

Speech Perception Theories

It should be evident from our previous discussion on perceptual cues to both vowels and consonants that a single phoneme may have different acoustic correlates depending on speaker, speaking rate, and phonetic context. As seen earlier, the acoustic correlates of the phoneme /d/ differ in /du/ and /di/. Conversely, two different phonemes may also have similar acoustic correlates due to the context. For instance, the acoustic correlates of the phoneme /p/ in /pi/ are similar to those of /k/ in /ka/ (Figure 10.6). A lack of invariant acoustic correlates to a phoneme (also see Figure 10.14) has prompted researchers to question the nature and the source of information used by listeners to perceive speech.

Two approaches have been proposed to deal with the issue. They differ in what they take to be the objects of speech perception. The first approach, represented by two prominent theories of speech perception, namely the motor theory and direct realism, take articulatory gestures to be the objects of speech perception. The second approach, the general auditory approach, believes that the objects of speech perceptions are auditory or acoustic events from the speech signal.

The Motor Theory

Failing to find acoustic invariants for a phoneme in their experiments, Liberman and colleagues at the Haskins Laboratory came to the conclusion that the articulatory gestures (coordinated movements of vocal organs) used to produce the phoneme are what listeners use to perceive speech. Unlike acoustic structures, gestures remain relatively stable from context to context. In the case of the /d/ phoneme in /du/ and /di/, the tongue touches the alveolar ridge in both syllables. However, while articulating gestures associated with the /d/, speakers anticipate and begin to articulate gestures for the following vowels, causing the overall acoustic pattern corresponding to the gestures for /d/ to change. To perceive the phoneme /d/, listeners must recover information about its articulatory gestures from the acoustic signal. According to the motor theory, the invariant cues to a phoneme are the articulatory gestures that produce them. This claim finds support in Liberman's early research.

However, there is evidence that, like acoustic signals, articulatory gestures are also context dependent. The same speech sound can be articulated with different gestures depending on its phonetic environment. The motor theory has since been revised. In its latest version, the revised motor theory, the neuromotor commands to the articulators (e.g., place the tongue at the alveolar ridge), also known as the intended gestures, are the objects of speech perception rather than the actual gestures. Through the acoustic medium, listeners do not perceive the actual movements of the articulators, but rather the neuromotor commands used by the articulators to actualize those movements. According to the revised motor theory, these neuromotor commands are invariant. That is, all /d/s are perceived as /d/ because their intended neuromotor commands are the same. The theory, however, does not offer an explanation of how listeners recover intended gestures or the neuromotor commands from the acoustic signals and how such skill is developed in children. Any mechanism proposed has to include the knowledge of the neuromotor commands, their effects on the context-dependent movements of the articulators, and their subsequent acoustic consequences. Nonetheless, the hypothesis that, unlike other auditory perception, the objects of speech perception are (intended) gestures or neuromotor commands is consistent with the claim that speech perception is special and requires speech-specific processes. It also allows the proponents of the motor theory to propose a close link between perception and production.

Early evidence suggesting that articulatory movements affect speech perception came from a speech perception phenomenon commonly known as the McGurk effect, named after its discoverer. The effect illustrates that audio and visual information are integrated during speech perception. For example, listeners report hearing /da/ or /ða/ when presented with a visual /ga/ syllable dubbed with an audio /ba/ syllable (see Role of Visual Information in Speech Perception below for more on this).

More recently, the discovery of a group of neurons in monkeys that fire both when the monkeys perform an action themselves and when they only hear the sound of the action, known as the mirror neurons, stimulated research into the link between speech perception and production. From this body of research, it is clear that neurons in areas of the brain associated with speech production are activated during speech perception. It has also been shown that activation of the speech motor system facilitates speech perception under adverse listening conditions, and that deactivation of neural networks controlling movements of speech production organs (e.g., lips) may degrade speech perception.

In Focus: Mirror Neurons and the Motor Theory

Mirror neurons are a class of visuomotor neurons that fire both when the monkey performs an action and when it observes another monkey or human doing the same action (Di Pellegrino et al., 1992; Gallese et al., 1996; Rizzolatti et al., 1996). Despite a lack of direct evidence, a mirror-neuron system is hypothesized to exist in humans (Rizzolatti & Craighero, 2004). The discovery of mirror neurons revived the motor theory of speech perception since the mirror neurons seem to "accomplish the same kind of one-to-one mapping between perception and action that MT theorizes to be the basis of human speech communication" (Lotto et al., 2009: 1). However, Lotto et al. argued that the "seeming correspondence is superficial" and that "mirror neurons are actually inconsistent with the core tenet of the motor theory," and their role in speech perception remains unclear.

Direct Realism

The direct realists posit that the objects of speech perception are actual rather than intended articulatory gestures. They also believe that the articulatory gestures are recovered directly from the rich structures of speech signals, without the assistance of special processing mechanisms. Just as our eyes directly perceive a visual object instead of the physical properties of reflected light, we directly perceive articulatory gestures through the physical properties (e.g., frequency, amplitude, duration) of the acoustic medium. This implies that each vocal gesture has a unique acoustic signature. There is evidence, however, that this is not the case. A single acoustic signal can be produced by multiple vocal tract gestures.

General Auditory Approach

Unlike the motor theory and direct realism approaches, the general auditory approach hypothesizes that the objects of speech perception are auditory or acoustic events present in the speech signals. According to this approach, speech perception relies on the same auditory and cognitive mechanisms that have evolved to perceive other sounds in the environment. To deal with acoustic variability in signals, listeners make use of multiple acoustic cues associated with phonemes. It is assumed that listeners' auditory processing systems become sensitive to statistical regularities in the distributions of acoustic properties as they co-vary with phonemic distinctions in different contexts, e.g., the different second formant onset frequency values and directions for /d/ in different vowel contexts. Through this experience, listeners learn to classify sounds into different functional categories or phonemes based on multiple acoustic attributes. Under this view, what's invariant is not a single, perfect acoustic cue but rather a unique combination of multiple imperfect cues.

There's evidence that listeners use multiple cues in speech perception. For example, it has been shown that listeners identify American English vowels in /bVb/ syllables most accurately when all three cues, namely vowel steady-state formant frequencies, vowel duration, and formant transitions, are present. Surprisingly, identification accuracy remains equally accurate without the vowel steady-state formants, but with formant transitions and duration cues intact, suggesting a reduced role for vowel steady-state formants. As expected, identification becomes less accurate when only one cue is present.

In sum, two main approaches have been proposed to account for the lack of a one-to-one correspondence between acoustic properties and an invariant perceptual unit (e.g., phonemes). Representing the first approach, the motor theory claims that either neuromotor commands to the articulators or intended gestures recovered from an acoustic medium are invariant and are the objects of speech perception. Direct realism, however, proposes that actual rather than intended vocal tract gestures, which can be directly perceived from the acoustic signals, are the objects of speech perception. The third approach suggests that the objects of speech perception are auditory or acoustic events. Through general auditory and cognitive mechanisms, listeners learn to associate complex and integrated cues to phonemic categories.

Role of Visual Information in Speech Perception

Speech is not only heard but seen. In verbal face-to-face communication, we see the speaker's lips, tongue, and jaw movements along with the sounds they produce. Studies show that visual information improves speech intelligibility in noisy listening conditions and when the acoustic signal is degraded (e.g., Benoit et al., 1994; Ross et al., 2007). The perception of foreign-accented speech is also enhanced with visual information (Kim & Davis, 2003).

Visual information also plays a role in speech perception development in infants. Research shows that young infants are sensitive to the congruence between the visual and audio components of natural speech (e.g., Kuhl & Meltzoff, 1984). Speech perception by audiovisual information also facilitates speech perception among hearing-impaired infants and cochlear-implanted deaf children (Arnold & Kopsel, 1996; Lachs et al., 2001; Geers et al., 2003).

Visual information is automatically integrated with audio information in audiovisual speech perception. The most dramatic demonstration of the integration of visual and auditory information in speech perception is the McGurk effect, mentioned briefly in our description of the motor theory above. This effect was named after Harry McGurk, who first reported the phenomenon in McGurk and McDonald (1976). In the demonstration, the listeners see incongruent audio and visual information, such as seeing someone mouthing syllables /ga-ga/ dubbed with a sound track /ba-ba/. Listeners reported hearing neither /ga/ or /ba/, but /da/, as illustrated in Figure 10.15.

Even more fascinating is the fact that listeners continue to experience the effects after they are told what's happening. Moreover, the effects have been reported even when there is a gender mismatch between the audio and visual information. Interestingly, in most cases, the audio information of the incongruent stimuli determines the perceived manner of articulation such as voicing or

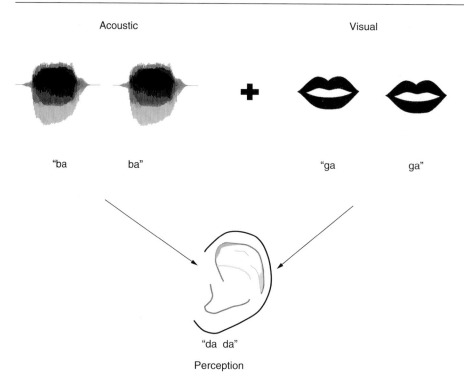

Acoustic   Visual

"ba   ba"   "ga   ga"

"da da"

Perception

Figure 10.15 The McGurk effect: the integration of visual and auditory information in speech perception

nasality whereas the visual information affects the perceived place of articulation (McGurk & MacDonald, 1976; Brancazio, 2004).

The size of the McGurk effect may depend on the auditory intelligibility of the signal. For example, it has been reported that very few McGurk illusions occur among Japanese listeners listening to Japanese syllables when the auditory signal is 100 percent intelligible, but that the effect is strengthened (e.g., increased reliance on visual information) when the audio signal is degraded in noise-added conditions (Sekiyama & Tokhura, 1991). This finding is consistent with the greater reliance on visual information reported among cochlear-implanted patients even after years of auditory recovery (Rouger et al., 2008).

The extent to which visual and audio information is integrated may also be language dependent. For instance, in comparison to native American English speakers, Japanese speakers relied more on audio information and exhibited a much weaker McGurk effect for clear Japanese stimuli, but the effect became stronger for foreign, English stimuli.

In sum, speech perception involves both visual and audio processes. Information from both modalities is automatically integrated in the perceptual process to enhance speech perception under non-optimal listening conditions among both normal listeners and patients with hearing impairment. However, the nature and the extent of the integration may be language and culture dependent.

Fun Fact: Skills Musicians Are Not Subject to the McGurk Effect

According to a study by Proverbio et al. (2016), forty musicians with at least eight to thirteen years of academic musical studies did not show a significant McGurk effect, suggesting the effects of intensive, long-term musical training on how the auditory cortex processes "phonetic information" (p. 1).

Role of Top-Down Information

Speech perception is determined not only by its acoustic nature (bottom-up information) but also by information from listeners' expectations (top-down information). For instance, research shows that perception of a phoneme is easier in words than in non-words. In 1976, Philip Rubin and colleagues from the Haskins Laboratory presented a series of short English CVC words, such as *sin*, *bat*, and *leg*, or non-words, such as *jum*, *baf*, and *teg*, and asked listeners to press a response key as quickly as possible when they heard an initial /b/ phoneme. They found that, on average, response time was faster (581 ms) when /b/ began a meaningful word than when it began a meaningless syllable, suggesting that both lexical meaning and phonological forms are accessed in speech perception.

Another example of the effects of meaning on speech perception was demonstrated by Warren (1970), who asked native American English college students to listen to the recorded sentence "The state governor met with their legislatures convening in the capital city," with the first 's' in "legislatures" removed and replaced by a cough or a tone of the same duration. The students reported hearing the absent phoneme and were not able to locate the position of the cough. This illusory perception of a missing phoneme is known as the **phoneme restoration** effect. Samuel (1981) found that perceptual restoration is more likely to occur when the replaced phoneme is acoustically similar to the replacement sound, such as /s/ and a hissing sound. Phonemic restorations also occur with deleted clusters of two to three sounds, and with any extra sounds besides a cough and a tone. Interestingly, Samuel (1996) further demonstrated the role of top-down processing in phonemic restorations by showing that the likelihood of phonemic restoration is increased in longer words. The extra context provided by a longer word appears to facilitate the perception of the masked phoneme. The fact that phonemic restorations occur more for a real word such as *prOgress* (with a masked /o/ vowel) than in a similar non-word such as *crOgress* provided additional evidence of the involvement of top-down processing in phonemic restorations.

The influence of lexical knowledge in speech perception is also attested in the "verbal transformation effect" (VTE), a perceptual phenomenon in which listeners report hearing illusory words when a spoken word is rapidly repeated for an extended period of time (Warren & Gregory, 1958; Warren, 1968; Pitt & Shoaf,

2002). For instance, the word 'spike' presented repeatedly at 500 ms intervals evokes illusory percepts of 'spy', 'spike', 'bike' etc. It is hypothesized that these illusory percepts result from the listener's perceptual regrouping of acoustic elements of the repeated utterance into separate streams. For example, listeners who experienced the illusory percept 'bike' from 'spike' reported hearing the plosive release burst of 'p' in 'spike' as a separate auditory stream from the preceding frication noise and could also generate the same 'bike' percept by separating the fricative noise of 's' from 'spike' (Pitt & Shoaf, 2002). More importantly, regrouping is influenced by whether the stimulus is perceived as speech or non-speech (Pitt & Shoaf, 2002), or as a word or non-word (MacKay et al., 1993).

Another intriguing example of top-down influences on speech perception comes from experiments exploring intelligibility of sine-wave speech (Remez et al., 1981). As shown in Figure 10.16, sine-wave speech is made up of sine waves that mimic the formant frequencies of an utterance. Independently, they are heard as non-speech whistles, reflecting the fact that they are harmonically unrelated sinusoids that are not perceptually coherent. However, if listeners are told the original identity of the utterance or that what they are hearing is speech, a clear and (somewhat) intelligible percept of a spoken utterance can be evoked.

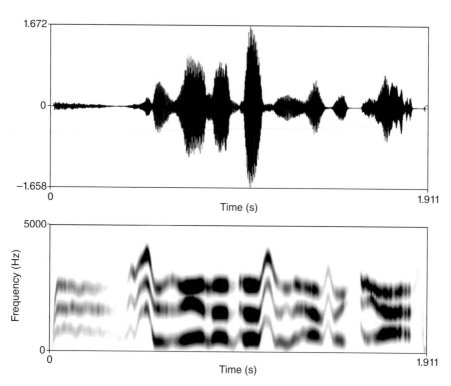

Figure 10.16 Original acoustic waveform (top) and its corresponding sine wave analog (bottom)

Speech Perception in Infants

Infants are born with the innate ability to discern the fine acoustic details used to group speech sounds into separate categories in the world's languages. It has been widely demonstrated that before the age of six months, infants are able to discriminate pairs of speech sounds from a wide range of non-native languages that adults find challenging. For example, like Hindi adults, 6–8-month-old English-learning infants are able to discriminate the voiceless aspirated–voiced aspirated [tʰɑ–dʰɑ] and the dental–retroflex [ṭɑ–ḍɑ] contrasts in Hindi (Werker et al., 1981) that English-speaking adults cannot. Patricia Kuhl, a well-known researcher on speech perception development, refers to infants at this stage as "citizens of the world."

However, during the second half of their first year of life, infants' perceptual systems undergo what's known as **perceptual reorganization** and become tuned to their native languages. Their initial sensitivity to the acoustic details of non-native phonetic segments declines while their sensitivity to the acoustic attributes used to separate sound categories or phonemes in their ambient language remains unchanged or is even enhanced. For instance, English-learning infants' good discrimination of Hindi and Salish at 6–8 months becomes poorer at 8–10 months and 10–12 months, whereas there is no such decline among Hindi- and Salish-learning infants. In addition, there's evidence that this age-related perceptual attenuation of non-native sounds begins earlier for vowels relative to consonants, suggesting an earlier bias toward steady periodic acoustic information (in vowels) over non-periodic acoustic characteristics (in consonants) in the speech signal.

By approximately the age of 5–7, all native sound categories are formed and knowledge governing their pronunciation in different positions in syllables, words, or utterances is fully mastered.

Speech Perception in Adults

Unlike infants, adults are language-specific listeners. They can no longer differentiate sound categories that are not contrastive in their native language. As shown in Figure 10.17, the ability to learn a new language declines with age (Johnson & Newport, 1989), and there is a time window commonly known as the **critical period** during which learning is optimal. For most learners, the critical period for language learning in general ends around puberty, but for the learning of sound contrasts, this critical period ends between five and seven years of age.

Several explanations have been proposed to account for the existence of the critical period. The biologically based approach suggests that a lack of brain or neuro plasticity is responsible for the learning decline. The cognitive-based approach, on the other hand, suggests that the pre-existing native-language sound system may hinder or facilitate the acquisition of non-native sound categories.

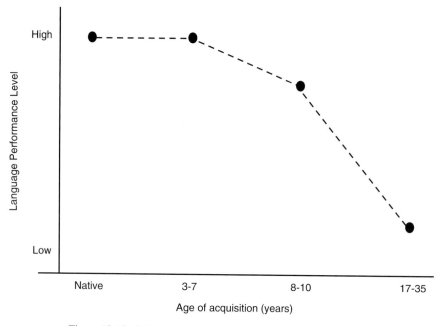

Figure 10.17 Critical period: optimal language learning ability declines with age of acquisition

According to Dr. Kuhl, the capacity to learn new sound categories is limited by the memories of native sound categories previously formed such that the perceptual salience of a new sound falling within the acoustic or auditory space of a native sound is reduced (Kuhl, 1991). That is, a native sound category acts as a magnet, pulling a non-native sound toward it. Perceptual distinction between the native and the non-native sounds is thus reduced. This is known as the **perceptual magnet effect**, illustrated in Figure 10.18.

This figure shows that [d̪] and [ʈ], which are allophones of two separate phonemes in Hindi, fall within the perceptual space of English /d/, causing them to sound like English /d/. This Hindi contrast is thus difficult for native English listeners to distinguish.

The native sound system has also been implicated in other accounts of cross-language and second language perception (L2), such as the speech learning model (SLM) (Flege, 1995) and the perceptual assimilation model (PAM) (Best, 1995). For both models, native-language (L1) sound categories play a crucial role in determining ultimate (SLM) or initial (PAM) levels of success in L2 speech learning. According to the SLM, new category formation is harder for L2 sounds that are perceived to be similar to L1 sounds than for L2 sounds that are perceived to be different or "new" from L1 sounds. For the SLM, L1–L2 perceptual comparison occurs at the position-sensitive allophonic level. PAM posits that L2–L1 perceptual mapping occurs at the articulatory gestural level.

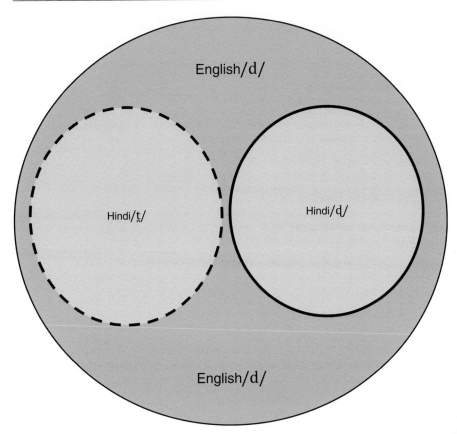

Figure 10.18 Perceptual magnet effect: Hindi and [ɖ] and [ʈ] fall within the perceptual space of English /d/

According to PAM, L2 sounds may be assimilated to L1 sounds in different ways and to different degrees, and assimilation patterns in turn predict the degree of difficulty L2 learners will initially have with L2 sounds. Specifically, PAM predicts that learners will have the most trouble distinguishing between two L2 sounds that are assimilated to a single L1 sound category (single-category assimilation). On the other hand, discrimination will be easiest when two L2 sounds are considered good exemplars of two different L1 categories (two-category assimilation). This is illustrated in Figure 10.19 (a) and (b) respectively.

In summary, there exists a critical time window for speech learning. By the age of six months, auditory sensitivity to the acoustic details that allow infants to distinguish speech contrasts in the world's languages is reduced to only those used to categorize sounds in the ambient language. Once established, the native-language sound categories may subsequently hinder or facilitate the acquisition of non-native contrasts.

Figure 10.19 (a) Single-category assimilation, (b) Two-category assimilation according to the perceptual assimilation model (PAM)

Perception of Suprasegmentals

In comparison to segments (consonants and vowels), relatively less is known about suprasegmental perception. With respect to categorical perception, similar to consonants and vowels, contrasts among contour tones are perceived more categorically whereas contrasts among level tones are perceived more continuously (e.g., Francis et al., 2003). Not surprisingly, lexical tone perception is more categorical among tonal than non-tonal language listeners (Hallé et al., 2004; Xu et al., 2006).

The effect of language background on lexical stress perception has also been examined. The results obtained suggest that native listeners of a language that lacks contrastive lexical stress such as French have trouble differentiating non-words based on stress location, a phenomenon known as "stress deafness" (Dupoux et al., 1997, 2001).

Perception of intonation is complex and relatively less is understood about it than perception of lexical tones and lexical stress. This is due in part to its lack of a universally accepted definition: for some, it is restricted to perceived pitch patterns, but for others, it may encompass other prosodic parameters that fulfill the same functions, such as pauses, relative loudness, voice quality, and duration. A consensus on the aim of intonation perception studies appears to also be lacking (Vaissière, 2005), with some considering grammatical distinction of intonation as primary (Pierrehumbert, 1980) while others consider it secondary to its emotion function (Bolinger & Bolinger, 1986). With respect to categorical perception, research has yielded inconclusive results. For instance, from three classical categorical perception experiments conducted to examine if the difference between "normal" and "emphatic" accent peaks in English is categorical, Ladd and Morton (1997) found an abrupt shift in the identification function from normal to emphatic, but without an associated corresponding discrimination peak. A similar finding was reported in Liu and Rodriguez (2012) on the difference between question and statement intonations in English, leading to the conclusion that intonation may be interpreted categorically but is not categorically perceived (Ladd & Morton, 1997). Interestingly, however, in a contextualized experiment (e.g., with a precursor utterance serving as a semantic frame), perception of intonation may become categorical (Kohler, 1987).

Unlike segments, how our perception of a language's prosodic system develops is also less known. However, what's known seems to be parallel to what we find on consonant and vowel perception. For instance, we learn that sensitivity to native-language prosodic patterns begins very early in life. Newborn infants preferred listening to the same story that had been read to them *in utero* than to a new story (DeCasper et al., 1994). As young as four days old, infants could distinguish utterances produced in their native language from those produced in another language. In addition, as early as five months of age (Mehler et al., 1988) infants have been shown to be able to discriminate the intonation contrast between declarative statements and yes–no questions (Frota et al., 2014).

Similar to vowel and consonant perception, perceptual reorganization also occurs for suprasegmentals. By 7.5 months, English-learning infants show preference toward the dominant, trochaic stress pattern of English in their segmentation of two-syllable words from a continuous stream of speech (Jusczyk & Aslin, 1995; Jusczyk et al., 1999). At nine months, English-learning infants could also segment words from a foreign language (e.g., Dutch) with similar prosodic patterns to English, but not from a language with a different prosodic system (e.g., French) (Houston et al., 2000). In addition, nine-month-old Spanish infants are able to distinguish between stress-initial and stress-final pseudo-words, while French infants of the same age cannot (Skoruppa et al., 2009).

Perceptual reorganization has also been found for lexical tone. Research (Mattock & Burnham, 2006; Mattock et al., 2008) shows that at six and nine months of age, Chinese-learning infants, for whom lexical tone is present in their ambient language, discriminate lexical tone and non-speech tone contrasts equally well. However, English-learning infants' discrimination of lexical tone contrasts, but not the non-speech tone contrasts, declined significantly between six and nine months, suggesting a lack of developmental phonetic representations for tone due to absence of lexical tone in English. A similar finding was also found for French-learning infants.

As with consonants and vowels, perception of a non-native prosodic system is difficult for adult listeners. For example, in comparison to native Spanish listeners, native French listeners are less sensitive to lexical stress contrasts (e.g., bópelo vs. bopélo) (Dupoux et al., 1997). However, studies also show that English-learning adults have some knowledge of the relationship between stress patterns and lexical class (noun and verb) and syllable structure in English and are able to extend stress patterns of known words to new words (Guion et al., 2003, 2004).

Non-native tone listeners also find lexical tone discrimination challenging. For instance, in comparison to Mandarin listeners, American English listeners' discrimination of Thai tones is significantly worse (Wayland & Guion, 2003). However, their performance improves with perceptual training (Wang et al., 1999; Wayland & Guion, 2004; Francis et al., 2008). The advantage of native experience on lexical tone perception varies as a function of the tonal contrasts involved. American English and French listeners discriminated Cantonese level-tone contrasts better than Mandarin listeners, whereas the opposite is true for contour-tone contrasts (Qin & Mok, 2011). This is likely due to a greater perceptual weight placed on pitch level among non-tone listeners, and on pitch contour among native tone listeners (Gandour & Harshman, 1978; Gandour 1983).

In these last three chapters, we have described speech sounds as acoustic outcomes of coordinated movements of the articulatory organs, and as auditory phenomena processed by the auditory system and perceived by the brain. In the next chapter, also the last, of the book, we discuss some tools available to directly and indirectly quantify articulatory movements during speech production. These tools have provided insightful information that could be used independently or in conjunction with the acoustic information to deepen our understanding and appreciation of the complexity of the speech production process.

Chapter Summary

- Vowels are generally more accurately perceived than consonants.
- The main acoustic cue to vowel perception is formant frequencies.
- Acoustic cues to consonant perception vary according to their place and manner of articulation, and voicing.
- The linearity problem and lack of acoustic invariance are two important theoretical issues in speech perception.
- Speakers and speaking rate are important sources of variation in acoustic speech signals.
- Listeners compensate for acoustic variation through the process of normalization.
- Humans are better at differentiating sounds drawn from two separate categories than those drawn from the same category.
- A number of theories have been proposed to account for the lack of invariant acoustic correlates to a phoneme.
- The motor theory claims that the neuromotor commands used to actualize phonemes are invariant and are the objects of speech perception.
- Direct realism proposes that actual articulatory gestures are the objects of speech perception.
- The general auditory approach contends that the objects of speech perception are the various auditory and acoustic events present in the

signal. Through experience, humans learn to associate a unique combination of these events to a phoneme.

- Infants are born with the capacity to perceive speech contrasts across the world's languages.
- Experience with the native language constrains adult listeners' ability to distinguish speech contrasts not present in their L1.

Review Exercises

Exercise 10.1: What are perceptual cues to place of articulation for plosive consonants?

Exercise 10.2: What are perceptual cues to the manner of articulation for plosives?

Exercise 10.3: What are perceptual cues to the place of articulation of fricatives?

Exercise 10.4: What is the "linearity" problem in speech perception?

Exercise 10.5: How do different speech perception theories deal with the "lack of acoustic invariance" issue?

Exercise 10.6: The two graphs (A and B) below show possible outcomes of an identification task (solid line) and a discrimination task (dash line) of a [sa–ʃa] continuum. Which graph shows that perception of this continuum is categorical? Explain your answer.

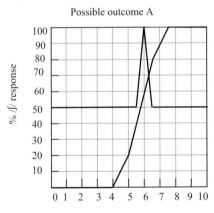

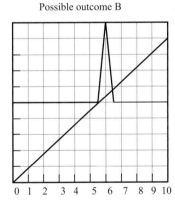

Possible outcome A   Possible outcome B

Exercise 10.7: Identify three sources of acoustic variation in speech signals.

Exercise 10.8: Discuss how acoustic variation may pose difficulty for speech processing or recognition by computers.

Exercise 10.9: Explain how the following factors affect speech perception:

  a. The perceiver's first language

  b. The presence of visual information

  c. The perceiver's expectation

Exercise 10.10: Describe an experiment that showed that perceptual reorganization has occurred in infants.

References and Further Reading

Arnold, P., & Kopsel, A. (1996). Lipreading, reading and memory of hearing and hearing-impaired children. *Scandinavian Audiology*, 25, 13–20.

Assmann, P. F., & Summerfield, Q. (1990). Modeling the perception of concurrent vowels: Vowels with different fundamental frequencies. *The Journal of the Acoustical Society of America*, 88, 680–697.

Benoit, C., Mohamadi, T., & Kandel, S. (1994). Effects of phonetic context on audio-visual intelligibility of French. *Journal of Speech, Language, and Hearing Research*, 37(5), 1195–1203.

Best, C. T. (1995). A direct realist view of cross-language speech perception. In W. Strange (ed.), *Speech Perception and Linguistic Experience: Issues in Cross-Language Research* (pp. 171–204). Timonium, MD: York Press.

Bolinger, D., & Bolinger, D. L. M. (1986). *Intonation and Its Parts: Melody in Spoken English*. Stanford, CA: Stanford University Press.

Brancazio, L. (2004). Lexical influences in audiovisual speech perception. *Journal of Experimental Psychology: Human Perception and Performance*, 30(3), 445.

Chalikia, M. H., & Bregman, A. S. (1989). The perceptual segregation of simultaneous auditory signals: Pulse train segregation and vowel segregation. *Perception & Psychophysics*, 46(5), 487–496.

Cutler, A., & Mehler, J. (1993). The periodicity bias. *Journal of Phonetics*, 21, 103–108.

DeCasper, A. J., Lecanuet, J. P., Busnel, M. C., Granier-Deferre, C., & Maugeais, R. (1994). Fetal reactions to recurrent maternal speech. *Infant Behavior and Development*, 17(2), 159–164.

Di Pellegrino, G., Fadiga, L., Fogassi, L., Gallese, V., & Rizzolatti, G. (1992). Understanding motor events: A neurophysiological study. *Experimental Brain Research*, 91(1), 176–180.

Dupoux, E., Pallier, C., Sebastian, N., & Mehler, J. (1997). A destressing "deafness" in French? *Journal of Memory and Language*, 36(3), 406–421.

Dupoux, E., Peperkamp, S., & Sebastián-Gallés, N. (2001). A robust method to study stress "deafness." *The Journal of the Acoustical Society of America*, 110(3), 1606–1618.

Eimas, P. D., Siqueland, E. R., Jusczyk, P., & Vigorito, J. (1971). Speech perception in infants. *Science*, 171(3968), 303–306.

Flege, J. E. (1995). Second language speech learning: Theory, findings, and problems. In W. Strange (ed.), *Speech Perception and Linguistic Experience: Issues in Cross-Language Research* (pp. 233–277). Timonium, MD: York Press.

Francis, A. L., Ciocca, V., & Ng, B. K. C. (2003). On the (non) categorical perception of lexical tones. *Perception & Psychophysics*, 65(7), 1029–1044.

Francis, A. L., Ciocca, V., Ma, L., & Fenn, K. (2008). Perceptual learning of Cantonese lexical tones by tone and non-tone language speakers. *Journal of Phonetics*, 36(2), 268–294.

Frota, S., Butler, J., & Vigário, M. (2014). Infants' perception of intonation: Is it a statement or a question? *Infancy*, 19(2), 194–213.

Gallese, V., Fadiga, L., Fogassi, L., & Rizzolatti, G. (1996). Action recognition in the premotor cortex. *Brain*, 119(2), 593–609.

Gandour, J. T. (1983). Tone perception in Far Eastern languages. *Journal of Phonetics*, 11(12), 149–175.

Gandour, J. T., & Harshman, R. A. (1978). Crosslanguage differences in tone perception: A multidimensional scaling investigation. *Language and Speech*, 21(1), 1–33.

Geers, A., Brenner, C., & Davidson, L. (2003). Factors associated with development of speech perception skills in children implanted by age five. *Ear and Hearing*, 24(1), 24S–35S.

Giguère, C., & Woodland, P. C. (1993). Speech analysis using a nonlinear cochlear model with feedback regulation. In M. Cooke, S. Beet, & M. Crawford (eds.), *Visual Representation of Speech Signal* (pp. 257–264). New York: John Wiley & Sons.

Guion, S. G., Clark, J. J., Harada, T., & Wayland, R. P. (2003). Factors affecting stress placement for English non-words include syllabic structure, lexical class, and stress patterns of phonologically similar words. *Language and Speech*, 46, 403–427.

Guion, S. G., Harada, T., & Clark, J. J. (2004). Early and late Spanish-English bilinguals' acquisition of English word stress patterns. *Bilingualism Language and Cognition*, 7, 207–226.

Hallé, P. A., Chang, Y. C., & Best, C. T. (2004). Identification and discrimination of Mandarin Chinese tones by Mandarin Chinese vs. French listeners. *Journal of Phonetics*, 32(3), 395–421.

Hillenbrand, J., Getty, L. A., Clark, M. J., & Wheeler, K. (1995). Acoustic characteristics of American English vowels. *The Journal of the Acoustical Society of America*, 97(5), 3099–3111.

Houston, D. M., Jusczyk, P. W., Kuijpers, C., Coolen, R., & Cutler, A. (2000). Cross-language word segmentation by 9-month-olds. *Psychonomic Bulletin & Review*, 7(3), 504–509.

Johnson, J. S., & Newport, E. L. (1989). Critical period effects in second language learning: The influence of maturational state on the acquisition of English as a second language. *Cognitive psychology*, 21(1), 60–99.

Jusczyk, P. W., & Aslin, R. N. (1995). Infants' detection of the sound patterns of words in fluent speech. *Cognitive Psychology*, 29, 1–23.

Jusczyk, P. W., Houston, D. M., & Newsome, M. (1999). The beginnings of word segmentation in English-learning infants. *Cognitive Psychology*, 39(3), 159–207.

Kim, J., & Davis, C. (2003). Hearing foreign voices: Does knowing what is said affect visual-masked-speech detection?, *Perception*, 32(1), 111–120.

Kohler, K. J. (1987). Categorical pitch perception. *Proceedings of the XIth International Congress of Phonetic Sciences* 5: 331–333.

Kuhl, P. K. (1991). Human adults and human infants show a "perceptual magnet effect" for the prototypes of speech categories, monkeys do not. *Perception & Psychophysics*, 50(2), 93–107.

Kuhl, P. K. (1994). Learning and representation in speech and language. *Current Opinion in Neurobiology*, 4, 812–822.

Kuhl, P. K. (2000). A new view of language acquisition. *Proceedings of the National Academy of Sciences of the United States of America*, 97, 11850–11857.

Kuhl, P. K., & Meltzoff, A. N. (1984). The intermodal representation of speech in infants. *Infant Behavior and Development*, 7(3), 361–381.

Kuhl, P. K., & Miller, J. D. (1978). Speech perception by the chinchilla: Identification functions for synthetic VOT stimuli. *The Journal of the Acoustical Society of America*, 63(3), 905–917.

Kuhl, P. K., Williams, K. A., Lacerda, F., Stevens, K. N., & Lindblom, B. (1992). Linguistic experience alters phonetic perception in infants by 6 months of age. *Science*, 255(5044), 606–608.

Lachs, L., Pisoni, D. B., & Kirk, K. I., (2001). Use of audiovisual information in speech perception by prelingually deaf children with cochlear implants: A first report. *Ear and Hearing*, 22(3), 236–251.

Ladd, D. R., & Morton, R. (1997). The perception of intonational emphasis: Continuous or categorical? *Journal of Phonetics*, 25(3), 313–342.

Ladefoged, P., & Broadbent, D. E. (1957). Information conveyed by vowels. *The Journal of the Acoustical Society of America*, 29(1), 98–104.

Liberman, A. M., Delattre, P., & Cooper, F. S. (1952). The role of selected stimulus-variables in the perception of the unvoiced stop consonants. *The American Journal of Psychology*, 65(4), 497–516.

Liberman, A. M., Delattre, P. C., Cooper, F. S., & Gerstman, L. J. (1954). The role of consonant-vowel transitions in the perception of the stop and nasal consonants. *Psychological Monographs: General and Applied*, 68(8), 1–13.

Liberman, A. M., Harris, K. S., Hoffman, H. S., & Griffith, B. C. (1957). The discrimination of speech sounds within and across phoneme boundaries. *Journal of Experimental Psychology*, 54(5), 358–368.

Liu, C., & Rodriguez, A. (2012). Categorical perception of intonation contrasts: Effects of listeners' language background. *The Journal of the Acoustical Society of America*, 131(6), EL427–EL433.

Lotto, A. J., Hickok, G. S., & Holt, L. L. (2009). Reflections on mirror neurons and speech perception. *Trends in Cognitive Sciences*, 13(3), 110–114.

MacKay, D. G., Wulf, G., Yin, C., & Abrams, L. (1993). Relations between word perception and production: New theory and data on the verbal transformation effect. *Journal of Memory and Language*, 32(5), 624–646.

Mattock, K., & Burnham, D. (2006). Chinese and English infants' tone perception: Evidence for perceptual reorganization. *Infancy*, 10(3), 241–265.

Mattock, K., Molnar, M., Polka, L., & Burnham, D. (2008). The developmental course of lexical tone perception in the first year of life. *Cognition*, 106(3), 1367–1381.

McGurk, H., & MacDonald, J. (1976). Hearing lips and seeing voices. *Nature*, 264, 746–748.

Mehler, J., Juscyzk, P. W., Lambertz, G., Halsted, N., Bertoncini, J., & Amiel-Tison, C. (1988). A precursor of Language acquisition in young infants. *Cognition*, 29, 143–178.

Miller, J. D., Wier, C. C., Pastore, R. E., Kelly, W. J., & Dooling, R. J. (1976). Discrimination and labeling of noise–buzz sequences with varying noise-lead times: An example of categorical perception. *The Journal of the Acoustical Society of America*, 60(2), 410–417.

Pierrehumbert, J. B. (1980). *The Phonology and Phonetics of English Intonation*. Doctoral dissertation, Massachusetts Institute of Technology.

Pitt, M. A., & Shoaf, L. (2002). Linking verbal transformations to their causes. *Journal of Experimental Psychology: Human Perception and Performance*, 28(1), 150.

Polka, L., & Werker, J. F. (1994). Developmental changes in perception of nonnative vowel contrasts. *Journal of Experimental Psychology: Human Perception and Performance*, 20(2), 421–435.

Proverbio, A. M., Massetti, G., Rizzi, E., & Zani, A. (2016). Skilled musicians are not subject to the McGurk effect. *Scientific Reports*, 6, 30423.

Qin, Z., & Mok, P. (2011). Perception of Cantonese tones by Mandarin, English and French speakers. In *Proceedings of the 17th International Congress of Phonetic Sciences (ICPhS)* (pp. 1654–1657).

Remez, R. E., Rubin, P. E., Pisoni, D. B., & Carrell, T. D. (1981). Speech perception without traditional speech cues. *Science*, 212(4497), 947–949.

Rizzolatti, G., & Craighero, L. (2004). The mirror-neuron system. *Annual Review of Neuroscience*, 27, 169–192.

Rizzolatti, G., Fadiga, L., Gallese, V., & Fogassi, L. (1996). Premotor cortex and the recognition of motor actions. *Cognitive Brain Research*, 3(2), 131–141.

Ross, L. A., Saint-Amour, D., Leavitt, V. M., Javitt, D. C., & Foxe, J. J. (2007). Do you see what I am saying? Exploring visual enhancement of speech comprehension in noisy environments. *Cerebral Cortex*, 17(5), 1147–1153.

Rouger, J., Fraysse, B., Deguine, O., & Barone, P. (2008). McGurk effects in cochlear-implanted deaf subjects. *Brain Research*, 1188, 87–99.

Samuel, A. G. (1981). The role of bottom-up confirmation in the phonemic restoration illusion. *Journal of Experimental Psychology: Human Perception and Performance*, 7(5), 1124.

Samuel, A. G. (1996). Does lexical information influence the perceptual restoration of phonemes? *Journal of Experimental Psychology: General*, 125(1), 28.

Samuel, A. G. (2001). Knowing a word affects the fundamental perception of the sounds within it. *Psychological Science*, 12(4), 348–351.

Sekiyama, K. (1997). Cultural and linguistic factors in audiovisual speech processing: The McGurk effect in Chinese subjects. *Perception & Psychophysics*, 59(1), 73–80.

Sekiyama, K., & Tohkura, Y. I. (1991). McGurk effect in non-English listeners: Few visual effects for Japanese subjects hearing Japanese syllables of high auditory intelligibility. *The Journal of the Acoustical Society of America*, 90(4), 1797–1805.

Skoruppa, K., Pons, F., Christophe, A., Bosch, L., Dupoux, E., Sebastián-Gallés, N., & Peperkamp, S. (2009). Language-specific stress perception by 9-month-old French and Spanish infants. *Developmental Science*, 12(6), 914–919.

Vaissière, J. (2005). Perception of intonation. In D. B. Pisoni & R. E. Remez (eds.), *The Handbook of Speech Perception* (pp. 236–263). Oxford: Blackwell.

Wang, Y., Spence, M., Jongman, A., & Sereno, J. (1999). Training American listeners to perceive Mandarin tone. *Journal of the Acoustical Society of America*, 106, 3649–3658.

Warren, R. M. (1968). Verbal transformation effect and auditory perceptual mechanisms. *Psychological Bulletin*, 70(4), 261.

Warren, R. M. (1970). Perceptual restoration of missing speech sounds. *Science*, 167(3917), 392–393.

Warren, R. M., & Gregory, R. L. (1958). An auditory analogue of the visual reversible figure. *The American Journal of Psychology*, 71, 612–613.

Wayland, R., & Guion, S. (2003). Perceptual discrimination of Thai tones by naïve and experienced native English speakers. *Applied Psycholinguistics*, 24, 113–129.

Wayland, R., & Guion, S. (2004). Training native English and native Chinese speakers to perceive Thai tones. *Language Learning*, 54, 681–712.

Wayland, R., & Li, B. (2008). Effects of two training procedures in cross-language perception of tones. *Journal of Phonetics*, 36, 250–267.

Wayland, R., Landfair, D., Li, B., & Guion, S. G. (2006). Native Thai speakers' acquisition of English word stress patterns. *Journal of Psycholinguistic Research*, 35(3), 285–304.

Werker, J. F., & Tees, R. C. (1983). Developmental changes across childhood in the perception of nonnative speech sounds. *Canadian Journal of Psychology*, 37, 278–286.

Werker, J. F., & Tees, R. C. (1984). Cross-language speech perception: Evidence for perceptual reorganization in the first year of life. *Infant Behavior and Development*, 7, 49–63.

Werker, J. F., & Tees, R. C. (1992). The organization and reorganization of human speech perception. *Annual Review of Neuroscience*, 15, 377–402.

Werker, J. F., Gilbert, J. H. V., Humphrey, K., & Tees, R. C. (1981). Developmental aspects of cross-language speech perception. *Child Development*, 52, 349–355.

Xu, Y., Gandour, J. T., & Francis, A. L. (2006). Effects of language experience and stimulus complexity on the categorical perception of pitch direction. *The Journal of the Acoustical Society of America*, 120(2), 1063–1074.

Zwicker, U. T. (1984). Auditory recognition of diotic and dichotic vowel pairs. *Speech Communication*, 3, 265–277.

11

Experimental Tools in Articulatory Phonetics

Learning Objectives

By the end of this chapter, you will be able to:

- Identify procedures used to measure contact areas between the tongue and the roof of the mouth, including:
  - Static palatography
  - Electropalatography (EPG)
- Distinguish techniques used to measure lip and face movements, such as:
  - Video imaging
  - Point tracking
- Recognize methods use to quantify vocal fold contact areas, namely:
  - Electroglottograh (EGG)
  - Endoscope
  - Photoglottography (PGG)
- Explain how the vocal tract geometry can be viewed and quantified:
  - MRI electroglottograph (EGG)
- Identify techniques used to examine tongue shape, such as:
  - Ultrasound
  - Electromagnetic midsagittal articulography (EMMA)

Introduction

Speech is largely invisible. Besides lip, jaw, and facial movements, most articulatory gestures that result in speech are hidden inside the vocal tract. In Chapter 8, we described the acoustic consequences of speech articulatory movements for vowels and consonants. Technological advancements have also afforded linguists and speech scientists the means to examine physical events associated with speech. In this chapter, we will survey a few tools used to quantify articulatory movements during speech production. Outdated techniques such as x-ray and overly invasive methods such as (intramuscular) electromyography (EMG) are not included. Data on articulatory movements are useful on their own and when considered in conjunction with acoustic and impressionistic data. Knowledge about articulatory movements and their acoustic output informs linguistic theories and provides a means to evaluate the effectiveness of pedagogical and clinical intervention techniques. For each technique, a brief overview of how it works is given, and its advantages and drawbacks are reviewed. Examples of research findings based on data collected with each method are also discussed.

Measuring Tongue Contact

We will begin our discussion with techniques used to quantify degrees of contact between the tongue and the roof of the mouth. The first method, static palatography, is simpler and more economical than the second method, electropalatography (EPG).

Static Palatography

Palatography is a collection of methods used to locate where the tongue makes contact with the roof of the mouth or the palate during speech production. For the **static palatography** (Figure 11.1) technique, a mixture of charcoal and vegetable oil is painted on the tongue of the speaker before a single repetition of a target speech sound is made, for example, a simple consonant plus vowel (CV) sequence [ta] or [ka]. Using an oral mirror, a photograph showing blackened areas where the tongue makes its contact with the palate is then taken.

The reverse of this method, with the charcoal mixture painted onto the roof of the mouth and the area of contact shown on the tongue, is called **linguography** (Figure 11.2). Both of these techniques are simple and are particularly useful in

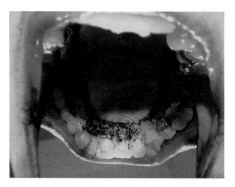

Figure 11.1 Static palatography

(Reused with permission from Jennifer Chard Hamano https://chamano.commons
.gc.cunyedu/research/.)

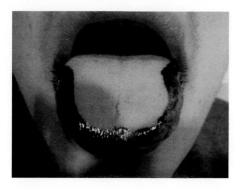

Figure 11.2 Linguogram
(Reproduced from https://chamano.commons.gc.cuny.edu/research/ with permission from Jennifer Chard Hamano.)

fieldwork situations where a quick check on the place of articulation of conso-nants, particularly the stops, fricatives, affricates, and clicks produced in the anterior region of the mouth, is needed. However, they provide the contact pattern of a single instance only. The tongue or the palate has to be cleaned and the mixture reapplied before another production.

Through static palatography, we have learned that in contrast to an approx-imant [ɹ]–[ɹa] 'bush', a trill [r]–[ra] 'worried' is produced with retroflexion (tongue curling) in Rongga, an endangered language spoken by about 4,000 people in south-central Flores, Indonesia (Arka, 2004). It has also been found that Nepalese retroflex plosives [ʈ, ʈʰ, ɖ, ɖʰ] are produced with the tongue tip curled to touch the post-alveolar region rather than simply raised toward the alveolar as previously claimed (Khatiwada, 2007). In Wari, spoken by about 2,000 people in Brazil, a dental plosive preceding a voiceless bilabial trill [t̪ʙ̥] is produced with full contact between the tongue and the upper teeth, including the front part of the alveolar ridge (Ladefoged & Everett, 1996). A more recent study of Korean suggests that younger speakers, those in their twenties, produce post-alveolar affricates as denti-alveolar affricates, and that female speakers use the tongue blade (laminal) rather than the tip and the blade area (apico-laminal) as male speakers do. See Figure 11.3 for apical, apico-laminal, and laminal tongue positions (Anderson et al., 2004).

Electropalatography (EPG)

The drawbacks of static palatography and linguography are overcome in **electropalatography** or **EPG**. This modern dynamic palatography involves a palatal insert similar to the one shown in Figure 11.4. An array of electrodes is attached to the palatal insert, with more electrodes located at the front than at the back of the palate in order to capture a finer contact pattern in this region. Contact points between the tongue and the electrodes are recorded hundreds of times per

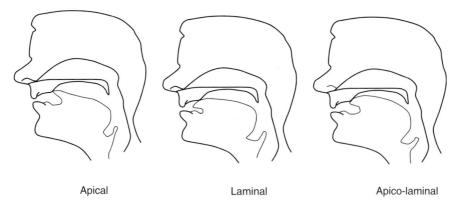

Apical   Laminal   Apico-laminal

Figure 11.3 Apical, laminal, and apico-laminal tongue positions

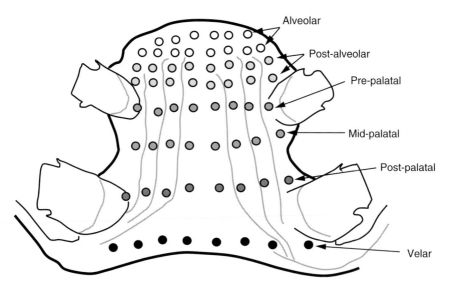

Figure 11.4 Palatal insert used in electropalatography

second, allowing for a fine-grained observation of rapid tongue-contact patterns over time (see Figure 11.5 for typical contact patterns for a number of consonants).

EPG has been used in research for several decades (e.g., Kydd & Belt, 1964; Hardcastle, 1972). The main drawback of EPG is the cost and time involved, as each palatal insert has to be custom built to fit each individual speaker. In addition, EPG is more sensitive to anterior distribution and duration of tongue–palate contact, and more suitable for consonants than vowels. The artificial palate may also compromise a speaker's natural speech production.

Besides its use in linguistic investigation, in recent years, EPG has been mainly used in the analysis and treatment of disordered speech (Mennen et al.,

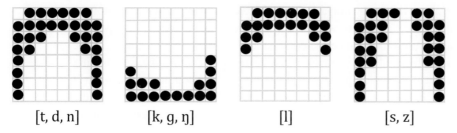

[t, d, n]   [k, g, ŋ]   [l]   [s, z]

Figure 11.5 Typical tongue-contact patterns from electropalatography for alveolar, velar, lateral, and fricative consonants

2010). For instance, it can be used to treat speech articulation disorders among cleft palate and deaf patients. Tongue-contact positions can be examined before and after an operation or therapy to assess their effectiveness.

Studies using dynamic palatography have yielded interesting results on movement of the tongue during normal speech articulation. For example, in Japanese, the tongue-contact pattern is the same for [t] and [d], but both the contact area and the duration is smaller and shorter for [d] (Shibata, 1968). In addition, tongue-contact patterns for Japanese flap [ɾ] were found to vary as a function of vowel context (Kiritani et al., 1982). American English [ɹ] is produced differently depending on whether it is in word-initial or word-medial position, and before a stressed or an unstressed vowel (Miyawaki, 1972). Interestingly, palatography data also suggests that a consonant produced before a stressed vowel shows a more characteristically distinct tongue movement than that before an unstressed vowel.

Dynamic palatography is a great tool for research on coarticulation. We learned, for instance, that, in Catalan, the production of a voiced palatal nasal [ɲ] and a voiced lateral palatal approximant [ʎ] in a VCV utterance (e.g., [iɲi], [iʎi]) differ from the sequence [nj] and [lj] (e.g., [inji], and [ilji]) in the duration of the time lag between the alveolar and the palatal closures, with a longer lag for the sequences. More interestingly, the V to C coarticulation effect is inversely correlated with this temporal lag: there is a greater degree of coarticulation for [ɲ] and [ʎ] than for the sequences (Ricasens, 1984).

Measuring Lip and Face Movements

Lip and facial movements during speech production may provide redundant but rich and salient information to help improve speech processing speed and accuracy, particularly in noisy listening conditions. In this section, we will discuss methods used to quantify degrees of lip and facial movements.

Video Imaging

Video imaging and point tracking are two methods used to examine lip and facial movements during speech production. Standard video captures spatial information about the face while a more advanced video technique can automatically measure face shape as well as the size and shape of the lip opening. Lipstick can be used to enhance the contrast and facilitate the tracking process. In addition, high-speed video imaging can be used to capture the fast-moving articulatory events of rapid lip movements during the production of a bilabial trill or the release of plosive consonants, for example. The main drawback of the high-speed video imaging technique is the amount of computer storage required.

Point Tracking

Point tracking is a more expensive alternative to the video imaging technique for recording lip and facial movements. Two slightly different point-tracking systems will be discussed here. The first one is a 3D optical point-tracking system that uses three single-axis cameras to track the movements of infrared-emitting diodes that are attached to the subject's face and lips (e.g., Optotrak). The diodes are connected to the system by wired or wireless connections. Optotrak provides high spatial and temporal resolution images. However, the system is expensive, and the diodes may heat up over time, limiting the duration of experiments. There is also a trade-off between the number of infrared markers and the spatial and temporal resolution. For an example of an Optotrak set-up, see www.haskins.yale.edu/featured/heads/KBS/kbsav.html.

Among the findings from studies using Optotrak is the report that jaw rotation and translation vary as a function of speaking rate and volume. The magnitudes of both types of movement are progressively reduced from speaking loudly to normal to fast speaking rate among both Japanese and English speakers. However, the difference in magnitudes for both rotation and translation is language specific: smaller for Japanese and English speakers, for example (Vatikiotis-Bateson & Ostry, 1995).

Instead of tracking the movements of infrared-emitting diodes, the second type of point-tracking system (e.g., Vicon MX), shines infrared light on light-weight reflective markers and tracks their movements, avoiding the over-heating issue of the first system. Nonetheless, it has some of its own drawbacks. Because the system cannot identify which markers are being tracked, the positions of the markers may not be reliably located from the proximity of the motion alone. In addition, reflective clothing and ambient light may interfere with the detection process. Finally, similar to the first system, there is a trade-off between the number of reflective markers and the spatial and temporal resolution of their movements.

Measuring Vocal Folds Contact Area

Despite its importance in the speech production process, the action at the larynx is not readily visible during the production of speech. Three relatively

non-invasive techniques used to quantify contact area between the vocal folds
during phonation are described in this section.

Electroglottography (EGG)

The electroglottograph (EGG), or laryngograph, is a non-invasive device used to
measure the contact area between the two vocal folds during phonation through a
display of electrical impedance patterns across the larynx. Two electrodes are
secured on the speaker's neck at the level of the larynx (Figure 11.6). A small,
but high-frequency electrical current is passed between the two electrodes and
the amount of electrical impedance is measured. Since the vocal fold tissue is a
better conductor of electricity than air, the amount of electrical impedance
decreases when the vocal folds are closer together (smaller glottis), but increases
when they are apart (larger glottis).

An EGG display known as the VFCA (vocal fold contact area), such as the one
shown in Figure 11.7, provides an easy way to see if the vocal folds are closed or
open. In addition, since the amount of electricity transferred increases with a
greater contact area, an EGG display also provides information on the degree of
closure during vocal fold cycles. EGG is a useful method of investigating vocal
fold cycles during different phonation types in the speech of normal speakers, as
well as among patients with voice disorders. Among the drawbacks of the EGG
method are its inability to provide information on the degree or the location of
the opening of the vocal folds. The EGG will also not work well if the larynx
moves above or below the range of the electrodes.

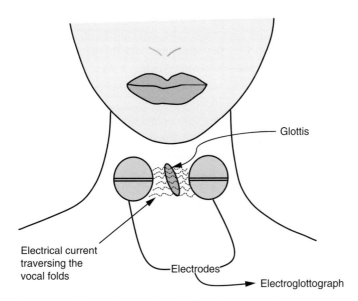

Figure 11.6 Electroglottography (EGG) or laryngography

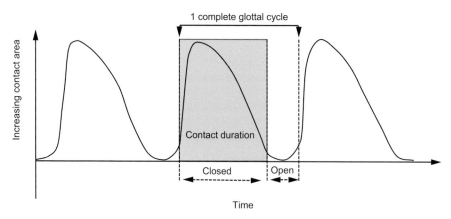

Figure 11.7 An EGG display of the vocal fold contact area (VFCA)

EGG has been used to examine vocal fold vibratory cycle details, vertical movement of the larynx, and voice fundamental frequency. In an interesting study, voice fundamental frequency measurement from EGG during continuous read speech obtained from third- to twelfth-grade boys in Copenhagen Singing School was found to correlate with measures of hormonal development and sex characteristics during pre-pubertal and pubertal periods (Pedersen et al., 1986).

Endoscopes

Information on the location and degree of vocal fold opening can be obtained through endoscopy, a family of methods used to video-record the larynx in action from above. Both rigid (Figure 11.8) and flexible (Figure 11.9) endoscopes involve inserting a tube attached with mirrors, a light, and camera into the mouth or the nasal cavity, respectively, to film the structures and the working of the larynx. However, both of these methods have drawbacks. A rigid scope makes speech production difficult and unnatural, and a flexible endoscope is invasive as its insertion into the nasal cavity requires local anesthetic.

Endoscopes have been used to study laryngeal control during speech production. In one study (Yoshioka et al., 1981), we learned that the glottal-opening gesture during a sequence of obstruent /s/ and /k/ production exhibits one, two, or more than two peaks depending on whether or not there is an intervening word boundary. For the /s#k/ sequence with an intervening word boundary (e.g., My ace caves), two glottal opening peaks were found, so the /k/ is aspirated, in comparison to one peak when a word boundary is absent (e.g., I may scale), with an unaspirated /k/. For geminates, /ss/ (e.g., My ace sales) or /kk/ (e.g., I make cave) exhibit only one glottal opening peak despite the presence of an intervening word boundary. On the other hand, when the initial aspirated [kʰ] is preceded by the word-final cluster /sk/ (e.g., I mask cave) or /ks/ (e.g., He makes cave), a bimodal pattern of glottal opening is observed, with the first

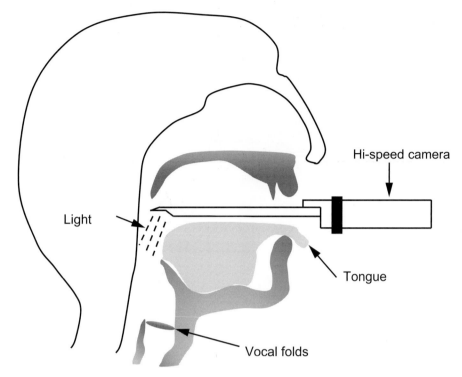

Figure 11.8 Rigid endoscope

maximum peak reached during the /s/ and the second around the burst of the aspirated stop. These results are consistent with the view that a separate glottal opening is required for the voiceless fricative and the aspirated stop to assure the aerodynamic requirements for generation of frication and aspiration for the two segments. Endoscopes have also been used to assess and treat laryngeal voice disorders.

Photoglottography (PGG)

Another endoscopic method used to examine vocal fold vibration is the trans-illumination of the larynx or photoglottography (PGG). PGG is an indirect measure of the size of the glottal opening during phonation. In PGG, a fiber-optic light source inserted through the mouth or nose is placed above or below the vocal folds. A light sensor located on the other side of the folds picks up the light and converts it into electrical voltage. Variation in the amount of light captured by the sensor corresponds to the size of the glottis (vocal fold opening): the greater the amount of light, the wider the glottis. However, only timing (i.e., not degree) of glottal activity during phonation such as points of initial, opening and closing within the cycle can be measured from a PGG signal as little to no

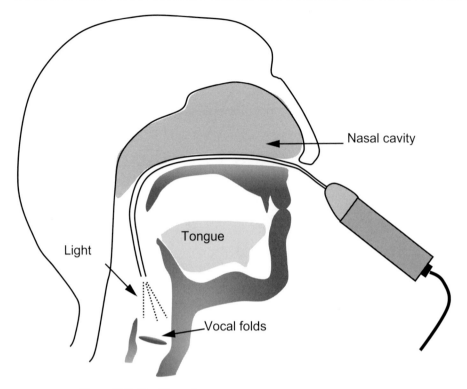

Figure 11.9 Flexible endoscope

light can pass through the vocal folds when they are closed. Figure 11.10 shows the PGG set-up. Due to its invasive nature, PGG has been used only in limited clinical settings to assess and treat voice disorders, for example.

Measuring Vocal Tract Geometry

Airflow movement inside the vocal tract is sensitive to the fine detail of vocal tract geometry. As such, information on the entire vocal tract shape during speech production is sometimes needed for a better understanding of the relationship between the vocal tract shape and its acoustic correlates to improve, for instance, speech synthesis and speech recognition systems.

Magnetic Resonance Imaging (MRI)

Magnetic resonance imaging or MRI is a tool used to obtain vocal tract geometry and tongue shape imaging without exposing speakers to the risks of radiation. In addition to information on the location of the tongue and the overall vocal tract shape, the vocal tract area function and volume can be directly calculated from MRI images. In earlier studies, due to the long exposure time (a few seconds)

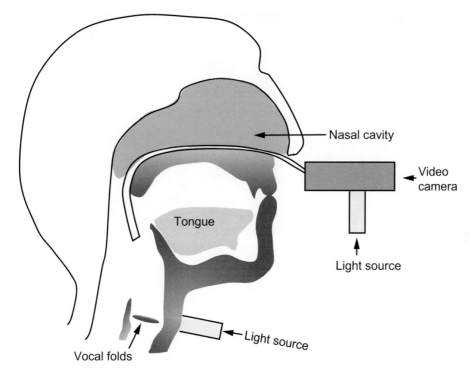

Figure 11.10 Photoglottography

required, only static images of the vocal tract shape during the production of prolongable sounds such as a sustained vowel or a nasal, liquid, or fricative consonant could be obtained. However, in recent years, researchers have attempted to acquire dynamic MRI sequences or movies by putting together single images taken from different times in the production of an utterance that is repeated over and over. Even though the resulting movie shows movements of the vocal tract organs with a good degree of temporal resolution, it is not a real-time recording of the movements of the speech event. More recently, attempts have been made to acquire faster or even real-time MRI (rtMRI) images (Figure 11.11). The faster image acquisition rate allows for quickly changing articulatory details, such as the transition from a consonant to the following vowel, to be captured.

Data on vocal tract shape and dimensions acquired using MRI techniques have been useful in understanding the vocal tract shape during the production of different vowels and consonants, their acoustic consequences, and the direction and degree of coarticulation. Besides being useful to linguistics research, MRI data obtained before and after an operation or therapy can be used to assess the effectiveness of clinical interventions among patients with speech or voice disorders. Additionally, information on vocal tract area functions and volume can enhance speech synthesis algorithms.

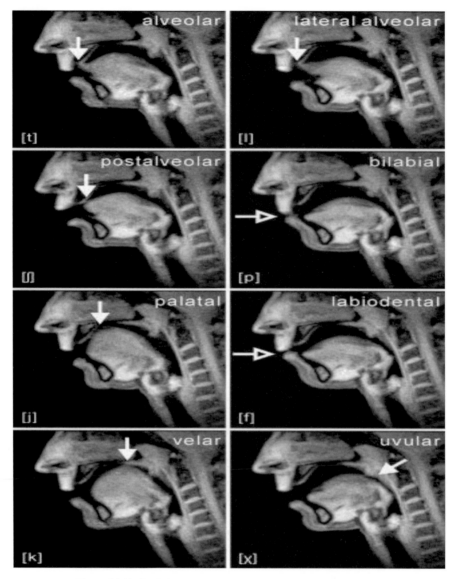

Figure 11.11 Real-time MRI of consonant production, demonstrating the place of articulation and the configuration of the articulators (arrows for tongue and lips) at the time of sound production.
(Reproduced from Niebergall, A., Zhang, S., Kunay, E., Keydana, G., Job, M., Uecker, M., & Frahm, J. (2013). Real-time MRI of speaking at a resolution of 33 ms: Undersampled radial FLASH with nonlinear inverse reconstruction. Magnetic Resonance in Medicine, 69(2), 477–485, with permission from John Wiley and Sons.)

The main drawback of the MRI technique in linguistics research is the high expense associated with using MRI equipment even when one is available. In addition, previous MRI studies have been mostly limited to vowels and a few sustainable consonants such as liquids, nasals, and fricatives. Furthermore, it has been suggested that the long (30 seconds or more) artificial sustaining causes the articulations to be hyperarticulated when compared to normally sustained articulation. Speakers also have difficulty holding articulations during artificial sustaining, leading to a backward movement of the tongue and a lack of velum control, for example. Sustained production is also different from real-time production in general, particularly in degree of coarticulation. Lastly, the speaker's supine position (facing upwards) during MRI data acquisition affects the position and shape of the tongue, leading to a decrease in the passage in the pharynx. This effect is particularly pronounced when the articulation is sustained artificially. Consequently, static MRI images should be complemented with other measurements to correctly replicate the articulatory movements and positions of running speech.

One area of research that has greatly benefited from MRI data is computer modeling of the speech articulation process and speech synthesis algorithms. The vocal tract shape obtained from MRI images along with their acoustic correlates allow us to better understand how the vocal tract acoustically shapes the sound sources generated both at the larynx (e.g., vocal fold vibration) and above (e.g., transient and noise generated inside the oral cavity) to produce distinct sounds.

MRI data is particularly useful for studying vowels. Of interest is the coordination of the tongue gesture and the velum-lowering gesture in nasal vowel production. Using real-time MRI techniques, a study revealed that during the production of the nasal vowel in the French word *pan* [pã] 'piece', the velum begins to lower right after the release of the initial [p] and is completely lowered by the time the tongue reaches its position for [ɑ] and stays open throughout the duration of the vowel. In contrast, the velum remains raised during production of the vowel [ɑ] in the word *panne* [pɑn] 'failure' and commences lowering only when the tongue tip begins to move toward the alveolar ridge target for the final [n]. Interestingly, in a manner similar to production of the French nasal vowel, the velum is fully lowered during articulation of the nasalized vowel [ɔ̃] in *Yvonne* [ivɔ̃n] produced by native American English speakers (Proctor et al., 2013).

Measuring Tongue Shape

The tongue is the most flexible organ of speech. Its position and shape are continuously changing during speech. Its fine and complex movements affect the amount and the direction of the airstream, and change the vocal tract's resonance properties.

Ultrasound

Ultrasound is a more affordable and portable imaging technique than MRI. It is designed to image soft tissue and has been used to acquire images of the tongue

during speech production in speech and linguistic research. An ultrasound
machine consists of a transducer or a probe, a processor, and acoustic and/or
video-recording tools. A transducer is a hand-held probe that makes contact with
the skin via a water-based gel. It transmits high-frequency sound waves ranging
from 3–16 MHz. Some of these sound waves penetrate through and get absorbed
by body parts while some hit a boundary (e.g., air, soft tissues) and reflect back
to the transducer. The machine processor uses the length of time it takes for the
sound waves to echo back to calculate the distance between the probe and
the boundaries. The intensity of the reflected sound waves and the distances
are displayed as one- or two-dimensional images. Figure 11.12 shows an ultrasound image of the tongue. The tongue surface is clearly visible in the image
because sound waves reflect off the air boundary (white line) just above it.

While portable, relatively affordable, and easy to use, the ultrasound technique
comes with some disadvantages, including difficulty with head movement,
transducer movement, and transducer contact with the skin. Using an

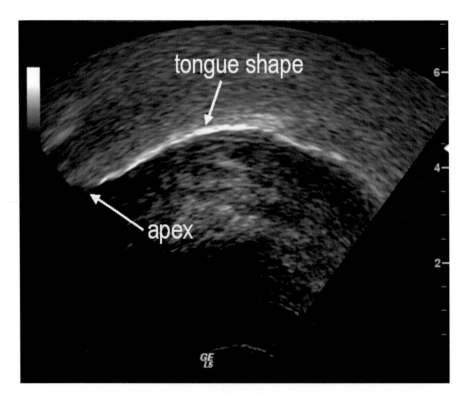

Figure 11.12 Two-dimensional ultrasound image of a tongue, with tongue tip
(apex) on the left. Tongue surface contour is shown as a white line

(Reused from Aron, M., Berger, M. O., Kerrien, E., Wrobel-Dautcourt, B., Potard,
B., & Laprie, Y. (2016). Multimodal acquisition of articulatory data: Geometrical
and temporal registration. The Journal of the Acoustical Society of America, 139
(2), 636–648, with permission from the Acoustical Society of America.)

appropriately shaped transducer and having the participant's head in a stationary position by leaning against a wall or being secured by a device may alleviate these problems. More importantly, ultrasound images are often too coarse or grainy, making it difficult to automatically detect the tongue's surface. This issue has been addressed by edge-tracking computer algorithms and statistical analysis tools. Finally, due to the shadow created by the sublingual cavity, the tongue tip is not easily captured. Additional transducer pressure may alleviate the problem.

Ultrasound imaging of the tongue has proven useful as visual articulatory feedback to improve pronunciation training among second language learners or clinical patients. A typical example is the teaching of the pronunciation of [ɹ], one of the most articulatorily complex sounds in English. It has been reported, for instance, that this technique improved pronunciation of [ɹ] among English-speaking adolescents who experienced delayed acquisition of this sound by breaking this sound into its simpler individual components and allowing the students to master them one at a time until full mastery was reached (Adler-Bock et al., 2007).

Electromagnetic Midsagittal Articulography (EMMA)

Electromagnetic midsagittal articulography (EMMA) is a point-tracking technique used to image the tongue position and movement during speech. In this technique, depending on the system, two or three transmitter coils are fixed on an apparatus (e.g., a helmet, a cubical structure in Figure 11.13a) surrounding the speaker's head, and receiver coils are placed on the speaker's tongue surface (see Figure 11.13b). An electrical signal is induced when the receiver coils receive an alternating magnetic field of different frequencies (about 10 kHz range) generated by the transmitter coils. The voltage of this electrical signal, captured at a

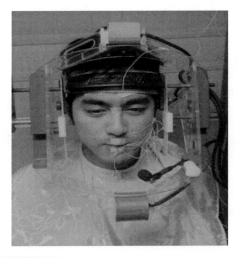

Figure 11.13a Electromagnetic midsagittal articulography apparatus

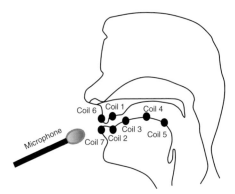

Figure 11.13b Receiver coil placements
Figure 11.13 Electromagnetic midsagittal articulography (EMMA) set-up
(Reproduced from http://site.hanyang.ac.kr/web/tcho/phonetics-lab, with
permission From Dr. Taehong Cho.)

200 Hz sampling rate, is proportional to (the cube of) the distance and orienta-
tion of the receiver coils relative to the transmitter coils. This relationship is then
used by a computer to calculate the position of the receiver coils as a function of
time. Tongue position and movements are then reconstructed from these data
points. However, because of the gag reflex and thus how far back the receiver
coils can be placed, information about the shape or motion of the tongue root is
difficult to acquire. In addition, the positions of the receivers affect the reconstructed tongue shape and it is possible that these positions are not optimal for all
sounds and that an important tongue shape occurring between two receivers is
not accurately reconstructed. Finally, the effects of irritation caused by the
receivers and the transmitter apparatus on the naturalness of speech articulation
are not known.

Using EMMA, the stability of the tongue, lip, and jaw movements of consonants were monitored in a study to see if they vary as a function of their syllable
affiliation. Specifically, it was hypothesized that the articulatory timing of two
consonants should be more stable when they belong to the same syllable (e.g., /f/
and /k/ in fak.tor) than when they belong to separate syllables (e.g., /f/ and /k/ in
fa.kor), whereas that of an intervocalic consonant that belongs to both syllables,
also known as an ambi-syllabic consonant (e.g., /k/ in fa[kk]el where /k/ is
simultaneously the coda of the first syllable and the onset of the second syllable)
should be somewhere in between. The hypothesis was disconfirmed by the data
(Schiller, 1997).

Another interesting use of EMMA is in an investigation of the effect of
Mandarin lexical tone production on tongue, jaw, and lower lip positions. The
result of a pilot study suggested that Mandarin tone 3 (low-falling-rising) shows
different articulatory and head positions from those of the other three Mandarin
tones (Hoole & Hu, 2004).

Chapter Summary

Various tools are available to obtain information on speech articulation from tongue-contact area to the shape of the entire vocal tract. Data obtained from these techniques have increased our understanding of the speech articulation process in the last decades. However, many of these tools are still too expensive for a typical phonetics laboratory. Data collection takes time and requires financial resources. Having an affiliation with a local hospital and securing external funding support are necessary.

References and Further Reading

Adler-Bock, M., Bernhardt, B. M., Gick, B., & Bacsfalvi, P. (2007). The use of ultrasound in remediation of North American English /r/ in 2 adolescents. *American Journal of Speech-Language Pathology*, 16(2), 128–139.

Anderson, V., Ko, I., O'Grady, W., & Choo, M. (2004). A palatographic investigation of place of articulation in Korean coronal obstruents. *Korean Linguistics*, 12(1), 1–24.

Arka, I. W. (2004). Palatography in a fieldwork setting: investigating and analysing alveolar continuant [r] and [ɹ] in Rongga. In I. W. Pastika (eds.), *Wibawa Bahasa* (pp. 40–50). Denpasar: Universitas Udayan.

Aron, M., Berger, M. O., Kerrien, E., Wrobel-Dautcourt, B., Potard, B., & Laprie, Y. (2016). Multimodal acquisition of articulatory data: Geometrical and temporal registration. *The Journal of the Acoustical Society of America*, 139(2), 636–648.

Badin, P., Bailly, G., Reveret, L., Baciu, M., Segebarth, C., & Savariaux, C. (2002). Three-dimensional linear articulatory modeling of tongue, lips and face, based on MRI and video images. *Journal of Phonetics*, 30(3), 533–553.

Bladon, R. A. W., & Nolan, F. J. (1977). A video-fluorographic investigation of tip and blade alveolars in English. *Journal of Phonetics*, 5(2), 185–193.

Byrd, D. (1996). Influences on articulatory timing in consonant sequences. *Journal of Phonetics*, 24(2), 209–244.

Davidson, L. (2006). Comparing tongue shapes from ultrasound imaging using smoothing spline analysis of variance. *The Journal of the Acoustical Society of America*, 120(1), 407–415.

Gick, B. (2002). The use of ultrasound for linguistic phonetic fieldwork. *Journal of the International Phonetic Association*, 32(2), 113–121.

Gick, B., Wilson, I., & Derrick, D. (2012). *Articulatory Phonetics*. New York: John Wiley & Sons.

Hardcastle, W. J. (1972). The use of electropalatography in phonetic research. *Phonetica*, 25(4), 197–215.

Hoole, P., & Hu, F. (2004). Tone–vowel interaction in standard Chinese. In *Proceedings of the International Symposium on Tonal Aspects of Languages: With Emphasis on Tone Languages*. Beijing: The Institute of Linguistics, Chinese Academy of Sciences.

Hoole, P., & Nguyen, N. (1999). Electromagnetic articulography. In W. J. Hardcastle & N. Hewlett (eds.), *Coarticulation–Theory, Data and Techniques, Cambridge Studies in Speech Science and Communication* (pp. 260–269). Cambridge: Cambridge University Press.

Khatiwada, R. (2007). Nepalese retroflex stops: A static palatography study of inter- and intra-speaker variability. *INTERSPEECH,* 1422–1425.

Kiritani, M. M. S. S., & Yoshioka, H. (1982). An electro-palatographic study of Japanese intervocalic /r/. *Annual Bulletin of RILP,* 16, 21–25.

Kydd, W. L., & Belt, D. A. (1964). Continuous palatography. *Journal of Speech and Hearing Disorders,* 29(4), 489–492.

Ladefoged, P., & Everett, D. (1996). The status of phonetic rarities. *Language,* 72(4), 794–800.

Mennen, I., Scobbie, J. M., de Leeuw, E., Schaeffler, S., & Schaeffler, F. (2010). Measuring language-specific phonetic settings. *Second Language Research,* 26(1), 13–41.

Miyawaki, K. (1972). A preliminary study of American English /r/ by use of dynamic palatography. *Annual Bulletin of the Research Institute Logopedics and Phoniatrics, University of Tokyo,* 8, 51–57.

Narayanan, S., Nayak, K., Lee, S., Sethy, A., & Byrd, D. (2004). An approach to real-time magnetic resonance imaging for speech production. *The Journal of the Acoustical Society of America,* 115(4), 1771–1776.

Pedersen, M. F., Møller, S., Krabbe, S., & Bennet, P. (1986). Fundamental voice frequency measured by electroglottography during continuous speech: A new exact secondary sex characteristic in boys in puberty. *International Journal of Pediatric Otorhinolaryngology,* 11, 11–27.

Perkell, J. S., Cohen, M. H., Svirsky, M. A., Matthies, M. L., Garabieta, I., & Jackson, M. T. (1992). Electromagnetic midsagittal articulometer systems for transducing speech articulatory movements. *The Journal of the Acoustical Society of America,* 92(6), 3078–3096.

Proctor, M. I., Goldstein, L., Lammert, A. C., Byrd, D., Toutios, A., & Narayanan, S. (2013). Velic coordination in French nasals: a real-time magnetic resonance imaging study. *INTERSPEECH,* 577–581.

Ricasens, D. (1984). Timing constraints and coarticulation: alveo-palatals and sequences of alveolar + [j] in Catalan. *Phonetica,* 41, 125–139.

Schiller, N. O. (1997). *The Role of the Syllable in Speech Production: Evidence from Lexical Statistics, Metalinguistics, Masked Priming, and Electromagnetic Midsagittal Articulography.* Doctoral dissertation, Radboud University, Nijmegen.

Shibata, S. (1968). A study of Dynamic Palatography. *Annual Bulletin of the RILP,* 2, 28–36.

Vatikiotis-Bateson, E., & Ostry, D. (1995). An analysis of the dimensionality of jaw motion in speech. *Journal of Phonetics,* 23, 101–117.

Yoshioka, H., Löfqvist, A., & Hirose, H. (1981). Laryngeal adjustments in the production of consonant clusters and geminates in American English. *The Journal of the Acoustical Society of America,* 70(6), 1615–1623.

Glossary

Active articulators: Parts of the vocal tract involved in speech production that move, including the tongue, the uvula, and the glottis.

Affricates: Consonants produced with a complete closure of a plosive followed by a slow release of a fricative such as the sound <ch> in 'church'.

Allophones: Predictable physical realizations of a phoneme in different positions of a word.

Allophonic rule: A generalization capturing the distribution of allophones.

Amplitude: The vertical height of a sound wave reflecting the extent to which sound pressure varies over time.

Analogous distribution: When two phones occur in nearly the same position in two different words with different meanings.

Anti-formants: Resonances of a side branch or a "shunt" resonator such as the oral cavity during a nasal consonant production.

Antinode: Points along a standing wave pattern where the amplitude is maximum.

Aperiodic wave: Oscillatory patterns that do not repeat at regular time intervals, such as transient and frication noise.

Band-pass filter: An acoustic filter that passes acoustic energy between a low and a high cut-off frequency.

Bark scale: A psychoacoustic scale of pitch perception based on the **critical band** theory formulated by Harvey Fletcher in 1940. The bark scale ranges from 1–24 barks, corresponding to the 24 critical bands along the basilar membrane. One bark distance on the bark scale is equal to the critical bandwidth which remains constant (~100Hz) for frequencies under 500Hz but logarithmically above that.

Breathy phonation: The mode of phonation produced with a low level of muscular tension, incomplete closure of the glottis, and relatively higher rate of airflow through the glottis.

Broad transcription: A type of phonetic transcription representing only necessary features that allow listeners to reproduce a recognizable word. It is sometimes used synonymously with phonemic transcription.

Cardinal vowels: A set of language-independent vowels.

Categorical perception: A phenomenon characterized by the ability to discriminate between two sounds earlier labeled as members of different categories.

Central approximants: Consonants produced with non-turbulent airstream released through the center of the vocal tract such as the <y> sound in 'yam'.

Clicks: Consonants produced with the velaric ingressive airstream. They are characterized by their distinctive and loud release, and are common in African languages such as Zulu and Xhosa.

Coarticulation: Articulatory overlaps between adjacent sounds.

Coda: Consonant(s) at the end of a syllable.

Complementary distribution: When two phones are found in different positions in two different words without a change in meaning.

Complex consonants: Consonants produced with simultaneous articulations with the same degree of constriction, such as [k͡p] in Ewe [k͡pɔ́] 'to see'.

Complex periodic wave: Periodic oscillations resulting from multiple harmonic movements.

Contour consonants: Consonants produced with two consecutive articulations, for example affricates.

Contrastive distribution: When two phones occur in the same position in two different words with different meanings.

Coronals: Consonants produced with tongue tip or blade, including typically (inter)dental and alveolar consonants but may also include post-alveolar (alveolo-palatal) and retroflex consonants.

Creaky phonation: The mode of phonation produced with a relatively slow and irregular rate of vocal fold vibration and thus, a relatively low rate of airflow through the glottis.

Critical period: A time window when learning is believed to yield optimal results.

Cut-off frequency: A frequency below or above which acoustic energy is allowed to pass or is blocked in an acoustic filter.

Cycle: Repetition of a pattern.

Damping: Amplitude reduction due to friction or other forces.

Decibel: Logarithmic units of sound intensity or pressure.

Decode: To translate coded information. The reverse of 'encoding'.

Digitization: The process of converting an analog signal into a digital form.

Diphthong: A vowel produced with tongue movement from one vowel to another within the same syllable, thus being perceived as having two qualities, such as the <uy> vowel in English 'buy'.

Direct realism: When applied to speech perception, direct realism posits that the objects of speech perception are actual rather than intended gestures.

Distribution: Environments a phone can occur in.

Dorsals: Consonants produced with tongue dorsum (back of the tongue), including typically palatal and velar consonants but may also include uvular.

Ejectives: Consonants produced with an abrupt release of a high-pressure air body trapped above the closed glottis and anterior closure (glottalic egressive airstream). It is characterized by a loud 'pop', cork-like release and is always voiceless.

Electroglottography (EGG): A non-invasive device used to measure the contact area between the two vocal folds during phonation through a display of electrical impedance patterns across the larynx.

Electromagnetic midsagittal articulography (EMMA): A point-tracking technique used to image tongue position and movement during speech.

Electropalatography: A method used to identify and quantify tongue-contact areas and locations during speech production using an inserted pseudo-palate with electrodes attached to capture rapid and fine-grained movements.

Encode: To convert information into a particular form.

Extrinsic vowel normalization: Vowel normalization based on acoustic information from other vowels in surrounding context.

Foot: A higher-order unit of speech containing a stressed syllable and any number of unstressed syllables.

Formant frequencies: Frequencies around which acoustic energy is concentrated as a result of the filtering action of the vocal tract, visible as prominent peaks in a spectrum.

Formant transition: Change in formant frequency before or after a segment.

Fourier analysis: The analysis performed to decompose a complex signal into its frequency components.

Free variation: When two phones can be interchanged without incurring a corresponding change in meaning.

Frequency: Number of periods or cycles per second. The unit of frequency is hertz (Hz).

Fricatives: Consonant sounds produced with a narrow channel formed by a near-complete closure of the articulators, resulting in audible hissing sound as a high-pressure airflow speeds through it, such as the <f> sound in 'fish'.

Fundamental Frequency (F0): The lowest frequency component in a complex periodic sound.

Glides: Vowel-like consonants including <w> and <y> as in English 'wig' and 'yak'.

Glottalic airstream: Airstream initiated from an air body trapped above the closed glottis and an anterior closure.

Glottis: Space between the vocal folds.

Harmonics: Frequency components of a complex periodic sound.

High-pass-filter: An acoustic filter that passes acoustic energy at frequencies above the cut-off frequency.

Implosives: Consonants produced with glottalic ingressive airstream. They are characterized by a small influx of air flowing into the oral cavity upon closure release due to lower-pressured air body inside the vocal tract. Implosives are mostly voiced.

Impressionistic transcription: A type of detailed phonetic transcription representing all discernible phonetic details without the influence of prior knowledge of the phonetic properties of the language being transcribed.

Intonation: The rise and fall of pitch over an utterance.

Intrinsic vowel normalization: An approach to vowel normalization that seeks to reduce the amount of overlap between vowel categories by representing their acoustic properties on an auditory scale or transforming them using different normalized metrics.

Lack of acoustic invariance: Refers to a lack of one-to-one mapping between acoustic properties and phonemes.

Lateral approximants: Consonants produced with non-turbulent airstream escaping through the side of the vocal tract such as the <l> sound in 'low'.

Lax vowels: Vowels produced with relatively less muscular effort, less extreme tongue position, and shorter duration, such as the <i> vowel in English 'bit'.

Length: When duration of a vowel or a consonant is used to contrast word meaning.

Linear predictive coding (LPC): The analysis performed on the signal to reveal the resonant properties of an acoustic filter (e.g., the vocal tract).

Linearity problem: Also known as segmentation problem. It refers to the difficulty in matching speech perception units (e.g., phonemes) to a corresponding, discrete portion of the acoustic signal.

Lip radiation factor: The amplification of high frequency relative to low frequency by approximately 6 dB per octave as sounds radiate out from the lips to the atmosphere.

Liquids: <r> and <l>-like sounds produced with the tongue in a raised position while allowing a constant volume of airflow through the vocal tract.

Loudness: Subjective sensation correlated with sound pressure.

Low-pass filter: An acoustic filter that passes acoustic energy at frequencies below the cut-off frequency.

Magnetic resonance imaging (MRI): In speech science, MRI is a tool that uses magnetic fields and radio waves to produce a detailed image of a vocal tract during speech production.

Manner of articulation: The size of the stricture made inside the vocal tract to produce a consonant.

McGurk effect: A perceptual illusion demonstrating that visual and audio information are integrated to derive a speech percept during perception.

Meaning: Concepts, actions, referents, and other information that the speaker intends to convey to the listener.

Mel scale: A subjective auditory scale expressing the relationship between frequency of sine tones and their perceived pitch.

Minimal pairs: A pair of words with different meanings that differ only in one phone; evidence for determining that two phones belong to different phonemes.

Modal voiced phonation: The neutral mode of phonation produced with the laryngeal muscle adjusted to a moderate level and a complete closure of the glottis during the closed phase, thus generating no audible frication.

Monophthong: A vowel produced with the same tongue position throughout the syllable that is perceived as having a single quality such as the <ee> vowel in English 'bee'.

Morpheme: The smallest meaningful linguistic unit.

Motor theory: A prominent theory in speech perception based on the premise that invariant cues to a phoneme are the neuromotor command or intended gestures used to produce it.

Narrow transcription: A type of phonetic transcription representing known phonetic details of a language as much as possible.

Narrow-band spectrogram: A spectrographic display highlighting changes in frequencies of individual harmonics in the voice source.

Nasal vowels: Vowels produced with airflows through the nasal and the oral cavities to signal a meaning contrast with oral vowels, as in French <bon> 'good' vs. <beau> 'beautiful'.

Nasalized vowels: Oral vowels produced with the velum in a lower position (nasalization) due to the presence of neighboring nasal consonants such as the <a> vowel in English 'ban'.

Neural impulse: Electrical signals traveling along a nerve fiber.

Node: Points along a standing wave pattern where the amplitude is minimum.

Nucleus: The center position of a syllable usually occupied by a vowel, but sometimes by a sonorant consonant.

Nyquist frequency: Frequency that is half of the sampling rate.

Obstruents: Consonants produced with a complete or near-complete obstruction of airflow through the vocal tract. These include plosives, fricatives, and affricates.

Octave: A 2:1 ratio difference in frequency. For example, a change from 100 Hz to 200 Hz or from 200 Hz to 400 Hz represents an octave.

Oral vowels: Vowels produced without velum lowering or nasalization.

Palatography: A collection of methods used to identify contact location between the tongue and the roof of the mouth during speech production.

Passive articulators: Parts of the vocal tract used to produce speech that don't move, including the upper lip, teeth, alveolar ridge, palate, velum, and pharynx.

Perceptual assimilation: The process whereby non-native sounds are perceptually mapped to existing native sound categories.

Perceptual reorganization: The process whereby the perceptual system becomes attuned to the ambient language input, making it difficult for infants to discriminate non-native contrasts. This occurs during the second half of an infant's first year of life.

Period: Duration of a cycle.

Perturbation theory: In phonetics, this refers to a model that accounts for the acoustic consequences of local perturbations (i.e., constrictions) on the resonant characteristics of an air body resonating in a tube.

Phon scale: A frequency-sensitive, psychoacoustic scale of perceived loudness of sine tones.

Phonate: To pass airflow through the glottis to produce sounds.

Phonation types: Ways that airflow passes through the glottis to make sounds. Common phonation types used to change word meaning in the world's languages are voiced, voiceless, breathy, and creaky.

Phonation: How air passes through the vocal folds to produce periodic vibrations.

Phoneme: Unpredictable, abstract units of sound that distinguish one word from another.

Phonemic transcription: Visual representation of abstract units of speech sounds (i.e., phonemes) stored in long-term memory.

Phonetic transcription: Visual representation of speech using a set of symbols such as the International Phonetic Alphabet (IPA).

Phonetics: A subfield of linguistics that studies the description of the physical, acoustic, and auditory properties of speech sounds.

Phonology: A subfield of linguistics that studies how speech sounds are structured and organized in the minds of speakers, and how they are used to express meaning.

Photoglottography (PGG): An endoscopic method used to measure the size of glottal opening during phonation.

Pitch-accent language: A language like Japanese where the meaning of words with identical strings of syllables is signaled by the location in the word where the pitch is lowered.

Pitch: Auditory impression correlated with frequency or rate of vocal fold vibration.

Pitch accent: A low or high pitch pattern placed over a syllable in an utterance to signal a focus or an emphasis.

Place of articulation: The locations within the vocal tract where a stricture is made to produce a consonant.

Plosives: Consonant sounds produced with a momentarily complete blockage of the airflow through the vocal tract before being later released, such as the <p> sound in 'put'.

Point-tracking: A method used to collect articulatory (e.g., lip and facial) movements in speech perception using cameras to track the movements of infrared-emitting diodes that are attached to the subject's face and lips.

Primary articulation: The basic place and manner of articulation of a consonant.

Primary stress: Highest degree of syllable prominence.

Prosody: The melody or tune of an utterance shaped by pitch level and pitch movement, acoustic intensity, and variation in phoneme and syllable duration.

Pulmonic airstream: Airstream initiated from the lungs.

Quantization errors: The difference in amplitude between the actual analog amplitude value of the continuous signal and the values represented in the digital signal.

Quantization rate: The number of amplitude values (measured in bits) available to record air-pressure level of the input signal during digitization.

Quantization: The process of converting pressure values at the sampling points into discrete values.

Resonance: The condition whereby vibrations of a physical body such as an object or an air column are amplified by an outside force of the same natural frequency (sympathetic vibration).

Rhotacization: Pronunciation of vowels accompanied simultaneously by an 'r' consonant quality. Vowels produced in this manner are also known as r-colored vowels.

Sampling rate: The rate at which pressure values are recorded during the digitization process, measured in hertz.

Sampling: The process of recording air pressure in a waveform at equally spaced time intervals.

Secondary articulation: Additional articulation simultaneously added to the primary articulation of a consonant such as lip rounding, as in how <sh> in English 'shoe' is pronounced.

Simple periodic wave: Periodic oscillations resulting from a simple harmonic movement.

Sine wave: A smooth, simple periodic waveform with constant amplitude corresponding to a sine function.

Sone scale: A subjective scale of perceived loudness between sine tones. A loudness of one sone equals to the loudness level of a 1,000 Hz tone at an intensity level of dB_{spl} or 40 phons. Doubling in sone value equals doubling in perceived loudness. The sone value doubles for every increase of 10 phons.

Sonorants: Speech sounds produced with a continuous and non-turbulent airflow. They are voiced and louder than other consonants. These include vowels, nasals, liquids, and glides.

Sonority scale: A hierarchy based on acoustic intensity, intra-oral air pressure, amount of airflow, duration, etc., among speech sounds.

Source–filter theory: A model of speech production characterized by a combination of a source energy modulated by the transfer function of a filter.

Spectrogram: A visual display of acoustic energy distribution as a function of frequency and time in a signal.

Speech spectrum: Visual representation of frequency components and their amplitudes of a signal.

Standing wave: A wave pattern that arises from the interference between two waves with the same frequency and amplitude moving at the same speed in opposite directions.

Stress: Relative degree of prominence among syllables in a word. For example, the first syllable is more prominent than the second in English 'baby'.

Suprasegmental features: Phonological patterning described in speech units larger than a segment. These include stress, tone, length, and intonation.

Syllabic consonant: A consonant that functions as the nucleus of a syllable.

Syllable: Smallest possible unit of speech.

Sympathetic vibration: A phenomenon whereby the vibration of a physical body causes another physical body to vibrate.

Tap or Flap: Consonants produced with a single and quick contact between the active and the passive articulator.

Tense vowels: Vowels produced with relatively greater muscular effort, more extreme tongue position, and longer duration, such as the <ea> vowel in English 'beat'.

Tone: Pitch variation on syllables that conveys contrasts in meaning. In a tone language like Mandarin Chinese, the same syllable conveys different meanings depending on the pitch level or contour in which it is produced.

Transients: Sounds characterized by a sudden change in pressure that is unsustained, such as bursts, taps, pops, clicks, etc.

Trill: Consonants produced with rapid vibrations of the active articulator against the passive articulator such as the <rr> sound in Spanish word *perro* 'dog'.

Ultrasound: A technique designed to image soft tissue that has been used in speech and linguistic research to acquire images of the tongue during speech production.

Velaric airstream: Airstream initiated from an air body trapped between the velum and an anterior closure.

Voiceless phonation: The mode of phonation produced with either fully closed vocal folds to completely block the airflow from the lungs or with the vocal folds far apart, so airflow can freely flow through the glottis.

Vowel normalization: A process by which listeners factor out acoustic variation across speakers in vowel production.

Waveform: A representation of how the pressure varies with time.

Wide-band spectrogram. A spectrographic display capturing individual vocal fold pulses and formant frequencies and how they change over time.

Windowing: The process of selecting a stretch of the signal for analysis.

Zero padding: The process of adding samples with zero amplitude to an otherwise short analysis window to increase frequency precision in the analysis.

Index